THE POLITICS OF
OBSCENITY

Recent Titles in
Contributions in Legal Studies

Lawyers, Courts, and Professionalism: The Agenda for Reform
Rudolph J. Gerber

John Marshall's Achievement: Law, Politics, and Constitutional Interpretations
Thomas C. Shevory, editor

Affirmative Action and Principles of Justice
Kathanne W. Greene

Unfounded Fears: Myths and Realities of a Constitutional Convention
Paul J. Weber and Barbara Perry

Protecting Constitutional Freedoms: A Role for Federal Courts
Daan Braveman

The Employment Relationship in Anglo-American Law: A Historical Perspective
Marc Linder

The Aristocracy of the Long Robe
J. M. Sosin

Equal Separation: Understanding the Religion Clauses of the First Amendment
Paul J. Weber, editor

Common Law in Southern Africa: Conflict of Laws and Torts Precedents
Peter B. Kutner

A History of the Anglo-American Common Law of Contract
Kevin M. Teeven

"We Have a Duty": The Supreme Court and the Watergate Tapes Litigation
Howard Ball

The Shaping of Nineteenth-Century Law: John Appleton and Responsible Individualism
David M. Gold

Comparative Constitutional Federalism: Europe and America
Mark Tushnet, editor

Church-State Constitutional Issues: Making Sense of the Establishment Clause
Donald L. Drakeman

THE POLITICS OF OBSCENITY

GROUP LITIGATION IN A TIME OF LEGAL CHANGE

Joseph F. Kobylka

CONTRIBUTIONS IN LEGAL STUDIES, NUMBER 64
PAUL E. MURPHY, Series Editor

GREENWOOD PRESS

New York • Westport, Connecticut • London

Library of Congress Cataloging-in-Publication Data

Kobylka, Joseph Fiske.
    The politics of obscenity : group litigation in a time of legal
change / Joseph F. Kobylka.
        p.   cm.—(Contributions in legal studies, ISSN 0147–1074 ;
no. 64)
    Includes bibliographical references and index.
    ISBN 0–313–26882–7 (alk. paper)
    1. Obscenity (Law)—United States. 2. Obscenity (Law)—United
States—Citizen participation.   I. Title.   II. Series
KF9444.K63   1991
345.73′0274—dc20
[347.305274]   90–46698

British Library Cataloguing in Publication Data is available.

Library of Congress Catalog Card Number: 90–46698
ISBN: 0–313–26882–7
ISSN: 0147–1074

First published in 1991

Greenwood Press, 88 Post Road West, Westport, CT 06881
An imprint of Greenwood Publishing Group, Inc.

Printed in the United States of America

Copyright Acknowledgment

The author and publisher are grateful to the following source for use of material:

Joseph F. Kobylka, "A Court-Created Context for Group Litigation: Libertarian Groups and
Obscenity," *The Journal of Politics* 49, no. 4 (November 1987): 1061–78.

To Janet
for her patience, understanding, and love

Contents

Tables   ix

Preface: Law, Politics, and Obscenity   xi

1: Introduction: Groups and Obscenity   1

2: The Groups and Their Interests   23

3: Organizational Adaptation: Exit   71

4: Organizational Adaptation: Continuance   97

5: Organizational Adaptation: Mobilization   125

6: Conclusion: A Court-Created Context for Organizational Litigation   155

Appendix A: Organizational Involvement in Obscenity Litigations before the Supreme Court   173

Appendix B: Citizens for Decency through Law Supreme Court Participation Not Counted in Appendix A   181

Appendix C: Participation of Groups in Supreme Court Obscenity Decisions: Pre- and Post-*Miller*   183

Appendix D: Table of Cases   185

Bibliography   193

Index   201

Tables

Table 1.1:   Outcomes of Obscenity Litigation before the
             Supreme Court, 1957–1987   8
Table 1.2:   Supreme Court Participation of Groups in
             Obscenity Cases, 1957–1987   9
Table 1.3:   Frequency of Group Participation in Supreme
             Court Obscenity Litigation, 1957–1987   17
Table 2.1:   Libertarian Group Involvement before the
             Supreme Court in Obscenity Cases, 1957–1987   27
Table 2.2:   Libertarian Groups Involved in Obscenity
             Litigation before the Supreme Court, 1957–
             1987   28
Table 2.3:   Pro-Decency Group Involvement before the
             Supreme Court in Obscenity Cases, 1957–1987   47
Table 2.4:   Pro-Decency Groups Involved in Obscenity
             Litigation before the Supreme Court, 1957–
             1987   48
Table 3.1:   ACLU Participation before the Supreme Court,
             Pre- and Post-*Miller*   75
Table 4.1:   Pro-Decency Group Participation before the
             Supreme Court, Pre- and Post-*Miller*   102
Table 4.2:   CDL Attempts to Participate in Obscenity
             Litigation before the Supreme Court, Pre- and
             Post-*Miller*   104

Table 5.1:   Participation of Material Groups before the
             Supreme Court, Pre- and Post-*Miller*   130
Table 5.2:   Incidence of Participation of Material Groups
             before the Supreme Court, Pre- and Post-*Miller*   131
Table 5.3:   Distribution of Participation of Material Groups
             in Obscenity Cases Decided by the Supreme
             Court, 1957–1987   133
Table 5.4:   Success of Material Groups in Obscenity Cases
             Decided by the Supreme Court, 1973–1987   143
Table 6.1:   Number of Supreme Court Appearances of the
             Five Most Frequent Libertarian Litigators,
             1957–1973   157
Table 6.2:   The Shift in Litigation Burden: Participation of
             Libertarian Groups in Supreme Court
             Litigation   158
Table 6.3:   Group Participation in Supreme Court
             Obscenity Litigation, Pre- and Post-*Miller*   161
Table 6.4:   The Increasing Density of Group Participation
             in Supreme Court Obscenity Litigation, Pre-
             and Post-*Miller*   162
Table 6.5:   Factors Conditioning Group Litigation Behavior   168

Preface: Law, Politics, and Obscenity

> Scarcely any political question arises in the United States that is not
> resolved, sooner or later, into a judicial question. . . . The language of
> the law thus becomes, in some measure, a vulgar tongue; the spirit of
> the law, which is produced in the schools and courts of justice, gradually
> penetrates beyond their walls into the bosom of society, where it de-
> scends to the lower classes, so that at last the whole people contract the
> habits and the tastes of the judicial magistrate.
> —Alexis de Tocqueville, *Democracy in America*

The politicization of the law, a subject of considerable discussion among
legal commentators, has been a fact of American life from the inception of
the nation. One need look no further than the tenure and decisions of Chief
Justice John Marshall to see the nexus between "legal" and "political" issues
and conflicts. "Modern" courts continue to work in this web; economic regulation, discrimination, religion, expression, abortion, and other social conflicts have all found their way to the judiciary for resolution. This
transformation of "legal" questions into the stuff of "ordinary politics" is
not uncommon. As de Tocqueville noted 150 years ago, the legal underpinnings of American politics invite it, especially in contentious policy areas.

This linkage between law and politics makes the courts a natural forum
for organizational action. In the last three decades, a literature has emerged

examining group litigation in a number of policy areas; but it has not treated the politics of obscenity. This is unfortunate in at least two senses. First, obscenity litigation witnessed wide participation by a variety of groups representing a broad spectrum of interests over a considerable period of time. In the 30 years since the Supreme Court's decision in *Roth* v. *U.S.* (1957), 24 groups with libertarian and conservative perspectives and political and material interests filed briefs at the apex of the judiciary. Second, after liberalizing the doctrine governing obscenity matters through the 1960s, the Court suddenly swung the law back to its late 1950s status with its decisions in *Miller* v. *California* (1973) and subsequent cases. The vastness and density of this litigation field, coupled with a longitudinal perspective sensitive to the Court's shift, provide an opportunity to assess the effect of a substantial legal change on the political dynamics of the group system. This is the focal point of *The Politics of Obscenity*.

Obscenity litigation is clearly a part of the ongoing politicization of the judiciary. Recent cover articles in national news magazines, reports of two presidential commissions, "feminist" antipornography statutes, and the removal of "men's" magazines from convenience stores have drawn public attention to the legal and political debate over obscenity. But though currently topical, obscenity politics has a much longer history. Drawing on English and colonial antecedents,[1] and at the urging of social reformers, American legislatures began to pass obscenity (more accurately, anti-obscenity) statutes after the Civil War.[2] Although these acts proscribed expression with sexual content, their constitutional status long went unchallenged. Indeed, the Supreme Court did not speak directly to the relevant First Amendment issues until 1957 when, in *Roth* v. *U.S.*, it held obscenity proscription permissible. Following *Roth*, however, ambiguity and instability characterized the Court's treatment of this issue as it struggled to define exactly what was beyond the constitutional pale. The Court, however, did not struggle in isolation; as in other areas of law and politics, groups mobilized to advance their interests.

Over the 30-year period covered in this study, the Supreme Court initially adopted a doctrinal posture intolerant of obscenity, eased away from this position to one of relative laxity, and then strongly reasserted the constitutionality of proscription. In its post-*Roth* decisions, the Warren Court narrowed the category of the obscene and reversed most of the lower court convictions on which it acted. This had two effects. First, it made convictions more difficult to attain and sustain, de facto liberalizing the law. Second, this liberalization gave sexual material a new legitimacy, and it became more prevalent. This increasing legitimacy and availability prompted outcry from defenders of "traditional" morality; the Court was attacked for undermining morality, the social climate, and American youth.[3] In 1968, public concern led President Lyndon Johnson to name a President's Commission on Obscenity and Pornography. In 1970, it recommended—consistent with the

Court's liberalizing decisions—"that federal, state, and local legislation prohibiting the sale, exhibition, or distribution of sexual material to consenting adults should be repealed" (President's Commission, 1970, p. 57). Three dissenting commissioners, two of whom were leaders of nationally prominent "pro-decency" organizations,[4] called this report "a Magna Charta for the pornographer" (*Report*, 1970:456).

As a presidential candidate, and as president, Richard Nixon blasted the permissiveness of the Warren Court, including its treatment of obscenity,[5] and his administration rejected the Johnson Commission's Report. Perhaps its most pointed statement on obscenity came from Vice President Spiro Agnew: "As long as Richard Nixon is President, Main Street is not going to turn into Smut Alley" (*New York Times*, 1 Oct. 1970). Nixon's four appointments to the Supreme Court provided an opportunity to act on this promise.[6] In *Miller* v. *California* (1973), "his" Court decisively reasserted the constitutionality of proscription and explicitly rejected the post-*Roth* liberalization. Judicial libertarianism waned. Thirteen years later, Attorney General Edwin Meese appointed another Commission on Pornography. Mixing the language of feminist antipornography critiques with traditional moralistic concerns,[7] this commission—with two antiporn organizational leaders prominent in its majority[8]—issued a proscriptionist report that stood in stark contrast to that of its predecessor. In a sense, the Court and the commission symbolically erased the legacy of the Warren Court in this area of law.[9] The group dimension of "modern" obscenity politics takes its structure from this legal ebb and flow.

By focusing on the struggle over the content of obscenity law, this study examines the behavior of a dense and varied group of organized litigators in an experimental setting; this approach allows the study to further our understanding of the vastness and dynamics of the group system. *Roth* and its aftermath ignited litigation by a wide variety of groups. Libertarian (opposing proscription) and *pro-decency* (favoring proscription)[10] groups battled to bend legal developments to their goals. Far from monolithic in focus, the libertarian camp included groups with interests ranging from political to vocational to commercial. The density and the heterogeneity of this litigation field facilitate analysis of a more complex group environment than those discussed in previous studies.

The design of this study allows it to examine the dynamism present in this field in a novel way. It views *Miller* v. *California* (1973) as an intervening factor in established litigation patterns and uses it to establish a "natural experiment" in which the behavioral effects of the interaction between group-specific and environmental factors can be assessed. In radically altering the context of litigation—in transposing the legally advantaged and disadvantaged (Cortner, 1968)—*Miller* created a new context for organizational activity. The decision moved pro-decency groups, whose arguments were not treated sympathetically during the Warren years, into an advantaged legal position. The opposite was true for libertarians: the Warren Court frowned on proscription; *Miller* made clear proscription would be accepted. How does this kind of role reversal—legally disadvantaged to legally advantaged and vice versa—affect the system of group litigation?

One would expect that groups would adapt their strategies and behavior to this new environment, but the literature on group litigation provides no pointed discussion of how this would occur. This study demonstrates the central role played by legal context in shaping both the configuration of litigating groups *and* the strategies they employ to secure their ends in times of legal change. To facilitate its analysis, this research draws on group theory to assess the factors—both group-specific and contextual—relevant to the adaptive responses observed. This assessment indicates that the litigation behavior of groups, the development of law, and group theory concepts can be woven into a framework that provides a more generalized basis for explaining the size and flexibility of the group system, especially as it incorporates litigation.[11]

The organization of the work is as follows. To set the context for the empirical analysis, the first chapter sketches the doctrinal twists and turns worked by the Supreme Court as it addressed the issues presented by obscenity proscription. This chapter then fits the analytical framework and concepts used in the study to make sense of the patterns of group litigation. Chapter 2 examines the groups—libertarian and proscriptionist, political and material, professional and commercial—that involved themselves in obscenity litigation. It discusses their range of interests, organizational modes and motives, goals, and strategies. The next three chapters treat the organizational response to the *Miller* shift. Chapter 3 examines the ACLU's de-emphasis of obscenity litigation and the reasons for this response. Chapter 4 discusses those groups that continued the political and litigation patterns they had established before the shift in constitutional doctrine. Chapter 5 assesses the group mobilization—predominantly those groups whose interests are libertarian and commercial—that occurred after the 1973 decision. The concluding chapter steps back from the specific empirical discussion to summarize the empirical findings of the study, to discuss the dynamism present in this litigation subsystem, and to suggest the utility of applying longitudinal research designs to densely populated litigation environments. It concludes that such an approach to the study of the organizational use of the courts can yield a more comprehensive, and less idiosyncratic, understanding of the vastness, dynamism, and fluidity of group politics—especially as those politics incorporate the judicial branch of government.

On a more personal note, I wish to acknowledge and thank a number of people who aided, in various ways, in the completion of this book. Frank J. Sorauf of the University of Minnesota served as my advisor on the preparation of this research in its dissertation phase. His insight, advice, and encouragement helped to shape not only this work but also my general academic style. I am deeply indebted to him, both personally and professionally. Professors Samuel Krislov and Paul L. Murphy, also of the University of Minnesota, provided thoughtful commentary on the early stages of this study. I owe my good friend and colleague Lee Epstein a huge debt of gratitude for the sage advice and criticism she tendered as I updated and revised the analysis presented here. I would also like to thank my chairman at Southern Methodist University, Dennis S. Ippolito, and my colleagues and students there, for fostering the kind of department that makes work fun. Finally, to my wife, Janet, and to my children, Keith and Jeff, thanks are due for their love, patience, and general support. Where my colleagues and students make it a pleasure to come to work in the morning, my family makes it a joy to go home at night. It is nice to have two such fulfilling lives.

NOTES

1. Obscenity was first held an offense under English common law in *Dominus Rex* v. *Curil* (1729). The first recorded American conviction was for the sale of *Fanny Hill* in *Commonwealth* v. *Holmes* (Mass., 1821).

2. On the proliferation of these statutes, see Schauer (1976), ch. 1; on the social and political pressures that led to their enactment, see Boyer (1968) and Pivar (1973).

3. For a sampling of such arguments, see the *New York Times* (hereafter *NYT*) of 23 May 1958; 14 and 24 April, 23 May 1959; 2 January, 7 and 16 March 1960; 2 May 1962; 6 May, 29 October 1963; 16 March and 7 August 1964; 23 October 1965; 2 May 1966; 23 April 1967; 8 January 1968; 2 October 1969; 23 August 1970; 8 July 1971; and 23 June 1973.

4. These were Father Morton A. Hill, the founder and president of Morality in Media and Charles H. Keating, Jr., the founder and president of Citizens for Decency through Law. These men, and their organizations, are discussed in more detail in chapter 2.

5. See his comments reported in the *NYT*: 10 October 1968, 9 February 1969, 3 May 1969, and 12 August 1970.

6. For the purposes of this study, the Nixon (or Burger) Court is defined as beginning with the 1972 term of the Court. It was not until then that all four of the Nixon appointees sat together for a complete term.

7. Because of their role in the drafting and enactment of "feminist" anti-pornography statutes (for example, see the discussion of the Minneapolis case in Brest and Vandenberg, 1987), the most often cited feminist critiques are those of Andrea Dworkin (1981, 1987) and Catherine MacKinnon (1984, 1985). For commentary on the work of the Meese Commission, see Downs (1987), Hertzberg (1986), Teachout (1987), Vance (1986), and West (1987).

8. Attorney General's Commission on Pornography, *Final Report* (1986). The commissioners noted are Father Bruce Ritter (the founder of Covenant House) and James C. Dobson (the president of Focus on Family).

9. Although this may be symbolically true, it is not empirically so. Not only have materials become more graphic in content, but their prosecution also has been less than systematic. See Obscenity Law Project (1976).

10. Leaders of anti-obscenity groups prefer the goals of their organizations to be described as *pro-decency* instead of *censorial*. They feel that the latter is a negatively charged label that does not adequately capture their concerns. In deference to these concerns, I will identify these groups in the text as *decency*, *pro-decency*, or *proscriptionist*.

11. The data sources used in this research include interviews and correspondence with group officials, legal briefs, group records and materials, judicial records, and popular literature. Obscenity cases were identified by Westlaw and Lexis searches and by a review of the obscenity sections of the *Modern Federal Practice Digest* and the *West Federal Practice Digest*.

1

Introduction: Groups and Obscenity

I do not believe freedom of the press means lewdness or pornography or obscenity.
                                                    —Rev. Billy Graham, 1958

What is pornography to one man is the laughter of genius to another.
                                                    —D. H. Lawrence

No action occurs in a vacuum. This is true of both political behavior and scholarly efforts to describe and explain it. Thus, before I examine group activity on obscenity issues, it is first necessary to describe the legal context in which this activity occurred, review the literature on group litigation, and discuss the orienting framework from which I will examine obscenity politics.

Understanding the ebb and flow of the Supreme Court's treatment of obscenity issues between 1957 and 1987 is crucial because this interpretational odyssey set the legal context for obscenity politics; the Court's manipulation of the law established incentives and disincentives for organizational action. After setting this legal context, I briefly address previous work on group litigation and group theory. These bodies of literature frame the perspective of the research reported here; this study integrates and applies concepts and insights drawn from them to assess the dynamics of ongoing organizational involvement in this area of law over a volatile 30-year period. In short, this chapter sets up the legal context and scholarly window

from which I will view the "natural experiment" afforded by the Court's
shift in *Miller* v. *California* (1973).

SETTING THE LEGAL CONTEXT: A THUMBNAIL
SKETCH OF THE OBSCENITY DECISIONS OF THE
SUPREME COURT

Although the First Amendment frames an absolute—"Congress shall make
no law . . . abridging the freedom of speech, or of the press"—the Supreme
Court has never held it to protect all expression. In the twentieth century
the Court has, de facto, divided expression into two categories: protected
and unprotected.[1] Regulation that touches on the former is presumptively
unconstitutional; limitation on the latter is generally permissible.[2] This
makes the Court's job definitional: What are the categories, and what expression fits into them? It is from this perspective that the Supreme Court
approached the obscenity issue.

From its first brush with obscenity issues in *Roth* v. *U.S.* (1957) to the
late 1980s, the Court was not uniform, consistent, or clear in its approach.
In *Roth*, it held obscenity to be a category of expression outside of the reach
of the First Amendment. In subsequent cases throughout the 1960s, while
never going so far as to grant obscenity constitutional protection, the Court
narrowed by fits and starts its definition of what counted as obscene. This
had the effect of lessening the ability of governments to successfully prosecute obscenity as a criminal offense. Indeed, with its decision in *Stanley* v.
Georgia (1969), the Court seemed to signal its inclination to discard the
obscenity exception to the First Amendment. In eight cases handed down
at the end of its 1972 term, however, a closely divided Court reaffirmed the
constitutional permissibility of obscenity regulation. With its decisions in
Miller (1973) and others, it firmly rejected the doctrinal liberalization that
characterized the law of obscenity it had inherited. In essence, the Burger
Court gave governments a green light to proscribe material they deemed,
under the *Miller* test, obscene.

Although the path charted by the Court through the obscenity thicket is
interesting in itself, its significance to this study is the context it set for the
interplay of the group forces under examination. The Court's decisions established the political and legal stakes that defined the obscenity debate and set
in motion the groups that came to dominate the politics of obscenity. To understand the group dynamics that the Court unleashed and conditioned, we
first need to lay out, albeit briefly, the path of its obscenity odyssey.

To Roth: Obscenity's Unquestioned Impermissibility

The United States Supreme Court did not write on a clean slate when it
first addressed the constitutionality of obscenity regulation. In *Regina* v.

Hicklin (1868), the British Court of the Queen's Bench held obscenity to be a crime, defining it as "whether the tendency of the matter charged as obscenity is to deprave and corrupt those whose minds are open to such immoral influences and into whose hands a publication of this sort may fall" (L.R. 3 Q.B. 360). The American obscenity odyssey, at least in its constitutional manifestations, began from this point. The federal Comstock Act (1873), named after the anti-vice crusader Anthony Comstock, prohibited the use of the mail to convey obscene material. The Supreme Court, albeit without an extended analysis of First Amendment implications, explicitly upheld the act in *ex parte Jackson* (1877) and *In re Rapier* (1892).

In the absence of any further doctrinal or definitional guidance from the Supreme Court, the *Hicklin* test served as the prevailing legal definition of obscenity in most American courts until *Roth* (Schauer 1976, p. 23).[3] Indeed, the Supreme Court's dicta in other decisions maintained its attachment to the underlying assumption of these early cases: obscenity was not a category of speech protected by the First Amendment. In *Chaplinsky* v. *New Hampshire* (1942), for example, it held:

There are certain well-defined and narrowly limited classes of speech, the prevention and punishment of which have never been thought to raise any constitutional problem. These include the lewd and the obscene.... It has been well observed that such utterances are no essential part of any exposition of ideas and are of such slight social value as a step to truth that any benefit that may be derived from them is clearly outweighed by the social interest in order and morality. (315 U.S., pp. 571–72)

Hicklin's vice grip on the law slipped when the Supreme Court directly confronted the constitutionality of obscenity proscription in its 1956 term. In *Butler* v. *Michigan* (1957), the Court, for the first time, reversed an obscenity conviction won under a statute forbidding the sale of books that would "tend to corrupt the morals" of youth. Writing for a unanimous Court, Justice Frankfurter held that the due process clause of the Fourteenth Amendment precluded legislative attempts to protect minors by prohibiting sales of material suitable for adults: "Surely this is to burn the house to roast the pig" (352 U.S., p. 383). *Butler* effectively shifted *Hicklin*'s focus from the most susceptible member to the average adult of a community (Henkin, 1963), but it did not explicitly reject *Hicklin* on First Amendment grounds.

The Court's decision in *Roth* v. *U.S.* (1957) more substantially altered the prevailing legal context.[4] Although reaffirming that obscenity was not "utterance within the area of protected speech and press" (354 U.S., p. 484), Justice Brennan—writing for a bare majority—rejected the *Hicklin* approach as unduly restrictive. In its place, he articulated a new test: "whether to the average person, applying contemporary community standards, the dominant theme of the material, taken as a whole, appeals to the prurient interest"

(354 U.S., p. 487). This test confined obscenity prosecution to a narrower category of material and, hence, was more sensitive to free expression values than that articulated in *Hicklin*. Indeed, lest his words be read to endorse proscription of all material treating sex, Brennan further noted that, "All ideas having *even the slightest redeeming social importance*... have the full protection of the [Constitution]. ... [S]ex and obscenity are not synonymous" (354 U.S., pp. 484, 487, emphasis added). In essence, Brennan and the *Roth* majority adopted a Meiklejohnian "two-level speech" approach to obscenity regulation (Krislov, 1968; Brennan, 1965), with some materials treating sex constitutionally protected, others not. The post-*Roth* problem was to decide where to draw the line separating protected and unprotected speech involving sex.

Brennan's opinion failed to persuade four justices. Chief Justice Warren concurred in the result, rejecting the constant or abstract definitional approach of the majority for a variable approach where "the conduct of the defendant is the central issue, not the obscenity of a book or picture" (354 U.S., p. 495). Justice Harlan concurred in the result in *Alberts* but dissented from that in *Roth*. He argued that under the Constitution, the states—not the federal government—were primarily responsible for enforcing public morality. Because of their absolutist interpretation of the First Amendment, Justices Black and Douglas dissented: "To allow the State to step in and punish mere speech or publication that the judge or jury thinks has an *undesirable* impact on thoughts but is not shown to be a part of unlawful action is drastically to curtail the First Amendment" (354 U.S., p. 509).

The Rocky Road away from *Roth*: The Rise of Libertarian Concerns

Harlan's separate opinion in *Roth* presaged the difficulties that were to plague the Court in its subsequent efforts to apply its new test.

The Court seems to assume that "obscenity" is a particular *genus* of speech and press, which is as distinct, recognizable, and classifiable as poison ivy is among other plants. ... But surely the problem cannot be solved in such a generalized fashion. ... [E]very suppression raises an individual constitutional problem, in which a reviewing court must determine for *itself* whether the attacked expression is suppressible within constitutional standards. (354 U.S., p. 497, emphasis in original)

Ultimately, the *Roth* approach frayed *precisely because* it required a close appellate review of convictions, and this review necessitated a judicial determination of the fit of the matter in question within the *Roth* framework. This required the justices to define the abstract entity that *Roth* placed beyond the pale in subsequent cases. To do this, they had to give meaning to the ambiguous central components at the heart of the test: *average* person, *contemporary community* standards, *dominant theme*, taken as a *whole*, and *prurient* interest. This proved to be no easy task. Just a term later, the Court summarily reversed four obscenity convictions on the new test's authority.[5] These reversals muddied *Roth*'s meaning because the Court failed to explain *why* the materials were outside of *Roth*'s definition of the obscene. This definitional conundrum—what was and was not obscene under *Roth*—threw the Court into a period of doctrinal dishevelment, but it also yielded a decisional libertarianism seemingly at variance with *Roth*'s proscriptionist thrust.

There were essentially two tracks to the Warren Court's liberalization of obscenity doctrine: procedural and substantive.[6] The procedural dimension contains cases treating issues such as *scienter* (the degree of knowledge of the obscenity of a material adjudged obscene required to find its seller criminally liable),[7] the proper warrant procedures for search and seizure,[8] the propriety of circuilating state-created lists of "obscene" works,[9] and the scope of permissible prior restraints.[10] In all of these cases (except one),[11] the Court made it more cumbersome to proscribe material believed to be obscene. One contemporary interpretation of these decisions stressed a perceived difference between the Court's procedural and substantive holdings. From this perspective, "the failure of the U.S. Supreme Court in its opinions between 1957 and 1966 to get across the idea that a reversal on procedural grounds was in no way a reflection of the majority's views on the obscenity of the subject matter, or the criminal culpability of the purveyors involved."[12] Another view, prevalent in law reviews[13] and adopted by the President's Commission on Obscenity and Pornography (1971), linked these decisions to the Court's evolving reading of *Roth* and contended that the Court was liberalizing obscenity law—more narrowly defining the abstract category of the legally obscene.

The Warren Court's substantive obscenity decisions—those that spoke directly to the standard for determining obscenity—complemented its procedural liberalization, albeit in an ungainly and confusing manner. At the core of this development were modifications of the *Roth* test. In *Manual Enterprises* v. *Day* (1962), a plurality—finding that materials suggesting homosexuality "cannot be deemed so offensive on their face as to affront current standards of decency" (370 U.S., p. 482)—held that works must be "patently offensive" to be obscene under *Roth*. In *Jacobellis* v. *Ohio* (1964), the Court reversed an obscenity conviction against a film (*The Lovers*). Justice Brennan, writing for a plurality, formally added "patent offensiveness" to the *Roth* standard and further required materials condemned as obscene to be "utterly without redeeming social importance" (378 U.S., p. 191). Two years later, in *Memoirs* v. *Massachusetts* (1966), a Brennan-led plurality reaffirmed the *Jacobellis* innovations and extended it by concluding that the community comprehended by the *Roth* approach was national in scope. In short, the libertarian dicta of *Roth* gradually seeped into the Court's subsequent applications of this formerly proscriptionist test.[14]

The post-*Roth* liberalization of the Court's obscenity doctrine, however, was not coherent, for the Court fractionalized on the appropriate test. Indeed, nine years after *Roth*, various justices subscribed to five different obscenity tests (Magrath, 1966). Brennan's *Jacobellis* reformulation, for example, never truly defined the law; Justice Goldberg endorsed it immediately, and Chief Justice Warren embraced it in *Memoirs*,[15] but it never commanded majority support on the Court. However, as long as Brennan held these justices to his test, Black and Douglas stuck to their absolutism,[16] and Stewart employed his "hard-core" standard,[17] Brennan's test was the constitutional least common denominator. This configuration of positions had the effect of loosening, de facto, *Roth*'s definition of obscenity, protecting a broadened range of sexual material, and making obscenity convictions more difficult to secure.

This awkward coalition of justices, and the doctrinal liberalization it yielded, characterized subsequent Warren Count decisions. In *Redrup* v. *New York* (1967), the Court reversed, per curiam, an obscenity conviction. The opinion admitted that the justices could not agree on a specific definition of obscenity but that under their various tests the material at issue was not obscene: there was no "pandering,"[18] no thrusting on nonconsenting adults, and no sale to children.[19] Over the next four years, the Court summarily reversed 32 cases simply by citing *Redrup*. These developments, combined with the logic of *Stanley* v. *Georgia* (1969),[20] moved the Court toward a rejection of *Roth*'s major premise—that there was a definable class of obscene material that lay beyond constitutional protection (Katz, 1969; Engdahl, 1969). The demise of the *Roth* approach seemed to be close at hand.

Miller's Reaffirmation of *Roth*: The Return of Proscriptionist Concerns

Richard Nixon effectively halted the Supreme Court's movement toward an "end of obscenity" (Rembar, 1968). He campaigned against the expansive holdings of the Warren Court[21] and, during his first term as president, filled four vacancies on the Court with appointments that weakened the Court's libertarian bloc.[22] In *Miller* v. *California* (1973)[23]—the Court's first obscenity case decided with all the new justices in place—Chief Justice Burger, joined by the other Nixon appointees and Justice White, held that the Warren Court had diverged from *Roth*, rejected its liberalization of obscenity doctrine, and reformulated the obscenity test:

(a) whether the "average person, applying contemporary community standards" would find that the work, taken as a whole, appeals to the prurient interest; (b) whether the work depicts or describes, in a patently offensive way, sexual conduct specifically designated by applicable state law; and (c) whether the work, taken as a whole, lacks serious literary, artistic, political, or scientific value (413 U.S., p. 24).

The *Miller* opinion, the first since *Roth* to articulate a definition of obscenity to which a majority of justices agreed, made three significant doctrinal changes. First, to facilitate increased prosecution, it substituted *local* for *national* community standards.[24] Second, it discarded the "utterly without redeeming social value" prong of *Jacobellis* and *Memoirs* and protected only work with "serious" value of specified types. This narrowed the net of protection into which sexual materials could fall and broadened the permissible scope of governmental regulation. Finally, in *Paris Adult Theatre* v. *Slaton* (1973), the Court refused to extend the consenting adults logic of *Redrup* and *Stanley*; obscenity could be proscribed regardless of the existence of a willing audience. In short, *Miller* signaled the Court's intention to leave the determination of obscenity to local authorities and thereby diminished the oversight role of the federal courts in this area of law.

Some scholars argue that *Miller* and its progeny did little to change obscenity law (Wasby, 1976; Schauer, 1976). This conclusion finds some support in Brennan's dissent in *Paris Adult Theatre*: "The differences between this [*Miller*] approach and the three-pronged *Memoirs* test are, for the most part, academic" (413 U.S., p. 95). However, in rejecting the *Miller* approach, Brennan also contended that the new test, although consistent in *form* with its predecessor, was "nothing less than a rejection of the fundamental First Amendment premises and rationale of the *Roth* opinion and an invitation to widespread suppressions of sexually oriented speech" (413 U.S., p. 97). Indeed, Brennan—following the logic of the Warren Court precedents—dissented in the 1972 term cases. By *Miller*, he (joined by Marshall, Stewart, and Douglas) had come to the conclusion that *any* suppression of what was arguably obscene material, unless forced on unconsenting adults or children, violated the values of the First Amendment, values that decision had failed to protect adequately.

Not all post-*Miller* decisions favored proscription,[25] but those that did not were exceptions. The Court's few libertarian decisions came at *Miller*'s margins; the doctrinal changes it worked were substantial and were strengthened by subsequent decisions.[26] Indeed, most of these decisions can be seen as dotting the *i*'s and crossing the *t*'s of the approach ushered in by *Miller*. The 1981 appointment of Justice O'Connor, whose proscriptionist vote replaced Stewart's libertarian one, further cemented these gains. Reagan's additions of Scalia and Kennedy have left *Miller*'s position secure.[27] In sum, by explicitly rejecting the doctrinal and decisional trends of the 1960s, the Burger Court returned obscenity law to the proscriptionist moorings of *Roth*.

An examination of the Court's treatment of obscenity issues before and after *Miller* demonstrates the empirical effect of its doctrinal change. Table 1.1 shows that the Warren Court supported libertarian claims in 78 percent

Table 1.1
Outcomes of Obscenity Litigation before the Supreme Court, 1957–1987

	Libertarian		Proscriptionist		Other	
	n	%	n	%	n	%
Warren Court (1957-71) (n=74)	58	(78%)	11	(15%)	5	(7%)
Burger Court (1972-87) (n=45)	10	(22%)	24	(53%)	11	(24%)

Total number of cases = 119
Individual cases and coding from appendix D

of its decisions, the Burger Court in only 22 percent.[28] It is arguable that this shift was prompted by the increased obscenity of the material reviewed by the Court,[29] but this ignores the doctrinal changes imposed by *Miller* and the minimal review function it mandates. In terms of doctrine and results, *Miller* had a lasting impression on the law and, as we shall see, the groups active in the litigation of obscenity issues.

OBSCENITY LITIGATION, GROUP THEORY, AND EXPECTATIONS

Over the 30 years covered by this study, 24 groups litigated obscenity questions (see table 1.2). Their orientation to these issues was dichotomous: before the Supreme Court they took positions that consistently either favored (pro-decency) or opposed (libertarian) proscription.[30] Beyond these similarities, the groups—especially those in the libertarian category—differed on other dimensions relevant to their political posture, for example, interest, focus, membership concerns, and maintenance needs. Given these differences, the density of the litigating field, and the "natural experiment" made possible by *Miller*, the use of group theory concepts allows this study to investigate the links between influencing factors and litigation choices more systematically than previous studies and to tie its findings to more general concerns with group behavior.

The Shape of Group Litigation: Scholarly Perspectives

Organizational litigation of obscenity issues is part of a larger phenomenon: the use of the courts by groups to achieve their goals. The systematic study of this phenomenon is of rather recent scholarly interest. Traditional legal

Table 1.2
Supreme Court Participation of Groups in Obscenity Cases, 1957–1987

	% cases in which group participated
Libertarian Groups	
Adult Film Association of America (AFAA)	6% (4 of 67)*
American Booksellers Association (ABA)	9% (11 of 119)
American Civil Liberties Union (ACLU)	25% (30 of 119)
American Library Association/Freedom to Read	
Foundation (ALA/FRF)	13% (15 of 119)
American Society of Journalists and Authors (ASJA)	1% (1 of 119)
Association of American Publishers (AAP)	21% (25 of 119)
Authors League of America (AL)	13% (15 of 119)
Council for Periodical Distributors Association (CPDA)	13% (15 of 119)
Direct Mail Advertising Association (DMAA)	1% (1 of 119)
Directors Guild of America (DGA)	1% (1 of 119)
First Amendment Lawyers Association (FALA)	5% (3 of 64)*
Media Coalition (MC)	35% (11 of 31)*
Motion Picture Association of America (MPAA)	6% (7 of 119)
National Association of Theater Owners (NATO)	3% (3 of 119)
Outdoor Advertising Association (OAA)	1% (1 of 119)
Video Software Dealers Association (VSDA)	10% (1 of 10)
Volunteer Lawyers for the Arts (VLA)	1% (1 of 67)*
Proscriptionist Groups	
Citizens for Decency through Law (CDL)	24% (29 of 119)
Covenant House/Institute for Youth Advocacy (CH/IYA)	5% (2 of 41)*
Freedom Council Foundation (FCF)	12% (1 of 8)*
Morality in Media (MM)	5% (5 of 107)*
National Institute of Municipal Law Officers (NIMLO)	1% (1 of 119)
National League of Cities (NLC)	1% (1 of 119)
National Legal Foundation (NLF)	12% (1 of 8)*

---

*Numbers in parentheses represent the number of cases in which the group participated compared with the number of cases in which it could have participated during this period. For AFAA (1969), CH/IYA (1972), FALA (1970), FCF (1983), MC (1973), MM (1962), NLF (1984), VSDA (1981), and VLA (1969). The latter numbers are smaller than for the other groups because they were founded after the Roth (1957) decision.

models find the subject incomprehensible and cannot provide an analytical framework for its examination: *individuals* bring cases to courts, and courts decide these cases through applications of *law* to *fact*. Early behavioral approaches, in focusing on the political preferences and characteristics of the *judges* deciding these cases, left little room for consideration of the effect of external factors on the resolution of judicial questions. Thus, for want of adequate focus and conceptual categorization, both traditional and behavioral approaches to legal study long neglected group pressure, as exerted through the courts. This is not to say, however, that the tools for mining the depths of group penetration of the judiciary were completely lacking. With the advent of the pluralist paradigm, it was only a question of time before the judicial activity of groups was unearthed and investigated.

Because it focuses on groups as the unit of analysis, the pluralist perspective invites a close examination of organizational involvement in the courts. The founder of this approach, Arthur Bentley, contended in his pathbreaking study, *The Process of Government*, that there were "numerous instances of the same group pressures which operate through executives and legislatures, operating through supreme courts" (1908, p. 338). This important insight suffered through an extended period of scholarly dormancy until it was resurrected by David Truman in *The Governmental Process* (1951, 1971). Although he did not examine this phenomenon empirically, Truman did hold that the group activity that animated American politics extended into the judiciary.

Relations between interest groups and judges are not identical with those between groups and legislators or executive officials, but the difference is rather one of degree than of kind. For various reasons organized groups are not so continuously concerned with courts and court decisions as they are with the functions of the other branches of government, but the impact of diverse interests upon judicial behavior is no less marked. (Truman, 1971, p. 479)

Gradually, students of the judiciary heeded Truman's invitation to investigate the linkages between groups and the courts. Initially, this work focused on high-profile issue areas in which politically disadvantaged groups (Cortner, 1968) sought to overcome recalcitrance in other governmental institutions. This early focus is readily understandable. It makes sense that groups lacking clout in more traditionally political institutions would turn to the courts in an effort to gain hearing for their concerns. Additionally, many "progressive" causes got their policy impetus in this manner. These orienting factors are amply displayed in the first study of this kind: Clement Vose's *Caucasians Only* (1959). Vose examined the successful litigation campaign waged by the NAACP to overturn state enforcement of restrictive covenants in the sale of private housing. With careful documentation and close analysis, Vose demonstrated that a group could—indeed, *did*—undertake a program of planned litigation to achieve its desired policy goal through the courts.

Despite the significance of Vose's study, scholarly analysis of group litigation did not explode in the 1960s. Although Morgan's work (1968) on the adjudication of church-state questions, Cortner's examination of reapportionment litigation (1968, 1970), and Barker's canvass of third-party litigation (1967) treated group participation in the judicial arena, broad-ranging investigation of this phenomenon was slow to take hold. Added to this was the "debunking" work undertaken by Nathan Hakman (1966). Taking the Truman-Vose pluralist view of the judicial process as the prevailing wisdom, Hakman concluded that group pressure on the courts was minimal and generally unimportant in conditioning the development of legal policy. He argued that, at least for the 1928–66 period he reviewed, group involvement in cases decided by the Supreme Court was nearly nonexistent; thus, the newly emerged conventional wisdom was merely "scholarly folklore."

Hakman's attempted debunking may, in fact, have spurred further examination of group use of the courts. In the 1970s, scholarly attention to this topic burgeoned. Vose again came to the fore with his *Constitutional Change* (1972), a work that discussed group-driven politics over a wide range of historical periods and issue areas. Kluger's (1975) compelling study of the NAACP's efforts to undermine the "separate but equal" doctrine of *Plessy* v. *Ferguson* (1896), at least as it applied to public education, announced a further resurgence of interest in this area. Cowan's (1976) piece on the ACLU's "Women's Rights Project" further nurtured this rebirth. But perhaps it was Sorauf's (1976) masterful chronicling of the web of groups entangled in establishment clause litigation that marked the return to scholarly focus on group litigation. Sorauf's rendering of this topic left little doubt that group pressures, from both the political right and left, were present and substantial in this contentious policy arena. Hakman's "folklore" was bowing in the face of these studies showing bountiful group involvement in the litigation of significant issues of public policy.

The conclusions pressed by Vose and Sorauf were reinforced by later studies of group-court linkages in other areas of law. O'Connor (1980) demonstrated that women's organizations had long used judicial strategies and tactics to advance their policy agendas. Rubin's (1987) study of abortion politics detailed the group pressures extant in that area, in both legal and more traditionally political institutions. The judicial activities of organized advocates of the rights of the handicapped were examined by Olson (1981, 1984). More generally, Epstein (1985) eschewing an issue-specific approach, showed that politically conservative groups also used the courts to advance political interests in a broad range of issue areas. Scholars who addressed group litigation from a more systemic perspective also demonstrated a concerted group penetration of the courts. For example, O'Connor and Epstein (1982) found a massive increase in amicus curiae participation as the 1960s gave way to the 1970s. Caldeira and Wright (1988) found substantial group involvement in the certiorari process and argued that the presence of organized litigants corresponds with a greater inclination of the Supreme Court to docket cases for plenary review. Thus, not only are groups active in litigation, but their presence seems to be important to the courts to which they appeal. Clearly, Hakman's folklore is, now, no more.[31]

These studies tell us much about group penetration of the courts and the politicization of the judicial process. We now know that groups regularly approach the judiciary for much the same reasons they court other branches of the political system: to pursue their organizational goals. Further, these goals vary over group and issue area. The literature articulates three distinguishable categories of these goals. Some groups seek *immediate victory*; that is to say, they enter into litigation largely to rectify a specific, present problem. Olson's (1981, 1984) treatment of handicapped rights groups and Cortner's (1968, 1970) examination of the coalitions challenging Tennessee's legislative apportionment scheme exemplify this litigation posture. Groups also enter the courts to facilitate their *organizational maintenance* and *development*. For example, Sorauf (1976) shows that Americans United for the Separation of Church and State joined the litigation fray in part to establish itself as the preeminent sectarian defender of the First Amendment. This, in turn, was intended to hold current group members and attract new ones. Pursuit of this goal implies a belief on the part of the group that its image and general information functions are at least as important as legal victory (Casper, 1972a; Kluger, 1975; Cowan, 1976).

Finally, groups can bring and join cases in an effort to establish broad-ranging *constitutional principles* generally protective of their interests. The civil rights litigation of the NAACP/LDF (Vose, 1959; Barker, 1967; Kluger, 1975) and the various civil liberties causes defended by the ACLU (Neier, 1979; Walker, 1990) are emblematic of this approach. This is the most weighty and dangerous goal that a group can seek: the most weighty because it has the potential to affect the largest population and is immune to legislative reversal; the most dangerous because an unfavorable decision not only loses the immediate case but also creates a precedent that may frustrate the future policy aspirations of a group. Although these categories are not mutually exclusive, they do provide convenient tools with which to analyze group litigation.

The judicial pursuit of these varied goals leads groups to develop a variety of litigation strategies. These strategies can be as elaborate as a comprehensive effort to seek out, sequence, and bring a series of cases to press legal development toward desired goals (Vose, 1959, 1972; Kluger, 1975; Epstein, 1985), as simple as waiting to join cases raising issues of importance to the group (Olson, 1981, 1984; Cortner, 1968, 1970), or somewhere in between (Sorauf, 1976; Epstein, 1985). The importance of these strategies is obvious: they structure an organization's judicial involvement—how, when, and to what degree it will participate in litigation (Wasby, 1983, p. 256).

Generally speaking, groups choose from three alternative litigation strategies: they can participate directly in litigation, come before the judiciary as an amicus curiae, or provide general support to the litigation of others with compatible interests and goals. Each of these approaches entails certain costs and benefits. Understanding these strategies, and the reasons for their selection, enables us to better understand and account for the extent and dynamics of the group litigation system.

Direct organizational involvement in public law litigation—what some term the *test case* strategy (Vose, 1959, 1972; Sorauf, 1976; Wasby, 1988)—provides a group its greatest opportunity to control and develop the direction of a legal policy area. Here, a group finds an aggrieved party, furnishes it counsel, and directs the litigation that results. By sponsoring a case (or a series of cases in a litigation campaign), a group can establish the factual context, the issue configuration, and, in some instances, the initial court environment (e.g., state or federal, jurisdictional) that it believes will best allow it to pursue its goals through the judiciary. The most renowned instances of this strategy, of course, are the campaigns of the NAACP/LDF in undermining and reversing unfavorable policy in areas such as housing (Vose, 1959) and public education (Kluger, 1975), but other groups—for example, the National Consumers' League which litigated in defense of its legislative victories establishing maximum hour and minimum wage statutes (Vose, 1972)—also followed this course. Groups were also instrumental in advancing death penalty (Meltsner, 1973), gender discrimination (Cowan, 1976; O'Connor, 1980), and abortion (Rubin, 1987) issues to the immediate attention of the Supreme Court.

Although direct sponsorship of litigation allows a group its greatest degree of say in the legal development of issues of organizational interest, this strategy also imposes substantial costs. Perhaps most obvious is the monetary expense of pursuing a case through its origination, trial, and appellate stages. Additionally, this approach requires a group to commit a substantial portion of its other resources (e.g, attorneys, staff, fund-raising efforts) to a single point of organizational concern, diminishing its ability to develop and pursue other items on its agenda. In short, the trade-off here is one between control and resource distribution and depletion.

Participation as an amicus curiae—literally, as a "friend of the court" and not an immediate party to the suit—provides groups another participatory avenue. Amicus curiae briefs originated in English judicial practice as a kind of "oral 'Shepardizing' " (Krislov, 1963, p. 695), a way of informing courts of legal developments of which they might otherwise be unaware. American legal practice, however, saw this kind of third-party participation evolve from "neutral" assistance to advocacy on behalf of one of the parties to the suit. Thus, by the early 1900s, a wide variety of actors—for example, governments, private citizens, interest groups—were able to present their concerns to the courts without assuming the immense costs of bringing cases themselves. Although the legal relevance and permissibility of this type of participation was a subject of some debate among Supreme Court justices, and although the practices surrounding the filing of amicus briefs formally underwent substantial restrictive revisions in 1937, 1949, and 1954, it is now commonplace for parties not directly connected to a specific case to express their positions to the courts as amici (Krislov, 1963). Indeed, the Court's acceptance of—perhaps even its invitation to—this type of participation is demonstrated by O'Connor and Epstein (1983), who found that between 1969 and 1981, the Court denied only 11 percent of the 832 petitions filed seeking amicus status.

The current rules governing participation as an amicus curiae are nicely summarized by Caldeira and Wright (1988, p. 1113).

To qualify as an *amicus curiae*, a nonparty must show that it has a substantial interest in the legal question and must file a motion and brief in a "timely" fashion. Governments may of course participate as *amici* without leave of the parties (Rule 36.4). Others may do so with the permission of the parties. If the parties refuse to permit a nonparty to submit a brief, the hopeful *amicus* may file for a motion with the Supreme Court for leave to submit a brief.

These Court-created rules go far toward explaining the attractiveness of amicus involvement to groups. By filing a brief in support of one of the parties to an established suit, a group can convey its concerns to the courts either of its own volition or at the request of one of the formal litigants. This participatory path presents a comparatively low-cost option for a group desirous of promoting its goals through litigation without the expense—monetary and organizational—of initiating its own litigation. To this end, the group can *endorse* the position of its favored litigant by repeating and amplifying the most important—from the group's perspective—arguments, or it can *supplement* arguments tendered by the formal litigant with those in which the group places primary importance (Krislov, 1963, p. 713). This tact has the further utility of informing a court of the range of interests affected by its decision, in essence making the court aware of the existence and concerns of an array of organized interests in the larger legal and political environment.

In confronting the courts with a group's goals and concerns, amicus participation accomplishes some of the ends of the sponsorship strategy. However, this approach is not without its own costs. The resource savings it affords come at the expense of a group's ability to develop the contours of the cases it joins—the factual setting and issues at the base of the legal controversy, the jurisdiction in which the case is pursued, and the arguments that shape the litigation both at trial and on appeal. In short, a group participating as an amicus curiae is fixing its argument to a wagon of someone else's design, and there is no guarantee that this wagon is the appropriate vehicle for the group to ride to achieve its goals. This deficiency, this lack of control over the comportment of the case, can limit a group's ability to guide or influence the development of judicial policy.

In addition to sponsoring test cases or participating in the judicial process as amici curiae, groups can also provide generalized support to the litigation of other organizations or citizens. The avenues for this kind of involvement are many. They include giving legal advice to others litigating in areas of group interest (Kluger, 1975), intervening on behalf of litigants with common concerns (Sorauf, 1976), providing data and testimony supportive of organizational goals (Vose, 1959, 1972), helping to fund the litigation of others

(Vose, 1981), and arranging and orchestrating publicity—both general (e.g., organizing "political" demonstrations, placing articles in newspapers, making group officials available to media outlets) and more targeted (e.g., lobbying governmental officials and opinion leaders, writing pieces for law reviews) (Vose, 1959; Scheingold, 1974; Kluger, 1975; Sorauf, 1976)—supportive of the group's concerns.

The attractiveness of this highly indirect participatory mode lies in its inexpensiveness: groups need not sink scarce resources into substantial litigation campaigns. The costs of this approach are, however, imposing: the group has minimal control over the development of the case as it makes its way through the courts. If a group has significant interests in the outcome of litigation, this type of judicial involvement may well prove insufficient to protect or advance them, unless the primary handlers of the case are extremely effective and sophisticated litigators. In general, therefore, the further removed a group's participation from the case itself, the less its control over a development and resolution consistent with organizational goals. Thus, groups with strong interests at stake in the judicial arena will seldom rely solely on this approach, using it to supplement the more active strategies of sponsorship and amicus participation.

As reviewed above, the emerging literature on group litigation is descriptively rich. We know that groups can and do use the courts as part of their organizational and political life, that different groups seek to advance different kinds of goals through this involvement, and that they develop strategies to guide their forays into the judiciary. In sum, groups have been an important part of the politicization of the courts and law. This being said, however, the literature is plagued by a lack of longitudinal and theoretical depth. It tends to focus on groups that are disadvantaged in more traditional political forums and that successfully attain their goals through the judiciary. Little consideration has been given to what groups do after they attain their goals or are stymied by hostile courts. Similarly underdeveloped is the litigation of what may be termed *advantaged* group actors—those with good access to the "usual" paths of politics.[32] Also unexamined is the behavior of organizational litigators in times of legal flux, in contexts marked by instability or change in judicial approach. In short, the extant literature provides analytic snapshots of group litigation, but it lacks an awareness of the dynamics— the give-and-take that characterizes a pluralist system—of that litigation over time. Indeed, we know little of the dynamics of group litigation *because we have looked for little that is dynamic* in it.

This deficiency is a part of a larger problem: few studies consciously integrate their empirical findings into a theoretical perspective. Factors that condition group behavior have been articulated, but they have not been placed into an organizing framework. This leaves us with a collection of isolated case studies and underplays the relationship between group behavior and the general context in which groups operate. The first problem renders the study of group litigation interesting, but not theoretically useful; the second causes scholars to miss an important aspect of the dynamics and vastness of this litigation. A more conscious use of group theory can mitigate these problems.

There is no monolithic group theory, but scholars since Olson (1965) have added to the sophistication of Truman's pluralism. A central insight of this recent work is that not all groups are intrinsically political; many exist for essentially private purposes. Two *organizational types* have been suggested. *Purposive* groups "work explicitly for the benefit of some larger public or society as a whole and not . . . chiefly for the benefit of members, except insofar as members derive a sense of fulfilled commitment or enhanced personal worth from the effort" (Wilson, 1973, p. 46). In essence, these groups are organized around inclusive interests that are explicitly political in nature. On the other hand, *material* groups exist to promote the exclusive interests of their members. Political activity is not their raison d'etre but is a by-product of organizational wealth (Olson, 1965). It stands to reason that these differences in group type would be reflected in the litigation posture of groups, but this hypothesis has never been tested systematically.

Both group types are present in obscenity litigation. For example, the American Civil Liberties Union (ACLU), Citizens for Decency through Law (CDL), and Morality in Media (MM) are purposive actors. Their member-ship incentives are purely political—the provision of public goods (appro-priate public policy) for all. For the ACLU, this means the protection of sexually oriented materials under a broad understanding of First Amendment freedoms; for CDL and MM, this entails the suppression of such (obscene) material for the long-term good of the moral climate of society. The material groups litigating obscenity fall into two sub-types: *commercial* and *professional*. The former—for example, the Adult Film Association of America (AFAA), the American Booksellers Association (ABA), and Media Coalition (MC)—exist to protect the economic profitability of their members. The latter—for example, the Association of American Publishers (AAP), the American Li-brary Association (ALA), and the Authors League of America (AL)—promote professional norms for specific occupational strata.[33] These groups differ from their purposive counterparts on two dimensions: their interest in obscenity politics is primarily exclusive (narrow), and their goals are essentially material (economic and vocational). This is not to say that the effects of their political actions are confined to their members but that they are undertaken for reasons that differ from those animating purposive groups. Again, it seems reasonable to suppose that these differences are relevant to their political behavior.

The group theory literature shows that different group types manifest different organizational relationships relevant to political action (Olson, 1965; Salisbury, 1969; Wilson, 1973; Moe, 1980, 1981), but this insight has not been incorporated into litigation studies. Although these self-consciously theoretical works largely focus on membership incentives and do not speak

Table 1.3
Frequency of Group Participation in Supreme Court Obscenity Litigation,
1957–1987

	Libertarian		Proscriptionist	
	n	%	n	%
Pre-Miller 1957-73 (n=88)	31	(35%)	17	(19%)
Post-Miller 1973-87 (n=32)	20	(63%)	17	(53%)
Total Group Participation (N=119)	51	(43%)	34	(29%)

N represents the total number of obscenity cases formally decided by the Supreme
Court.

to the *kinds* of actions that groups undertake, they do suggest a focal point
for the analysis of that behavior. Organizational type, in orienting a group
to its general environment, *should* condition the group's political (including
judicial) decisions. For example, purposive groups might act differently than
those organized on the basis of material incentives. Given the *Miller* shift
and the large number of groups it affected, obscenity litigation presents a
unique opportunity to explore some of the linkages between group type and
behavior in a context of legal change. An examination of this rich and dynamic
issue area, then, promises to advance our understanding of both group litigation *and* the larger context into which its study fits. This, in turn, can
provide more substance and theoretical depth to our understanding of an
important development in the conduct of American politics: the growing
politicization of the judicial process.

Groups and Obscenity: Descriptive and Theoretical Concerns

The groups examined in this study use litigation as a tool to influence the
development of obscenity law. Table 1.3 notes the frequency of their participation (sponsor or amicus) in cases decided by the Supreme Court. These
data do hide some important information. First, they speak only to Supreme
Court cases and say nothing about lower court litigation. Second, the pre-
Miller count includes 46 summary dispositions of obscenity cases—decisions
on the merits without formal argument.[34] As a result, interested groups may

have lacked adequate opportunity to participate in these cases. If so, the data undercount organizational interest. Third, the data do not count participation in cases denied certiorari. This particularly discounts the efforts of CDL, the preeminent pro-decency litigator.[35] These caveats registered, the data *do* demonstrate three things: there was substantial group participation in this litigation; these groups represented the political right and left; and the rate of participation increased after *Miller*.

Given these findings, several questions are suggested. Why did the post-*Miller* surge in litigation occur? Was it consistent over all groups? Was it present only in Supreme Court litigation, or did it permeate other levels of the judiciary? Did *Miller* alter the goals, strategies, or activities of litigating groups? If so, how and in what ways? What factors influenced this adaptation? In short, what effect does a major environmental upheaval have on group litigation? Because previous studies did not use longitudinal designs to examine dense litigation fields, they could not address these and related questions. Obscenity—because of its high levels of group involvement and the natural experiment created by *Miller*—affords an excellent opportunity to analyze questions arising out of the dynamism of ongoing organizational litigation.

Groups had three possible responses to *Miller*: continuance, mobilization, and exit. Continuance can take one of two forms: groups can continue their previous behavior, or they can adapt their goals and strategies to the new context. Mobilization entails the actualization of latent groups or the activation of those previously uninvolved. Exit allows groups to leave or de-emphasize one issue area and participate in others, or not at all. Group reaction to *Miller* includes all three adaptive responses. What factors conditioned these choices? A useful distinction is between those internal (group-specific) and external (contextual) to a group.

Because it orients a group to its environment, organizational type is an internal factor central to group behavior. It organizes other group-specific variables: purpose, interests, maintenance needs, and goals. We might expect groups with narrower and more specific interests to mobilize in the face of a threat, and those with more broadly based political concerns to turn to others when one could not be attained. This should be especially true for purposive groups, which, because of their public focus, tend to pursue broad judicial pronouncements. However, continuance or mobilization might be the response of purposive groups if the relevant issue is critical to their maintenance. Material groups would be expected to go to court only when threats to their specific, exclusive interests emerge. For groups that do not perceive an increased threat, the continuance of established behavior would be expected.

Group-specific factors interact with the environment to condition behavior. Threat is an important part of this environment. We would expect extant groups, for which start-up costs are not an issue, to mobilize in order to defuse threats directed at them. Threat is a function of social, legal, and political context, the existence of other active litigators, and the deportment of the courts. Once a threat to a group's interests is defused, the group would presumably exit; an ongoing threat would induce continued litigation.

This study uses these group-specific and contextual factors to examine group participation in obscenity litigation during a time of extreme legal change to assess litigation choices and explain the dynamics of the resulting behavior. This enables it to address questions left unanswered by studies that focus on areas of law less densely populated and more doctrinally stable. The *Miller* shift opened new possibilities to organized litigators; it also provides an opportunity to study the fluidity of the group litigation system and the factors that account for that dynamism. This study exploits this opportunity in an effort to broaden our understanding of the forces working on group litigation patterns.

CONCLUSION

In addition to exploring a neglected area of group litigation, this study seeks to demonstrate two things: the dynamism and vastness of the group litigation system and the centrality of legal context to its operation. To this end, it uses the natural experiment created by the *Miller* decision as a window through which to observe the dynamics of organizational litigation. It incorporates concepts central to group theory to clarify the factors, and the relationship between those factors, that give structure to systems of organizational litigation.

This approach allows us to separate idiosyncratic behavior from that of a more generalized nature and provides a more systematic base from which to analyze litigation as a component of group behavior. It also suggests a framework for the comparative study of the interaction between groups and the Warren and the Burger-Rehnquist courts in other unstable policy areas—for example, criminal justice or civil rights and liberties. Such studies could extend our understanding of the contours of the group system and the fluidity that exists within it and could put the empirical study of group litigation back where it belongs—in the rubric of group theory.

The literature shows that groups pursue their goals through the courts, but it does not discuss the effect of a radical change in legal context on this behavior. The design of this study, the variety and number of groups involved in this litigation, and the intervention of *Miller* allow this research to fill this gap. Its findings identify some group-specific and contextual factors that condition group litigation choices and suggest the need to incorporate the dynamic interplay between these factors and group behavior into our thinking. The development of a conceptual framework integrating group-specific and contextual factors relevant to organizational actions would provide a hub for a more systematic study of group litigation and a basis for a more generalized explanation of this phenomenon.

NOTES

1. Although this division is a simplistic summary of the development of First Amendment doctrine, it is sufficient for the purposes of this study. On such distinctions, see Meiklejohn (1948, 1961), Brennan (1965), and Bork (1971).

2. Two common examples of unprotected categories of expression are "fighting words" (*Chaplinsky* v. *New Hampshire,* 1942) and libel (*New York Times* v. *Sullivan,* 1964). Commercial speech was another such area until it was given First Amendment protection in *Virginia State Board* v. *Virginia Citizens Council* (1976).

3. Some federal judges did attempt modifications. See Judge Learned Hand, *U.S.* v. *Kennerley* (1913) and *U.S.* v. *Levine* (1936); Judge Woolsey, *U.S.* v. *Ulysses* (1933); and Judge Augustus Hand, *U.S.* v. *Dennett* (1930).

4. *Roth* upheld a conviction under the Comstock Act. Also decided by this opinion was a companion case, *Alberts* v. *California* (1957), which sustained a state law prohibiting the sale of obscene material.

5. *Mounce* v. *U.S.* (1957), *Times-Film* v. *Chicago* (1957), *One* v. *Olesen* (1957), and *Sunshine Books* v. *Summerfield* (1957).

6. In making this distinction, I am not unaware of the persuasive argument of Professor Laurence Tribe (1980). The distinction between procedure and substance is somewhat artificial, and Tribe is quite correct in noting the substantive underpinnings of procedural mechanisms. However, the distinction is useful for present purposes insofar as it parallels the path traveled by the Court. Indeed, the Warren Court's liberalization of the "procedural" aspects of obscenity proscription had a substantive impact in practice—it made the prosecution of obscenity increasingly difficult, thus extending the constitutional protection afforded this expression.

7. See *Smith* v. *California* (1959).

8. See *Marcus* v. *Search Warrant* (1961) and *Quantity of Books* v. *Kansas* (1964).

9. See *Bantam Books* v. *Sullivan* (1963).

10. See *Times-Film* v. *Chicago* (1961) and *Freedman* v. *Maryland* (1965).

11. In *Times-Film* v. *Chicago* (1961), the Court held, 5–4, that not all prior restraints on movie presentation were unconstitutional. However, in *Freedman* v. *Maryland* (1965), it held that such restraints, absent strict safeguards to protect First Amendment interests, were impermissible. This ruling, blunting the decision in *Times-Film,* was later reiterated and broadened in *Teitel Films* v. *Cusak* (1968) and *Interstate Circuit, Inc.* v. *Dallas* (1968).

12. Amicus curiae brief of Citizens for Decent Literature in *Memoirs* v. *Massachusetts* (1966).

13. See, for example, Note (1966a, 1966b), Katz (1969), Note (1969–70), and Engdahl (1969). For a gleeful libertarian perspective, see Rembar (1968). Interestingly, the "Legal Panel" of the President's Commission on Obscenity and Pornography (1970) came to this conclusion as well in building its case for limiting obscenity regulation to unconsenting adults and minors.

14. This development—the doctrinal evolution away from the initial statement of the *Roth* test—was noted by, among others, Justices Clark and White. In *Memoirs,* they dissented, holding that the "utterly without social value" language in *Roth* was intended as a way to *define* obscenity, not as part of the test to *determine* it.

15. Justice Marshall, Goldberg's replacement, also endorsed the *Memoirs* test. See

his opinion in *Stanley* v. *Georgia* (1969) and his votes in the "Redrupping" sequence of cases.

16. This was first articulated in their *Roth* dissent.

17. Stewart introduced his approach to obscenity in *Jacobellis* (1964): "I shall not today attempt to define the kinds of material I understand to be embraced within that short-hand definition, and perhaps I could never succeed in intelligibly doing so. But I know it when I see it and this is not that" (378 U.S., p. 197). "It" was "hard-core" pornography.

18. The pandering concept was developed in *Ginzburg* v. *U.S.* (1966). Although that decision, as well as *Mishkin* v. *New York* (1966), was proscriptionist, they both are best understood as a reaction to public clamoring against the liberalizing trend of the law. See Pritchett (1968).

19. Sale to children was defined as a dimension of obscenity in *Ginsberg* v. *New York* (1966). See Krislov (1968).

20. In *Stanley* (1969) the Court held First Amendment and privacy interests to preclude criminalization of private possession of obscenity in one's home. Although formally distinguishing *Roth*, the decision called it into question; it gave obscenity, at least in this context, constitutional protection.

21. See his comments as reported in the *NYT*, 10 October 1968, 9 February 1969, 3 May 1969, and 12 August 1970.

22. In Nixon's first term, Hugo Black, Abe Fortas, and Earl Warren—all 'Redruppers"—were replaced by Lewis Powell, Harry Blackmun, and Warren Burger.

23. *Miller* is but the most prominent of the eight obscenity decisions—*Paris Adult Theatre* v. *Slaton*, *Kaplan* v. *California*, *U.S.* v. *12 Reels*, *U.S.* v. *Orito*, *Heller* v. *New York*, *Roaden* v. *Kentucky*, and *Alexander* v. *Virginia*—handed down at the end of the Court's 1972 term. All of these holdings rejected, 5–4, libertarian claims.

24. Local standards were later defined to be those of the vicinage from which the jurors in the trial would be drawn. See *Hamling* v. *U.S.* (1974) and *Smith* v. *U.S.* (1977).

25. For example, *Jenkins* v. *Georgia* (1974) reversed a Georgia state court obscenity conviction of the movie *Carnal Knowledge*; *Southeastern Promotions* v. *Conrad* (1975) reversed a city's denial to lease its theater to a traveling production of *Hair* on the grounds of the show's obscenity; and *Erznoznik* v. *Jacksonville* (1975) reversed a public nuisance conviction for an outdoor showing of a film containing nudity.

26. For example, *Hamling* v. *U.S.* (1974), *Young* v. *American Mini Theatres* (1976), *Smith* v. *U.S.* (1977), *New York* v. *Ferber* (1982), *Renton* v. *Playtime Theatres* (1986), and *Pope* v. *Illinois* (1987).

27. Scalia, although generally supportive of obscenity regulation, may be somewhat uneasy with *Miller*. Note his separate concurrence in *Pope* v. *Illinois* (1987) in which he concluded, "All of today's opinions, I suggest, display the need for reexamination of *Miller*" (106 S.Ct., p. 1923). Should Scalia ultimately reject the *Miller* formulation, this would still leave the Court supportive of its standard by at least a 5–4 margin. David Souter's replacement of William Brennan will probably further cement the *Miller* test.

28. This counts only formally decided cases where the Court rendered a substantive decision. This includes cases decided by full opinion and summary disposition. Certiorari denials are not counted because they lack legal substance.

29. The explicitness of these materials did increase over time. See Obscenity Law Project (1976), p. 889.

30. This dichotomization is not intended to imply that all proscriptionists or libertarians agree on all obscenity issues but merely to show a general similarity in perspective. Intracategory differences are present and are relevant to adaptive strategies.

31. It bears noting that Hakman's argument may have been incorrect, or at least incomplete, even when it was written. To note only two of its problems, it treated only amicus curiae participation; it did not address litigation sponsorship or the various indirect ways groups seek judicial influence (e.g., monetary grants to litigators, public demonstrations, authorship of law review articles, nomination of judges, etc.). Further, it weighted all cases equally; that is to say, it treated all cases as equivalent in policy importance. This is clearly not true, for even minimal group intervention in a few important issue areas (e.g., civil rights and civil liberties) can substantially alter public policy.

32. By *advantaged*, I mean essentially the opposite of Cortner's disadvantaged concept: groups that have easy access to (and legitimacy in) other governmental branches.

33. The material interests of commercial and professional groups are distinct but not, in all cases, mutually exclusive. One obvious point of overlap is that professional organizations *do* have commercial interests. The chapters that follow, however, note that the distinction tendered here has both empirical and conceptual content and utility.

34. See appendixes A, B, or C for a listing of these cases.

35. See chapter 2 and appendix C.

2

The Groups and Their Interests

Liberty, as a principle, had no application to any state of things anterior to the time when mankind have become capable of being improved by free and equal discussion. . . . But as soon as mankind have attained the capacity of being guided to their own improvement by conviction or persuasion . . . compulsion, either in the direct form or in that of pains and penalties for non-compliance, is no longer admissible as a means to their own good, and justifiable only for the security of others.
—John Stuart Mill, *On Liberty*

John Stuart Mill, if alive today, would realize that we do not live in the relaxed calm of the steamboat era.
—James J. Clancy, amicus curiae brief for Citizens for Decency through Law, *Jacobellis* v. *Ohio* (1964)

With a treasury of such titles as "Oriental Babysitter," "China Doll," "Oriental Treatment," "China Cat," and with U.S.-Red China trade opening up, there could be a lot of won-ton in the coffers of Adult Film Association producers-distributors. And that's American enterprise.
—David F. Friedman, Chairman of the Adult Film Association of America, 1979

Obscenity has long been on the agenda of American politics. Pro-decency groups began to spring up in the United States in the mid-nineteenth century.[1] This movement was more than an attempt to eradicate "dirty" books from city streets, and it centered on no single person. In fact, the proscription of obscene material was but one facet of a multipronged campaign by well-financed groups to build a more perfect society— a "City on the Hill"—in America. Two social historians on these aspects of this era, Paul S. Boyer (1968) and David J. Pivar (1973), argue that this movement arose from the ashes of the Civil War in response to generalized fears of urban drift and moral decay.

Initially energized in the postwar period by obscene materials and prostitution, nineteenth-century pro-decency organizations—for example, the Woman's Christian Temperance Union, the Boston Society of Morals and Religious Instruction of the Poor, the American Association for the Prevention of Licentiousness and Promotion of Morality, and various Sunday School societies—gradually broadened their focus to include the education and protection of women and children and the prevention of crime. These and other groups worked through private and governmental channels to improve the moral tone of society. Anthony Comstock's Society for the Suppression of Vice, founded in 1873, is perhaps the most famous of these pro-decency organizations. Comstock and this group were the moving forces behind the first significant federal anti-obscenity legislation, an act barring the use of the mails to convey obscene materials. Passed in 1873, and surviving today with alterations and additions, the Comstock Act went through one hour of congressional debate and prompted complementary legislation in the states.[2]

In many ways, Comstock was the prototype progressive. In addition to fighting obscenity,[3] he used his group to battle prostitution, abortion, gambling, lotteries, liquor, and quack medicine. Although New York newspapers ridiculed his more overzealous actions—the suppression of aesthetic nudes, art school manuals, and "classic" literature—they generally supported his work. Indeed, at the time, groups like Comstock's were seen by many to be the vanguard of philanthropic reform.[4] Thus, it is a mistake to view such groups, historically speaking, as a haven for the politically right-wing.

The religious underpinnings of the pro-decency movement came to its fore in the 1930s as two agencies of the Catholic Church—the National Legion of Decency (NLD) and the National Office for Decent Literature (NODL)—formed to promote further moral appropriateness. Founded in 1933, the NLD was to preserve a wholesome motion picture industry. This agency and its local units coded films on their moral content and made these ratings available to the general public. The NODL, established in 1938, produced lists of books that it deemed acceptable and unacceptable for children.[5] These ratings and lists had no formal legal status, but libertarian critics such as the American Civil Liberties Union (ACLU) charged that these materials were informally given such status when used by police and prosecutors in the enforcement of obscenity laws.[6]

The first concerted challenge to proscriptionist domination of the law came in the late 1950s.[7] By this time the influence of the Catholic Church was waning in the face of profound societal changes. Legally, the Warren Court served notice in cases such as *Brown* v. *Board of Education* (1954), *Yates* v. *U.S.* (1957), and *Mapp* v. *Ohio* (1961) that it would actively protect its version of constitutionally guaranteed rights and liberties. Politically, the cautious conservativism of Dwight Eisenhower was giving way to the pragmatic liberalism of John Kennedy, and the civil rights movement stood poised to change the face of the nation. Socially, rock and roll and the beat generation symbolized a new restiveness and sense of alienation in American youth. In short, the comfortable conservativism of the 1950s ebbed as that decade rolled into the sixties. These social, political, and legal trends came together in, among other places, obscenity politics.

It was in this context that the modern politics of obscenity—its transformation from unchallenged morals regulation to contentious policy battles—began in the courts. With the assistance of groups such as the ACLU, the Association of American Publishers (AAP), and the Authors League of America (AL), *Butler* v. *Michigan* (1957), *Roth* v. *U.S.* (1957), and *Alberts* v. *California* (1957) were taken to the Supreme Court. In questioning the permissibility of obscenity regulation given the First Amendment's protection of speech and press, these groups ushered before the Court what became "the intractable obscenity problem" (*Manual Enterprises* v. *Day*, 1962, opinion of Harlan, J.). These and subsequent group actions put obscenity on the national political agenda. The legal successes (and their concomitant social effects) of these libertarian groups stimulated the organization and mobilization of national pro-decency groups—groups whose members and donors previously sat quietly in the early 1950s consensus on the "obvious correctness" of obscenity proscription. These libertarian and proscriptionist camps have dominated the organizational dimension of obscenity politics ever since.

Over the period covered in this study (1957–88), the pitch of this battle between the forces of freedom (permissiveness) and decency (suppression) grew more shrill.[8] In part this was a function of sociopolitical changes. Initial libertarian successes in the courts opened the door to greater availability of sexual material. This fed, and was in turn fed by, an increasingly open and morally tolerant society. Feeling their backs against the wall, proscriptionist groups mobilized and escalated their rhetoric and actions to stave off the "Romanization" of America. Concomitantly, libertarians pushed harder to fulfill their agenda—the end of state regulation of obscenity. As America and its politics grew more conservative in the 1970s and 1980s, and as proscriptionist concerns gained renewed credence in and out of government, libertarians scrambled to protect vestiges of their prior successes while pro-decency groups tried to stuff sexually explicit material back into the closet. In this effort, the latter received assistance from a new source—elements of the largely left-wing women's movement. With this, the language of sexual oppression was added to that of decency in opposition to the arguments of

conventional liberalism. This altered the dimensions of the conflict and escalated its rhetorical tenor.

The sociopolitical context, however, accounts for only a portion of the
rhetorical shrillness and political activity that characterize this policy debate:
economic factors also come into play. Once the Court opened the door to
liberalized expression, the production and provision of sex-oriented materials
became a multibillion-dollar business. Indeed, estimates of the yearly "take"
from one segment of this enterprise—theater presentation of X-rated films—
range as high as $500 million.[9] This kind of money virtually insures that
involved individuals and companies will continue production until forced to
stop, and gives them a strong incentive to fight efforts to restrict their commercial freedom. The advent of the videotape recorder, which provides a
means to view sexual videos in the privacy of one's home, further enhances
the commercial promise of these materials. Indeed, even today—when legal
barriers to the prosecution of obscenity are the lowest since the 1950s—
proscriptionists fear (and commercial purveyors hope) that their fight may
be lost if home use of these materials becomes socially accepted and legally
tolerated. As such, they continue to work to close the door while libertarians—for both philosophic and economic reasons—work to keep it open. The
legal and political battle, now over 30 years old, continues to rage.

To understand the dynamics that undergird group activity here, and to
assess the effect of the environmental upheaval occasioned by the Supreme
Court's conservative redefinition of obscenity in *Miller* v. *California* (1973)
on that activity, we first need to sketch in brief the interests and characteristics of the various libertarian and proscriptionist groups that have dominated
modern obscenity politics. The proscriptionists, because their concerns are
clearly and completely political and social, are all purposive—politically organized and committed—organizations. Their fight is to promote and preserve a preferred way of life for American society. The group interests
represented in the libertarian camp are more diverse, and this diversity—and
that in the factors relating to the organizations themselves—strongly condition their actions (or lack thereof). It is to these groups that we now turn.

LIBERTARIAN ORGANIZATIONS

Table 2.1 describes the involvement of libertarian groups in the Supreme
Court's obscenity decisions. An examination of all formal decisions, including
per curiam reversals tendered without benefit of oral argument, reveals group
activity in slightly less than half the cases. There was heavy participation—
two or more groups appearing in a given case—in more than a quarter of
these decisions. When we exclude summary judgments, organized libertarian
participation occurred in over 60 percent of these cases, with a heavy group
presence in slightly more than 40 percent of the Court's formal decisions.

Table 2.1
Libertarian Group Involvement before the Supreme Court in Obscenity Cases, 1957–1987

Number of Groups Appearing in Each Case	All Cases*		Not Counting Summary Reversals**	
	n	%	n	%
None	68	57%	29	38%
One	18	15%	16	21%
Two	9	8%	8	10%
Three or More	24	20%	24	31%
Total	119	100%	77	100%

* Includes all cases formally decided by the Court.
** Does not count the 42 cases summarily treated by the Court. Also does not include group activity in three of those cases -- Times Film (1957), Sunshine Books (1957), and Aday (1967).

Clearly, the organized libertarian activity in this area was substantial; it also was varied.

As table 2.2 indicates, the 17 groups working against restriction of sex-oriented materials are not monolithic in vision, interest, or behavior. A variety of different organizational types compose the libertarian camp: some are based on individual membership; others are trade associations. The modes of these groups also vary: two organizations have purposive bases of organization—they exist to promote a vision of a liberal individualist society—and 15 are organized around essentially material concerns. Further, not all material interests are conceptually equivalent: five groups are primarily moved to involvement by vocational concerns with political principles, and ten participate to protect commercial interests. Because group characteristics orient groups—both internally toward their constituents and externally toward their environment—the characteristics subsumed under these typological headings help to account for the varying levels of litigation involvement among these groups, both absolutely and before and after the *Miller* decision; they also aid in explaining the different strategies and tactics one sees in this policy area.

A Purposive Actor: The ACLU

Purposive groups, as defined in the literature (Wilson, 1973; Moe, 1980, 1981), come into existence to pursue public, political concerns. Although factors such as organizational maintenance are relevant to their strategic

Table 2.2
Libertarian Groups Involved in Obscenity Litigation before the Supreme Court, 1957–1987

	Organizational Type	Organizational Mode	% Participation*	Type of Participation
Adult Film Association of America (AFAA)	Trade Assoc.	Material-Com.	6%**	Amicus, Spons.
American Booksellers Association (ABA)	Trade Assoc.	Material-Com.	14%	Amicus, Spons. (and through MC)
American Civil Liberties Union (ACLU)	Ind. Memb.	Purposive	35%	Amicus, Spons.
American Library Association/Freedom to Read Foundation (ALA/FRF)	Ind. Memb.	Material-Prof.	19%	Amicus, Spons., Grants
American Society of Journalists and Authors (ASJA)	Trade Assoc.	Material-Prof.	1%	Amicus
Association of American Publishers (AAP)	Trade Assoc.	Material-Prof.	31%	Amicus, Spons., (and through MC)
Authors League of America (AL)	Ind. Memb.	Material-Prof.	19%	Amicus
Council for Periodical Distributors Association (CPDA)	Trade Assoc.	Material-Com.	19%	Amicus, Spons. (and through MC)

Direct Mail Advertising Association (DMAA)	Trade Assoc.	Material-Com.	1%	Amicus
Directors Guild of America (DGA)	Ind. Memb.	Material-Prof.	1%	Amicus
First Amendment Lawyers Association (FALA)	Ind. Memb.	Material-Com.	5%**	Amicus
Media Coalition (MC)	Trade Assoc.	Material-Com.	35%**	Amicus, Spons.
Motion Picture Association of America (MPAA)	Trade Assoc.	Material-Com.	9%	Amicus, Spons.
National Association of Theatre Owners (NATO)	Trade Assoc.	Material-Com.	4%	Amicus, Spons.
Outdoor Advertising Association (OAA)	Trade Assoc.	Material-Com.	1%	Amicus
Video Software Dealers Association (VSDA)	Trade Assoc.	Material-Com.	10%*	Amicus
Volunteer Lawyers for the Arts (VLA)	Ind. Memb.	Purposive	1%	Amicus

* Percentage includes only those cases formally decided after oral argument.

** Factors date of establishment (AFAA, 1969; VLA, 1969; FALA, 1970; MC, 1973; VSDA, 1981) into percentage calculation.

choices, their animating avenue of activity is the provision of public policy
goods they deem desirable for a population beyond active group members.
Two such groups participated in obscenity litigation between 1956 and 1987:
the American Civil Liberties Union (ACLU) and the Volunteer Lawyers for
the Arts (VLA). Because the participation of the VLA—a New York–based,
NEH-funded organization providing free legal aid to those involved in art-
related matters—in obscenity litigation was minor,[10] the following discussion
focuses on the ACLU.

Over the 30-year period covered in this study, the ACLU was the dominant
libertarian group active in obscenity politics. Its involvement ranged from
testimony before legislatures and commissions to direct involvement in litigation. Indeed, it is the organization most responsible for the heyday of
libertarian claims: the Supreme Court's serious flirtation with a "consenting
adults" limitation on proscription and the 1971 Obscenity Commission's
endorsement of a similar minimal regulation stance. Obscenity, however, is
not the ACLU's primary interest; in fact, its relevance to the group has
shifted with the times and with the press of other issues within the group's
areas of concern.

Perhaps the most obvious initial factor to consider in any treatment of the
ACLU is the incredibly broad range of its interests. As described in its
constitution, the ACLU seeks to "maintain and advance civil liberties, including the freedoms of association, press, religion, and speech, and the
rights to the franchise, to due process of law, and to equal protection of the
laws for all people throughout the United States and its possessions." Even
when we discount for rhetorical excess, the group's activities historically
touch all of these issues. Not only has it litigated in these disparate areas,
but it has established various "projects"—for example, "Women's Rights
Project," "Military Project," and "Coalition Against Censorship"—to promote and extend its interests. Additionally, one of its national counsels
devotes full-time attention to racial issues. This diversity of interests, given
a scarcity of resources, factors into its allocation of organizational attention
to any specific legal question.

Because of the stretch of the ACLU's interests, its political goals are best
understood in terms of three levels of abstraction. At the most general level,
the group promotes and protects an understanding of a liberal individualist
society with minimal constraint on personal choice. In advancing this end,
the group claims that it takes cases regardless of the political posture of those
who seek its assistance. Alan Reitman, its associate director, points to the
ACLU's defense of the Skokie Nazis and notes, "We hold our noses all the
time." The point is that the group defends noble principles, not necessarily
noble people.[11] This "defense" includes legislative and executive lobbying
and public relations work in addition to participation in litigation.

The diversity of the ACLU's interests runs not only across the Bill of
Rights but within particular amendments as well. In the First Amendment

alone, the group is concerned with issues such as libel, prior restraint, political speech, free assembly and association, church-state matters, and censorship. The general organizational goal remains the same at this issue level, but its specific content—the principle advocated—varies with the subject matter at hand. For example, the group seeks a stark separation of church and state in religious matters while pursuing unconstrained expression in speech and press matters. This is not to say that these principled goals are inconsistent; clearly they are not. It is only to note that different issues of organizational interest require different articulations of overarching goals.

Nested in the issue goals of the ACLU are its subject goals. These speak to the position the group takes on specific subjects within a more general issue area. This division allows the group to adjust the goals it pursues when it treats subjects within an issue area (e.g., "fighting words" and obscenity) and to develop different specific goals for similar, but distinct, subjects. The distinction between issue and subject goals also allows the latter to change while the former remain consistent as the group's perception of its external environment changes. The actuality of this distinction is manifest in the ACLU's evolution on the subject of obscenity.

The ACLU's goal on First Amendment matters has long been the establishment of a strict interpretation of its guarantees. This is probably best understood as a mix of Justice Black's absolutist and Justice Brandeis's "clear and imminent danger" approaches.[12] However consistent this issue goal, its application to obscenity matters evolved over time. In the civil liberties thaw following World War II, the ACLU began to address obscenity seriously.[13] The initial attacks were sporadic and tended to focus on prior restraints. In *Burstyn* v. *Wilson* (1952), for example, it successfully argued against a New York City commissioner's decision to deny a theater license to Roberto Rossellini's *The Miracle*, a film the commissioner found "blasphemous" (Walker, 1990, pp. 231–32). Similarly, in *ACLU* v. *Chicago* (1954), the Illinois CLU unsuccessfully challenged the constitutionality of a city ordinance requiring a permit as a prerequisite to the exhibition of any film. Here the group contended that the conditions under which the prior restraint was authorized were insufficient to meet the strictures imposed by *Near* v. *Minnesota* (1931). The narrowness of these arguments—they posed no general challenge to obscenity regulation per se—stands in stark contrast to the position advocated by the group in the early 1960s: without a showing of individualized harm, obscenity statutes could not pass constitutional muster. The evolution in the group's obscenity subject goal exemplifies the fluidity of the relationship among the three goal levels discussed above and frames the principled dimension of the ACLU's subsequent participation in obscenity politics.

Although the ACLU's public participation in the obscenity debate began with *Roth* and other decisions of the Supreme Court, its board—on the recommendation of its newly established Censorship Committee—adopted the group's initial position on obscenity earlier in 1957. "To be constitutional, an obscenity statute at the very least must meet the requirement of definiteness and also require that, before any material can be held to be obscene, it must be established beyond a reasonable doubt that the material represents a clear and present danger of normally inducing behavior which validly has been made criminal by statute."[14] After the 1957 decisions of the Court, the committee appointed a subcommittee charged with preparing a comprehensive memorandum on obscenity in light of these new developments. After circulation to state and local affiliates, the memorandum came to the full committee for discussion in April 1960.

The subcommittee's report urged the ACLU to adopt a more libertarian position on obscenity. It contended that most expression portraying sex was constitutionally permissible: only "hard-core" pornography was unprotected by the First Amendment; and special limitations could be applied only to the distribution of obscenity to children. In a contentious discussion of this draft, Harriet Pilpel, Elmer Rice, and Ephraim London secured, by a vote of 8–5, deletion of the hard- and soft-core distinction on the ground that it was too vague to protect First Amendment values adequately. On 28 May 1962, the ACLU's board of directors approved and announced its revised position: first, "limitations of expression on the ground of obscenity are unconstitutional"; second, prosecutions undertaken on the basis of present statutes must be based on clear proof of a demonstrable nexus between obscenity and specific criminal behavior; and third, the circulation of sexual material to children could not be restricted unless "its effect . . . would have led to behavior that would violate a criminal statute."[15] Thus, over a five-year span, reacting to the flow of events after *Roth*, comments from its affiliates, and its own perception of the weaknesses of its prior position, the ACLU moved from a position tolerant of obscenity laws to one holding them unconstitutional. This remains the subject goal of the organization.

This goal set the ACLU's internal philosophic and legal context; this context, in turn, informed the formulation of its strategies. Foremost was the development of a layered set of litigation goals to achieve its obscenity policy goals. The preferred end of its efforts was the establishment of First Amendment absolutism. Since the Supreme Court had never embraced the absolutist position, the group set and pursued "fall back" positions consistent with its overarching obscenity goal. One such "minimal" litigation goal was the reversal of *Roth*. To this end, its attorneys argued that the vagueness of the 1957 test led to due process problems in addition to "chilling" expression entitled to constitutional protection.[16] Securing the reversal of *Roth*, although not exempting all "obscenity" from prosecution, would at least extend to it the same protection afforded other expression. Failing this, the group sought a judicial broadening of the *Roth* test so that almost all sexual material would be adjudged non-obscene.[17] The strategy here was to secure an expansive interpretation of *Roth*'s "utterly without redeeming social value" language so that the test, though technically intact, would apply to a considerably smaller body of material.[18] If the ACLU could secure either of these minimal litigation goals, it would be in a position to use them as a base from which to push for the absolutism it truly wanted.

Although the ACLU had a coherent goal structure on obscenity, it never developed a formal litigation strategy designed to bring these issues systematically before the courts to realize its goals. Despite its massive involvement in this area of law—between 1957 and 1987 it (and its state and local affiliates) participated in 25 percent of the obscenity cases decided by the Supreme Court, 35 percent if per curiam reversals are not counted[19]—the ACLU entered obscenity litigation without a preconceived plan tying its goals to a series of "test" cases. Organizational officials attribute this to three factors. First, as with all organizations (especially those with wide-ranging interests), the ACLU faced significant resource constraints. These—available staff, time, and money—limited its ability to orchestrate planned litigation programs in all areas of organizational interest. Although planning did occur in a few areas,[20] it was the exception rather than the rule. Obscenity, despite the intragroup attention given it, never ranked as an exception. Second, the organization's federated nature made planned strategies difficult to conceive and execute. It was hard for the national office to direct affiliates (which are autonomous and which often face different immediate problems in their own areas) to pursue certain types of cases. Finally, the dense litigation field— the large number of other group actors and the diversity of their obscenity interests and goals—worked against the execution of a coherent litigation strategy. As a result, the ACLU's participation in obscenity litigation, although frequent, was largely ad hoc and limited to relatively inexpensive amicus curiae briefs.

This being said, it is important to note that the absence of a specific litigation plan does not mean that a group has no judicial strategy; it merely means that it is not managing a *series* of cases in a particular area of law as did, say, the NAACP in the school segregation area. Since it had a coherent goal structure, the ACLU did have strategic decisions before it—for example, case selection, mode of participation, nature of argument, and wisdom of appeal—in the obscenity area. Although its leaders never instructed its counsel or affiliates to seek out obscenity test cases, the group articulated a policy to guide its selection of cases: "[The ACLU] will not enter every legal proceeding involving obscenity, but will confine its intervention to those cases that offer an opportunity for the protection and extension of the right of freedom of expression provided for in the Bill of Rights."[21] This vague statement, in practice, amounted to a willingness to file amicus briefs in federal appellate cases (especially those before the Supreme Court) when their fact settings would facilitate ACLU arguments undermining the existence or enforcement of obscenity law.

Before *Miller* (1973), this judicial strategy led the ACLU to file in cases extending the "social value" prong of *Roth* to increasingly explicit material[22] and in those carving exemptions from general enforcement. The most obvious instance of the latter was its effort to extend the logic of *Stanley* v. *Georgia* (1969)—consenting adults cannot be prosecuted for using obscene materials in their homes—to cases raising questions of private shipment and importation of obscenity and those regarding the prosecution of "adult" theaters.[23] Along similar lines, the ACLU sought to limit the applicability of the *Roth* test by promoting procedural hurdles to its successful prosecution; these included the strict interpretation of *scienter* requirements, the impermissibility of prior restraints, the need for civil determinations of obscenity prior to criminal prosecutions, and the requirement that states demonstrate the link between exposure to obscenity and illegal behavior in individual cases. In urging the last, the group used empirical studies that suggested there was no causal nexus between obscenity and antisocial behavior and, hence, no basis for state regulation of its dissemination to consenting adults. The President's Commission on Obscenity and Pornography *Report* (1970), a panel dominated by ACLU members and sympathizers,[24] added support and legitimacy to this argument. After *Miller*, with neither the law nor the Court supportive of these kinds of arguments, the ACLU's interventions stressed the importance of limiting the range of the new test's application.[25]

The ACLU's participation in obscenity litigation was significant in terms of both the frequency of its involvement and the success of its arguments. This activity was intended to extend broad First Amendment protection to sex-related expression—a subject goal consistent with the ACLU's position on other expression issues and with its general goal of broadening individual freedom from governmental interference. To this end, it modified its stance on obscenity in the early 1960s and acted to ingrain its goal in the law. In deciding *Miller* in a manner at odds with late Warren Court decisions and previous ACLU arguments, the Burger Court changed the field on which obscenity politics were played. As I will discuss in the next chapter, this shift provided the occasion for the ACLU to de-emphasize obscenity and dramatically altered the group dynamics of libertarian litigation.

Material Groups

Although the ACLU was the dominant libertarian litigator of obscenity questions, it was not the only one. Other groups, whose interest in this issue was sparked by its nexus with facets of their members' livelihoods, also joined this litigation. The variation in interests, goals, and participation levels among these groups was large, as is demonstrated in table 2.2. However diverse their specific motivations and behavior, the interest of these groups in obscenity was animated by a common perspective: the groups had formed to watch over particular, narrow, and exclusive material interests of defined sectors of society. In short, the motive behind their formation was not public or political but private and exclusive. The focus of some of these groups was professional (those whose obscenity interests were tied to their larger vocational concerns), whereas that of others was more commercial (those who engaged in this litigation essentially to protect their economic interests). Although these subcategories are not mutually exclusive—the professional Association of American Publishers (AAP) obviously has an economic interest in broadening the market for printed material, and the commercial Adult Film Association of America (AFAA) couches defense of its members in terms of First Amendment principles—this categorization corresponds to differences in interest and focus as well as argumentational and behavioral differences.

The ACLU never monopolized organizational input into obscenity litigation: the AAP and the AL, professional groups, also filed amicus briefs in *Butler* v. *Michigan* (1957) and *Roth* v. *U.S.* (1957). Over the period under study, these groups participated in a large portion of the obscenity cases decided by the Supreme Court: the AAP in 21 percent (31 percent not counting summary reversals), the AL in 13 percent (19 percent not counting summary reversals). Of the other three professional groups active in this area, only the American Library Association (ALA)—with the affiliated Freedom to Read Foundation (FRF)—was involved in a substantial percentage (13 percent, 19 percent not counting summary reversals) of the Court's obscenity decisions. The Directors Guild of America (DGA) and the American Society of Journalists and Authors (ASJA) participated in only one case apiece.[26] In total, professional groups participated in 25 percent of the Court's obscenity decisions and in 38 percent of those decided after argument. These figures are strikingly similar to those for the ACLU (25 percent and 35 percent).

The sectoral concerns of these groups are different and distinct. The AAP defines its primary tasks as expanding the book publishing market, establishing a forum for the advancement of publishing interests, assisting members in corporate management and administration, providing members with information on governmental activities and social movements that touch on publishing interests, and speaking authoritatively for the industry it represents.[27] The AL, the umbrella group for the Authors Guild and the Dramatists Guild, works to advance the development of "a flourishing community of authors" in the United States through disseminating information on, among other things, contract negotiations, copyright matters, and royalties.[28] The ALA seeks to promote the career of library service, to set strategies, standards, and practices for library maintenance and growth, and to emphasize the importance of libraries in American society.[29] Although the concerns of these groups vary, they cluster around a common element: providing a broad array of information to the public. It is this that connects these groups to First Amendment concerns and, more pointedly, to obscenity politics.

Because of the material nature of the interests that prompted the organization of these groups, the range of issues they treat is both broader and narrower than that of their purposive counterpart, the ACLU. It is broader in the sense that it subsumes both material and political concerns. None of these groups exist to enter political affairs; the basis of their organization is material. As such, their relationship to government and policy is closely moored to issues that link pointedly to the specific and tangible concerns of the vocational sectors they organize. The interests of these sectors, though not strictly exclusive—not all publishers, authors, and librarians are actual group members, and the political victories won by these groups benefit these free riders as well as dues-paying members—are not public or inclusive by design; they are borne and felt most pointedly by the affected professionals. It is in this vocational and political sense that the interests of these groups are substantially narrower than those of the ACLU: where the latter is concerned with a broad range of political interests independent of particular material concerns, the AAP, AL, and ALA are oriented to politics by and *precisely because of* the vocational interests they represent. This limits and defines the scope of their political concerns.

One of the concerns common to these groups is obscenity. Governmental restriction (or prohibition) of materials treating sexual themes is related to the material interests of their members because pursuit of their vocations may run them afoul of federal and state laws. This potential for prosecution poses group members two problems. First, it could entail legal action against them. For example, in *St. Martin's Press* v. *Carey* (1979), the AAP filed an amicus brief before the United States Court of Appeals for the Second Circuit challenging the "child pornography" law later upheld as constitutional by the Supreme Court in *New York* v. *Ferber* (1982). In this case, a preemptive challenge by the publisher of *Show Me*—an illustrated children's sex education book that was arguably obscene under the statute—the AAP argued that the law was so broadly written as to threaten legitimate works of value and those (such as its members) who publish them. This, it concluded, would "chill" protected speech by forcing publishers to avoid works dealing frankly with sex under fear of prosecution and the negative publicity and potential fines that could result from it. A similar concern is held by the ALA, which occasionally assists in the legal defense of librarians who refuse, for example, to remove "objectionable" books from collections.[30] Thus, group members may be in danger of prosecution for pursuing their "legitimate" vocational activities, and these organizations seek protection of those in the profession as a class.

The second problem obscenity statutes pose these groups is more generic: a threat to the information distribution system of which their members are functionally a part. It is here that First Amendment concerns directly tie into organizational interests. Perhaps because of their training, or perhaps because of pre-professional interests that led them to pursue careers in these fields, the members of groups such as the AAP, AL, and ALA have a deep and abiding faith in the sanctity of the marketplace of ideas. This belief parallels twentieth-century doctrinal development in First Amendment law; this link buttresses the understanding by organizations of their role in the system of free expression and of the threat posed by governmental intervention in speech and press.

The principled—as opposed to purely material—concerns of these groups predate the Supreme Court's treatment of obscenity issues. For example, in 1953 the ALA and the AAP jointly issued a policy statement entitled "Freedom to Read," which called for the provision and maintenance of a wide diversity of viewpoints by publishers and libraries. This seven-point statement, reaffirmed in 1971, is explicitly premised on Millian concerns:

The freedom to read is essential to our democracy. It is continuously under attack. . . . We are deeply concerned about these attempts at suppression . . . [which] rest on a denial of the fundamental premise of democracy: that the ordinary citizen, by exercising his critical judgment, will accept the good and reject the bad. . . . Books are among our greatest instruments of freedom. . . . They are the natural medium for the new idea and the untried voice from which come the original contributions to social growth. . . . We believe that every American community must jealously guard the freedom to publish and circulate, in order to preserve its own freedom to read. We believe that publishers and librarians have a profound responsibility to give validity to that freedom to read by making it possible for the readers to choose freely from a variety of offerings.

The ALA and the AAP developed and maintain organizational arms to promote this position: the ALA's Office of Intellectual Freedom and the AAP's Freedom to Read Committee. Additionally, these groups cooperated in the 1969 establishment of the Freedom to Read Foundation (FRF), a privately funded, semiautonomous (it is housed at the ALA) group dedicated to these principles. Although the AL does not operate a similar apparatus, its litigation interest in obscenity also began prior to the Supreme Court's entry into this field,[31] and its amicus briefs articulate beliefs similar to those propounded by the AAP and the ALA in stressing "maturity of judgment," not governmental assessment of value, as the factor that should govern an individual's reading choices (amicus brief in *Roth*).

The nature of the interests of these professional groups—its narrowness in terms of vocational grounding and its breadth in terms of the philosophical bases of their perspectives—structures their political goals. At the general level their goals revolve around protection of the integrity and vitality of the vocational sector they organize. This leads them to pursue public policies that protect the specific interests of their members. Because their vocations differ, so too do some of the issue goals they adopt to advance these general goals. For example, the AL is active in legislation and litigation involving tax, contract, and copyright issues; in all of these areas it seeks to enhance the economic and legal well-being of authors. Indicative of this focus is the fact that the group is more politically active on copyright issues than any other area of organizational interest (Karp, 1977, pp. 1,12). The AAP's issue goals touch on many of the areas treated by the AL, although the different perspectives of publishers and authors occasionally lead them to advocate different positions. Among the issue goals of the ALA is obtaining "the federal support necessary for libraries to flourish" (ALA "Fact Sheet"). Although vocational concerns lead these groups to pursue a variety of issue goals, all of them are active in expression issues relevant to the professional lives of their members. Obscenity is one area of common interest, and here their goals are identical.

The specific goals of these groups reflect a balance between the philosophical and the vocational concerns that animate their political activities. Although none of them were ever favorably inclined to obscenity regulation, it is the AL that has been the most consistent (and most libertarian) in its specific goals. In its amicus brief in *Butler* (1957), it contended that prohibition of books "containing" obscenity was unreasonable. This position was further elaborated in the AL's *Roth* brief. Here the group argued that "present judicial interpretations of obscenity are unconstitutional because they are unduly restrictive of freedom of expression in their operation"; obscenity could not be defined in a way protective of other speech interests. The brief held regulation of works with sexual content to be illegitimate unless enforcement was confined to protection of minors or exposure to unwilling adults. The AAP and the ALA were initially less bold in the positions they advanced, with the former urging the Court to apply extant doctrine—the clear and present danger test—to material charged as obscene (*Roth* and *Butler*, 1957) and the latter calling for some evidence of a specific harm to an individual or society to justify successful prosecution (*Smith*, 1959). In the early 1970s, after the announcement of the *Report* of the President's Commission on Obscenity and Pornography, the AAP and the ALA came around to the AL's position that the provision of any expressive material to consenting adults was protected by the guarantees of the First Amendment.[32]

The litigation paths forged by these groups reflected this specific goal. Like the ACLU, they developed a layered set of litigation goals to promote their specific goals. There was, however, an important difference: the layers were crafted in ways that would, if adopted by the Court, protect the vocational interests of their members. Thus, the primary litigation goal, shared by all the groups, was the reversal of precedents that tolerate the prosecution of anyone involved with providing sexually oriented material to consenting adults. Failing this, the groups sought constitutionally grounded procedural protections to limit the harmful effect of unfavorable precedents and existing legislation. The "technicalities" pursued vary somewhat by vocational area but include extending the applicable prong of the current constitutional test ("utterly without redeeming social value" or "serious literary, artistic, political or scientific value") to protect more sex-oriented material, narrowing the applicable conception of *scienter* (knowing provision of illegal material), requiring a civil hearing to determine a material's obscenity prior to any criminal prosecution, and securing a specific typology of obscenity—the AL flirted with Justice Stewart's *Ginzburg* distinction between "hard-core" and "soft-core" material[33]—to lend some clarity to the legal definition of obscenity. The importance of the secondary litigation goals increased after the *Miller* decision, as a strong majority of justices committed the Court to the unquestioned constitutionality of obscenity proscription.

In pursuit of these goals, the AAP, AL, and ALA turned to the courts. This most frequently took the form of amicus participation—in only one case, *Bantam Books* v. *Sullivan* (1963), did one of them (AAP) directly argue a case. They base their preference for amicus participation on their resources (money, staff), interests (for all of these groups obscenity was a concern but not a group-defining one), and effectiveness. The AL speaks to the latter: "The *amicus curiae* brief is the only opportunity for organizations representing authors, publishers, or film companies to present their members' views to a court before it judicially 'legislates' broad principles that will affect their copyrights, contracts, or freedom of expression" (Karp, 1977, p. 4). After *Miller*, however, these groups, while still presenting amicus briefs, began— through the newly established Media Coalition (MC)—to involve themselves directly in litigation at all federal and state judicial levels. The expressed reason for this participation, and the arguments tendered in these courts, was concern for the material and vocational interests of their members: they painted themselves as "legitimate" enterprises trying to do business without running afoul of the law.

The switch from reliance on political or principled opposition to that of vocational concern with the effect of obscenity law enforcement was neither arbitrary nor inconsistent with the previous behavior of professional groups. Regardless of the breadth of the arguments they employed, these groups— with the exception of the AL—always entered cases with a close connection to the material interests of their members. For example, of the 12 Supreme Court cases in which the AAP participated prior to *Miller*, 11 involved printed materials and 10 were books. All of the ALA's four pre-*Miller* amicus briefs came in cases involving books.

Compared with the other professional groups, the AL demonstrated a somewhat broader subject-matter focus: two of its briefs were filed in cases treating films, seven came in cases litigating printed materials. This broader vision persisted after the decision in *Miller*. In part, this is a function of the scope of the material interests represented by the AL and its constituent parts (the Authors Guild and the Dramatists Guild); this suggests a focus that would extend beyond a particular medium. However, the greater range of AL activity also is a function of the vision of its general counsel, the man who decides in which cases to intervene, Irwin Karp. Not only was the AL the first of them to adopt—on Karp's suggestion—the extreme libertarian goal of protecting all expression conveyed to "consenting adults," but he also believes that a group litigating to protect its interests cannot particularize its participation in legal development by the specific vocational area it represents: "the obscenity decisions did have serious First Amendment consequences. . . . [P]rinciples established by a decision often apply generally, and are not limited to the parties" (Karp, 1977, p. 4). This understanding of doctrinal development and application led Karp to file for the AL in cases dealing with a wide range of media. It also led him to develop a thinly disguised disdain for groups that entered only that litigation *directly germane* to the functional interests they represent. This feeling, although it extends to the AAP and the ALA because they came late (1971) to the AL's "consenting adults" position, is most obviously manifest in Karp's remarks about his dealings with the commercially oriented Motion Picture Association of America (MPAA).

The MPAA has been active in cases involving films; parochial elsewhere. I have filed briefs at the request of the Association, for the League: e.g. *Interstate Theaters* v. *Dallas* (1968), *Jenkins* v. *Georgia* (1974), and *Erznoznik* v. *Jacksonville* (1975), all involving films; the MPAA has not shown a comparable interest in cases involving books or the theater (e.g. *Southeastern Promotions Ltd.* v. *Conrad*, 1975), and no interest in other First Amendment areas such as schoolbook-banning, libel and invasion of privacy, broadcasting of offensive language (*Pacifica* v. *FCC*, 1978) etc.[34]

The interests of the remaining libertarian groups, although material, differ from those of the professional groups, and they differ in the way suggested above by the AL's Karp. Their concerns are best described as commercial; an organizational impulse to protect a business climate conducive to the production, distribution, and sales of the goods of their members. The nexus with obscenity issues is obvious: sex sells, and because it does there is an industry that sells it in varying degrees of explicitness. The components of this industry are organized around their relevant commercial sectors: film, books, periodicals, distributors, and exhibitors.

A brief glance at table 2.2 indicates that commercial groups are the most numerous libertarian litigators of obscenity claims, with ten participating in cases decided by the Supreme Court between 1957 and 1987. As with their professional counterparts, the frequency of their participation varies substantially. Some groups, especially those with very narrow obscenity concerns, litigated in a very few cases: the Direct Mail Advertising Association (DMAA), the Video Software Dealers Association (VDSA), and the Outdoor Advertising Association (OAA) filed as amicus curiae in one case apiece; the National Association of Theatre Owners (NATO) participated in 3 percent of the Court's decisions (4 percent not counting summary reversals). Two groups closely associated with the "adult materials" industry—the Adult Film Association of America (AFAA) and the First Amendment Lawyers Association (FALA)—were directly involved in 5 and 6 percent of the formal decisions of the Court between their establishment in the late 1960s and the present, but this measure fails to capture their indirect influence on the judiciary. The AFAA maintains a staff counsel of five attorneys who have considerable experience in obscenity litigation, and who advise members (and their attorneys) on legal matters including litigation. The FALA, an association of defense attorneys active primarily in the obscenity area, acts as an information clearinghouse through which expertise, strategies, and tactics are shared.

Without question, however, the most active organized commercial participants are the American Booksellers Association (ABA)—9 percent of the Supreme Court's obscenity decisions, 14 percent not counting summary reversals; the Council for Periodical Distributors Association (CPDA)—13 percent, 19 percent not counting summary reversals; the Motion Picture Association of America (MPAA)—6 percent, 9 percent not counting summary reversals; and the Media Coalition, a group formed by the ABA, CDPA, MPAA, and the professional AAP after the *Miller* decision—35 percent. All told, commercial groups formally participated in 24 percent of the Court's obscenity decisions, 40 percent of those decided after oral argument. These figures demonstrate substantial commercial involvement in the Court's obscenity docket and are comparable to those for professional groups and the ACLU.

Like the interests of their professional counterparts, the interests of commercial organizations are varied and not primarily political. Essentially, they exist to promote and protect an economic environment conducive to their business dealings. Some examples help to clarify the scope of their interests. The AFAA is a trade association of companies that produce sexually explicit films. It functions as something of an alternative MPAA, as a promoter of the products of its members. In addition to providing legal advice to members' attorneys, the AFAA compiles statistics on the production and marketing of "adult" films and sponsors the annual "Erotic Film Awards." The ABA is composed of over 4,000 booksellers including national "chain" operations. It seeks to improve and maintain favorable relationships between sellers and publishers of printed materials, increase the sales of such materials, and improve the efficiency and profitability of its members. The CPDA consists of wholesale distributors of newspapers, periodicals, and paperback books. It works to advance the commercial interests of its members by improving merchandising methods, extending markets, and facilitating exchange of information and expertise. The other groups in this category are similarly oriented to sector-based, commercial issues and concerns.

None of the above-noted organizations exists for political purposes, but they all became active in obscenity politics to protect member interests. In one sense, MC is an aberration to this pattern. It is a creature of the trade associations that established it, but its sole purpose is political: to protect the commercial interests of its members from infringement by obscenity prosecutions. This political vision, however, is directly tied to the specific goals of its members. Because of this, the scope of its obscenity interest is subject to sudden change. For example, the MPAA, a co-founding member, left MC after Supreme Court decisions in *Jenkins* v. *Georgia* (1974)[35] and *Young* v. *American Mini Theatres* (1976)[36] made it relatively clear that the new obscenity doctrine was not to be construed to apply to the releases of major motion picture studios. After the MPAA departure, MC narrowed its attention to obscenity cases involving printed media. Thus, its interest range not only is flexible but also is purely driven by the commercial interests of its member organizations. As such, its participation in obscenity litigation is as "parochial" as that of other commercial groups.

The commercial nature of these groups' interests conditions the goals they pursue. At the general level, these goals concern the maintenance of an environment conducive to the occupational practices of their members. Although this most often turns their attention to private avenues of activity (e.g., assessing market conditions, sharing information on efficiency techniques, etc.), it occasionally leads them to the political system. Here they develop issue goals consistent with the general interests of their members.

As was true for their professional counterparts, the different occupational interests of these material groups often lead them to adopt different, largely sector-based issue goals. For example, the interests of MPAA members extend to questions of major motion picture production and distribution. These interests include economical film production, the distribution of the films of members to the widest possible theatrical and cable television audience, and the "pirating" of movies onto videotape. The issue goals of the ABA differ from those of the MPAA because their members work in a different commercial sector. This leads the ABA to be concerned with political affairs of particular interest to booksellers—tax laws regarding inventories, for example. The DMAA's interest is focused exclusively on the domain of its operations: the U.S. mail. This focuses it on issues pertaining to mailed advertisements, such as postage rates. In short, these groups formulate issue goals that correspond to the commercial sector they organize. Although these narrowly material concerns lead them into different areas of organizational activity, they occasionally coincide. This happened in the instance of obscenity.

The subject goals of the various commercial groups show considerable variation, but they share a central focus: the protection of the wares of members from prosecution as obscenity. This goal was sought in a number of ways. Prior to *Miller*, for example, the AFAA and the FALA essentially endorsed the position tendered by the ACLU—"no law" means no law restricting the expression of sexual ideas and images. The obscenity goals of other commercial groups were narrower and, perhaps, more parochial. NATO, for example, never challenged the legitimacy of obscenity regulation, instead arguing that statutes must precisely define the obscene and require a civil hearing on the obscenity of any film prior to criminal action against its exhibitor (amicus brief in *Rabe*, 1972). The CPDA adopted the same tact. In its amicus brief in *Gent* (1967) it noted that its members were "anxious to prevent the dissemination of obscene material" but went on to argue that they were "also concerned that the freedom of speech guaranteed by the First and Fourteenth Amendments may be negated by over-restrictive criminal obscenity legislation." Having set this context of concern, the CPDA brief articulated the specific concerns of its membership:

First... the local wholesaler handles thousands of publications, and it is unjust to hold him criminally accountable for selling a book which he could not have possibly read and may not have seen.... Second, local magazine and paperback wholesalers, such as members of CPDA, are not criminals in any sense of the term, and are usually responsible community leaders.... Whether the local wholesaler wins or loses the criminal action, his good name is besmirched by its mere commencement. (CPDA *amicus* brief, Gent, 1967)

It is this material focus that serves to unite the obscenity goals of these groups. Regardless of their specific preferences—MC's general counsel, Michael Bamberger, prefers the tripartite *Memoirs* approach as does the MPAA's president, Jack Valenti;[37] some feel comfortable with the *Miller* approach (at least when narrowly construed and applied); and others long for the "consenting adults" position adopted by Justice Brennan in *Paris Adult Theater* (1973)—all of these groups seek, first and foremost, to protect the commercial well-being of their members. This "least common denominator" is why, after *Miller*, these organizations were able to function in the new legal environment without substantially modifying the arguments they made before the courts. Indeed, they shared this ability to focus on the least common denominator with the professional groups, which were, by vocational focus, much more inclined prior to *Miller* to argue against the logic of any effort to control obscenity through governmental regulation. MC was self-consciously established, by both professional and commercial groups, on the basis of these least common denominator concerns. Legal and philosophical principles may be of interest to these groups, but in the end, they organize material interests, and it is these interests they seek to protect.

As noted above, the commercial focus of these groups allows them to pursue goals that accommodate a desire both to undermine the *Miller* approach and to live within its confines. The fact that these groups can tolerate two different legal outcomes lets them develop and maintain ambiguous goals. This affects the way they orient themselves to the political arena. Nowhere is this ambiguity, and its effect on a group's political strategy, more clearly drawn than in the case of the AFAA.[38] Members of the AFAA produce 35-millimeter movies and videocassettes. The group's obscenity goal is to protect these materials from prosecution. Publicly it calls for the abolition of obscenity laws aimed at consenting adults; this would free its members from potential legal harassment. The parochial nature of its commercial interests, however, muddies this goal at the operational level; there the end of obscenity could cause significant problems for AFAA members. First, this would allow inexpensive 16-millimeter short films to flourish—competition that the AFAA would prefer to avoid. Second, it would permit the major motion picture studios to produce films graphically portraying sex. Some believe that this could threaten the profitability of AFAA members because MGM and others would make "better" films. Third, it would remove the illicit nature of the product of its members, something that group officials believe to be one of its major drawing points. This ambiguity in goals has, in part, contributed to the ill-focused nature of the AFAA's obscenity actions; its members have been able to survive quite profitably in the twilight of the *Miller* decision,[39] and this gives them little incentive to mobilize to push the law to more libertarian extremes.

The litigation goals adopted by commercial groups reflect their specific goal of protecting the market interests of their members. These organizations face an immediate problem: keeping their members free from legal prosecution. Because of this, they do not rely heavily on arguments drawing on abstract philosophical principles of democratic theory. Rather, their legal arguments—and the goals those arguments seek to achieve—are more earthbound and tangible: the protection of the businesses they represent. This is a distinctly different tack from that taken by professional groups and the purposive ACLU, which seek a change in social and legal order in addition to the protection of more exclusive interests. After *Miller*, however, the professional groups joined their commercial counterparts in emphasizing their common, material concerns.

The litigation goals sought by commercial organizations remained relatively constant over the period of this study. In general, groups in this category sought to confine the application of obscenity laws on the grounds of vagueness and overbreadth,[40] procedural requirements,[41] and definition of community standards.[42] Significantly, the arguments that spin off of these goals, as is true of the goals themselves, are parochial—they are narrowly tailored to the sector represented by the group and reflect concerns that are exclusive rather than inclusive, material rather than philosophical, sectoral rather than societal. Rhetoric to the side, these groups enter this political arena, as they would enter any political arena, to protect their economic interests.

The strategies adopted by commercial groups reflect their narrow, economic focus. Prior to the *Miller* decision, they essentially were free riders on the rising tide of liberalization fostered by the Warren Court and the heavy judicial involvement of the purposive ACLU and the professional—but principle-driven—AAP and AL. With expression protected by doctrine favorable to their economic interests, these groups entered litigation only occasionally, and most frequently at the level of the Supreme Court. After the Burger Court rejected the doctrinal underpinnings of the Warren Court liberalization—on which the ACLU and professional groups based their judicial intervention—commercial organizations became extremely prominent in obscenity politics, boosting their participation before the Supreme Court— from involvement in 28 percent of its decisions (not counting summary reversals) to 52 percent.

The expansion of commercial group litigation was not confined to the Supreme Court; these groups, most prominently through MC, also entered lower federal and state court proceedings to protect economic interests. The goals of MC at this level were the same as those it pursued in appellate courts—to demonstrate the practical problems that overbroad and vague obscenity legislation poses to legitimate businesses. For example, it successfully litigated state "minor's access" laws—laws prohibiting the plainview sale of materials that, though not legally obscene for adults, are such for children. In *ABA, et al.* v. *McAulliffe* (1981), it prevailed in its argument that a Georgia statute of this type was unconstitutionally overbroad in restricting access to materials that adults have a right to purchase. The group used "expert witnesses" to show that placing these materials in a back room substantially reduces their sales because most purchases are generated by visual contact with the material.[43]

More recently, MC challenged the constitutionality of the Indianapolis "feminist" anti-pornography ordinance in *ABA, et al* v. *Hudnut* (1984). This ordinance—similar to one vetoed by the mayor of Minneapolis, Minnesota— defined pornography as "the graphic sexually explicit subordination of women, whether in pictures or in words." It was meant to apply to materials that presented women (or men, children, or transsexuals):

as "sexual objects who enjoy pain or humiliation or . . . rape"; "as sexual objects tied up or cut up or mutilated or bruised or physically hurt, or as dismembered or truncated or fragmented or severed into body parts"; "as being penetrated by objects or animals"; "in scenarios of degradation, injury, abasement, torture, shown as filthy or inferior, bleeding, bruised, or hurt in a context that makes these conditions sexual"; or "as sexual objects for domination, conquest, violation, exploitation, possession, or use or through postures or positions of servility or submission or display." (*Hudnut*, 771 F.2d, p. 324, 1985)

As in *McAulliffe*, MC successfully argued that this ordinance ran afoul of the obscenity standard established in *Miller* and was unconstitutionally overbroad and vague.

Summary

The libertarian groups canvassed here all entered obscenity litigation to advance the interests they represented, but their particular interests were,

in many instances, different. Some groups sought the end of obscenity proscription per se; others simply wanted to protect their members from prosecution under otherwise legitimate legislation. To a significant degree, these
differences in goals corresponded to differences in organizational type. The
ACLU, a purposive group, waged a legal campaign to bring obscenity into
the fold of traditional First Amendment jurisprudence. This required the
Supreme Court to abandon the approach it initially adopted in *Roth* (1957).
Although the professionally oriented among the groups ultimately endorsed
the ACLU position, organizations with material concerns sought protection
of the vocational and commercial status and viability of their members. This
led them to accept, or at least work within the confines of, both the *Roth*
and the *Miller* approaches. As such, the litigation strategies they adopted
were more parochial and less constitutionally ambitious than that of their
purposive counterpart, the ACLU.

The Supreme Court's decision in *Miller* (1973) substantially altered the
political environment in which these groups pursued their goals. In decisively
rejecting the absolutism of the ACLU, the Court established a legal context
that, for the first time in over a decade, was favorable to the proscription of
obscene materials. The effect of this Court-induced environmental shift on
the actions of libertarian groups is the subject of the chapters that follow.
However, the libertarians did not tilt with the courts in an organizational
vacuum. Their initial success, and the concomitant increase in the availability
of sexually oriented material, prompted the organization of groups opposed
to their agenda.

PRO-DECENCY (PROSCRIPTIONIST)
ORGANIZATIONS

Table 2.3 describes the involvement of pro-decency organizations in obscenity cases formally resolved by the Supreme Court. The data it presents
reveal proscriptionist participation in about 29 percent of all cases decided
by the Court, and in nearly 42 percent of those cases decided with a full
hearing. Unlike the libertarian case, these groups evinced little tendency to
"bunch" their litigation efforts—in only seven of the 34 cases in which they
appeared (about 21 percent) did more than one group participate. However,
these data demonstrate that proscriptionist participation in obscenity litigation, though less frequent than that of their libertarian counterparts, was
substantial. Although both camps were deeply involved in this litigation,
the pro-decency side did not manifest the variety of interests found among
the libertarian groups.

As noted in table 2.4, the interests of the seven pro-decency groups involved in the judicial processing of obscenity issues can be described only
as political and purposive. Whereas the bulk of libertarian actors in this area
approached these issues as something of a sidelight—they were organized

Table 2.3
Pro-Decency Group Involvement before the Supreme Court in Obscenity Cases, 1957–1987

Number of Groups Appearing in Each Case	All Cases*		Not Counting Summary Reversals**	
	n	%	n	%
None	85	71%	45	58%
One	27	23%	25	33%
Two	3	3%	3	4%
Three or More	4	3%	4	5%
Total	119	100%	77	100%

* Includes all cases formally decided by the Court.

** Does not count the 42 cases summarily treated by the Court. Also does not include group activity in two of those cases -- Aday (1967) and Cain (1970).

around other, primarily material, concerns—the proscriptionists, with the possible exceptions of the National League of Cities (NLC) and the National Institute of Municipal Law Officers (NIMLO), exist to promote the public policy interests of their members and donors. Indeed, the preeminent pro-decency litigators, Citizens for Decency through Law (CDL) and Morality in Media (MM), devote themselves exclusively to enhancing the prosecutory climate related to obscenity. Thus, unlike their libertarian counterparts, the proscriptionist groups active in this litigation were generally consistent in focus and concern. This focus gives their arguments and strategies an air of homogeneity.

The distribution of the legal activity of pro-decency groups also differs from that of libertarian litigators. Whereas the latter saw a number of groups heavily involved in obscenity litigation, this pattern does not hold for the former. Of the seven groups that supported proscriptionist outcomes in briefs filed with the Supreme Court, four—Freedom Council Foundation (FCF), National Legal Foundation (NLF), National League of Cities (NLC), and National Institute of Municipal Law Officers (NIMLO)—appeared in only one case apiece. These groups are, by and large, tangential players in the obscenity game. NIMLO, NLC, and FCF all filed as amicus in *Renton* v. *Playtime Theatres* (1986), a case involving zoning regulations as applied to adult theaters. NLF filed an amicus brief in *Virginia* v. *American Booksellers Association, et al.* (1988), a case addressing the constitutional permissibility of state-mandated protective coverings for "adult" magazines on sales displays. Another group, the Covenant House/Institute for Youth Advocacy (CH/IYA), filed as amicus curiae in only two cases, *New York* v. *Ferber* (1982)

Table 2.4
Pro-Decency Groups Involved in Obscenity Litigation before the Supreme Court, 1957–1987

	Organizational Type	Organizational Mode	% Participation*	Type of Participation
Citizens for Decency through Law (CDL)	Ind. Memb.	Purposive	38%	Amicus, lit. assistance
Covenant House/Institute for Youth Advocacy (CH/IYA)	Ind. Donors	Purposive	5%**	Amicus
Freedom Council Foundation (FCF)	Ind. Memb.	Purposive	12%**	Amicus
Morality in Media (MM)	Ind. Memb.	Purposive	7%**	Amicus, lit. assistance
National Legal Foundation (NLF)	Ind. Memb.	Purposive	12%**	Amicus
National League of Cities (NLC)	Corp. Memb.	Purposive	1%	Amicus
National Institute of Municipal Law Officers (NIMLO)	Ind. Memb.	Purposive	1%	Amicus

* Percentage includes only those cases formally decided after oral argument.
** Factors date of establishment (MM, 1962; CH/IYA, 1972; FCF, 1983; NLF, 1984) into percentage calculation.

and *Virginia* (1988). CH/IYA provides counseling to be sexually abused youth of New York's Times Square, and both *Ferber* (child pornography) and *Virginia* (protective coverings) were related to the "refuge" work undertaken by this organization.

The two remaining groups, Citizens for Decency through Law (CDL) and Morality in Media (MM) are the preeminent proscriptionist organizations active in obscenity litigation. In many respects—type of organization, range of interests, goals, and general vision for the attainment of those goals—these groups are remarkably similar. In one central respect—the specific organizational strategies used to achieve these goals—these groups differ dramatically. Whereas MM concentrates on providing information to local prosecutors combating obscenity, CDL, although also active here, places a greater premium on active organizational involvement in the litigation process itself.

The circumstances of the founding of these groups are remarkably similar. Both began as organizations dedicated to proscribing the availability of obscenity in their immediate locales. CDL was organized in Cincinnati, Ohio, in 1957. The context for its creation was described in an admiring article that appeared in *Reader's Digest*.

[Charles H.] Keating's concern over the flood of printed poison was galvanized one day in 1956, when he noticed youngsters at a newsstand snickering over a display set apart from the rest of the magazines and paperbacks. Moving over for a look, Keating was shocked. Besides the "girlie" magazines featuring nudes in suggestive poses, dozens of publications depicted not only raw sex but stories of abnormal sex behavior. . . . The same fare was available on other stands, Keating found. At Cincinnati's police headquarters he was told, "Sure, there's a law against it . . . but we make arrests, bring these smut sellers into court, only to find ourselves pitted against high-priced legal talent, hired by well-heeled publishers, yowling about 'censorship' and freedom of the press. The public is nowhere around to back us up." (Hall, 1964)

In response, Keating formed CDL (initially Citizens for Decent Literature) and ran it out of his law office. He took the group "national" in 1959 by spawning state affiliates and local chapters to aid local police efforts at proscription with the expertise of a battery of attorneys who volunteered their time to the national office of CDL. It was not until 1967 when DeWitt Wallace, the publisher of *Reader's Digest*,[44] gave CDL $36,000 that the group hired a full-time national director to guide and coordinate its activities.[45] Until the early 1980s, the national organization was largely the creature of Keating, who was prominently assisted by two associates—James J. Clancy (a cooperating attorney) and Raymond P. Gauer (its first salaried national director). Indeed, Keating's prominence was such that, in 1969, he was appointed to the President's Commission on Obscenity and Pornography by President Richard M. Nixon.

Morality in Media (MM), until 1968 "Operation Yorkville," was founded in the fall of 1962 in response to the increasing availability of sexually oriented material in New York City. The catalyzing event occurred when two Manhattan schoolchildren were discovered with "salacious publications in their possession."[46] MM's founders were three Manhattan-area clergymen who were concerned about the ready availability of this kind of material to youth and the effect this would have on family relationships. At first it was citywide in scope, but it gradually expanded to become a statewide and ultimately a national organization.[47] By 1968, its visibility was such that one of its founders, a Jesuit priest named Morton A. Hill, was appointed a member of the President's Commission on Obscenity and Pornography by President Johnson. Father Hill, the Charles H. Keating, Jr., of MM, remained the group's leader throughout the period under examination here.

CDL and MM are both purposive organizations—the incentives they offer to members and donors are purely political. These groups exist solely for the purpose of assisting governmental authorities in combating the easy availability of sexually oriented material, a policy that they believe to be in the public interest. Both groups are moved to action by the fear that this availability will undermine public morality by divorcing it from its traditional Judeo-Christian roots. Because it cheapens, debases, and objectifies the act of love and the human beings who engage in it, pornography threatens these traditional values and teaches citizens that people are little more than instruments and objects. The gratification of desire, not the promotion of public virtue, is thus fostered as normal behavior. This irrevocably tears the seamless web of society and diminishes the greatness of a nation and its people. This degeneracy—similar to the sort to which past civilizations have succumbed—is not seen to be inevitable, but its advance can be checked only by active opposition. These groups define their role as assisting in this opposition. As such, they are not only purposive but also, in the sense articulated by Wilson, ideological organizations.

An ideological organization is one that exposes a systematic critique and program . . . for man in all aspects of his life or for society as a whole. . . . The goals it favors are seen by it as having an important interrelationship and being derived from fundamental assertions about the nature of man and society. . . . Their principal focus is on the reconstruction of society in general or the redemption of men generally. . . . [They are] conversionist movements, which seek to alter radically the lives of others, rather than adventist or agnostic movements, which seek to perfect, redeem, or specially enlighten the lives of their own members. (Wilson, 1973, pp. 46–47)

Thus, although CDL and MM offer members and donors minimal material benefits (e.g., membership cards, newsletters, car decals), and though the local affiliates and chapters of the groups may provide members certain solidaristic benefits, the primary good they offer their benefactors is that of an organization pursuing a political agenda of agreed-upon importance.[48]

The range of interests held by proscriptionist groups is substantially narrower than that characterizing the libertarian camp. Of the seven appearing before the Supreme Court, two—NLC and NIMLO—are concerned with general governmental policies relating to the varied functions their members fulfill—NLC, those relating to local governance and NIMLO, those relevant to local law enforcement generally. Significantly, these groups' only brush with obscenity litigation came in the *Renton* (1986) case involving the zoning authority of city governments. Two other pro-decency litigators, NLF and FCF, are "non-profit corporation[s] organized to defend, restore, and preserve religious liberties, family rights, and other freedoms guaranteed by the Constitution" (FCF amicus curiae brief in *Renton*, p. ix). These groups, which share the same executive director (Robert K. Skolrood), are related to Pat Robertson's Christian Broadcasting Network. Their church-state focus—the FCF, for example, filed amicus curiae briefs in *Lynch* v. *Donnelly* (1984) and other religion-clause cases—makes obscenity an area of peripheral but occasional group activity. A similar conclusion can be drawn about CH/ IYA. Its primary concern is aiding the street youth of New York. It will involve itself in obscenity litigation only as amicus and only in cases that touch on the nexus between youth and obscenity (e.g., *Ferber*, *Virginia*). All of this is not to say that these groups will not become more active in this area of litigation in the future; it is merely to explain their somewhat limited involvement in the litigation the Court has treated to date.

In contrast to the broader agendas of these groups are the very focused interests of CDL and MM. Although leaders of both groups define them as "pro-family," their raison d'être is obscenity. Indeed, the explanation these groups give for this focus is similar. CDL's general counsel, Bruce A. Taylor, a former ACLU member and a former prosecutor in Cleveland, Ohio, said that his group was "busy enough with obscenity to be wholly occupied." Paul J. McGeady, MM's general counsel, noted that although his group is also concerned about drug abuse and abortion, the pursuit of other interests would spread the group "too thin." However, even though these groups are narrowly and intensely focused on obscenity questions, they have entered litigation on related issues. For example, CDL filed as amicus in *Cohen* v. *California* (1971)—involving the prosecution of a man for wearing a jacket displaying the legend "Fuck the Draft"; *Papish* v. *Board of Curators* (1973)— printing political obscenities and indecencies in a college newspaper; *Ballew* v. *Georgia* (1978)—using five-person juries in criminal trials; and *Board* v. *Pico* (1982)—removing "objectionable" books from a school library. The explanation for this apparent straying from organizational concerns in *Cohen* and *Papish* stems from the group's understanding of obscenity: it sees obscenity as a variable concept, the definition of which varies with the object, the audience, and the context. *Ballew*, although it turned on the jury question, involved a prosecution of the movie *Behind the Green Door*. Thus, only *Pico* stands out as an anomaly, but even here, given the variable conception of obscenity, the group's participation is easily explicable, especially in light of the school board's request that CDL file in support of its position.

The only instance of MM involvement in litigation not directly raising obscenity issues was its participation in *FCC* v. *Pacifica Foundation* (1978)— regulating "indecent" speech on commercial radio. Again, however, this involvement is easily linked to the group's larger interests, which extend to protecting youth from exposure to sexual immorality. Thus, CDL and MM are unique among proscriptionist groups in the intensity of their focus on obscenity questions.[49] In fact, the only analog to their posture in this arena is the libertarian MC, and even here the parallel is imperfect, given the material-commercial concerns of that group.

As is true for their libertarian counterparts, the nature of the interests of the pro-decency groups structures the goals they seek. The narrowness of these interests—their relative homogeneity—makes for another point of distinction between the two litigating camps. The general goals pursued by the proscriptive groups are compatible, but not identical. All of them, except for NLC and NIMLO, can be considered to have a "pro-family" orientation. They seek, generally speaking, to accomplish two tasks: to inform and educate the public on the threats posed to traditional values by an increasingly liberal social climate, and to take action to stem those threats. Because the liberalization of the past few decades—aided and, in some cases, prompted by Supreme Court decisions—forms the core of what they oppose and consequently seek, their general goals are compatible. These goals are stated in different ways by the different groups. MM, for example, is pledged to oppose the "ideology of pornography: sex anytime, anywhere, and with anyone." Put positively, this translates to the "promotion of decency" through the establishment of "media based on love, trust, and good taste."[50] CDL phrases its commitment somewhat differently; it is dedicated to "the promulgation of decency and the ideals of a Judeo-Christian civilization."[51] This dissatisfaction with the perceived liberal excesses of recent American policy defines the perspective from which these groups approach the political system.

The issue goals spawned by the general goals of these groups are somewhat less homogeneous. FCF and NLF are primarily interested in fostering governmental accommodation of religion, especially as it touches public life. This issue goal generally leads them into other areas of First Amendment litigation and away from involvement in obscenity issues, although when those issues touch on schools[52] or the access of minors to alleged obscenity (*Virginia* 1988), they will file as amici. CH/IYA, given its general goal of assisting youthful "victims" of the "sex industry," is activated by obscenity issues touching on minors. It made this focus clear in its amicus brief in *Ferber* (1982): "The constitutional guidelines for meaningful regulation of sexual exploitation of children in the pornography industry are at this time so murky as to be useless. . . . Thousands of children, finally, have paid and will pay the price for such confusion—selling their most private personal dignity, then living with the consequences of knowing the sale is endlessly available for public viewing" (p. iii). The issue goals of CDL and MM are more pointedly related to obscenity matters per se. The position of these groups is that obscenity is not expression protected by the First Amendment. Both organizations embrace a variable notion of obscenity and work to insure that communities be allowed to enforce *their* understanding of decency through their law and courts. From here, however, their issue foci diverge somewhat: CDL is active in all areas of obscenity law; MM, though attentive to these questions, concentrates most of its attention on child pornography and issues relating to broadcast and cablecast media.

These issue goals drive not only the litigation behavior of the proscriptionist organizations, but their more broadly political activities as well. CDL and MM provide good examples of this phenomenon. CDL maintains a speakers bureau, produces a newsletter, conducts conferences and seminars on obscenity law for prosecutors and police, produces films on the evils of obscenity, writes model obscenity statutes, organizes letter-writing campaigns and public demonstrations to promote the prosecution of obscenity statutes, and lobbies legislatures on obscenity matters. Its officials also occasionally write articles for publications such as *Reader's Digest* and *Parents Magazine*.

In a somewhat more visible effort, CDL actively lobbied against the elevation of Justice Abe Fortas to the chief justiceship. James Clancy and Charles Keating appeared before the Senate Judiciary Subcommittee on Judicial Nominations to argue against Fortas's promotion. They leveled two charges against him. First, it was noted that he helped to prepare Greenleaf Publishing Company's amicus curiae brief in *Roth* and had further legal ties with a publisher of sexually explicit materials, William Hamling. Second, CDL produced a film containing exhibits of materials that had been found obscene by lower courts but that had been "Redrupped" by the Court with Fortas voting to reverse the convictions. Because it never came to a vote, it is impossible to gauge precisely the effect of CDL's actions on the demise of the Fortas nomination. However, the *New York Times* reported that, "one key Senate source said that some 'middle of the roaders' who viewed the film had said that they were revolted by what they saw and hinted that they might oppose Mr. Fortas on that issue alone" (*New York Times*, 6 Sept. 1968). As it turned out, Fortas's loss was CDL's gain—Warren Burger was far more sensitive to its concerns than was Fortas.

MM engages in many of the same general activities employed by CDL. One point of difference, however, is the National Obscenity Law Center (NOLC) it established in 1976 to act as an information clearinghouse on all aspects of obscenity law. Subscribers to this service have access to its files on legal memoranda, articles, statutes, ordinances, and briefs. They also receive the NOLC *Obscenity Law Bulletin*—a monthly digest of cases, statutes, and new legal developments relating to obscenity. CDL provides a similar service, but given its focus on litigation involvement, it is far less formalized.

Another area of common organizational activity was the President's Commission on Obscenity and Pornography appointed by President Johnson in 1968. MM's Father Hill was an original appointee to the commission, and CDL's Keating was appointed as a replacement for a commissioner who resigned to take an ambassadorship, thus overcoming a slight of considerable magnitude—Keating and CDL had been calling for such a commission since 1961. These men helped to detract from the legitimacy of the final report, which recommended the rejection of obscenity regulations aimed at consenting adults. Both wrote stinging dissents denouncing the final report— Hill dubbed it "a Magna Charta for the pornographer" (President's Commission, 1970, p. 456)—dissents that were seized on by politicians eager to distance themselves from the report's recommendations. Keating's work against the product of the commission was yet more extensive. He was appointed to the body by President Nixon, a man very uncomfortable with the direction the commission he had inherited was moving. As such, Keating functioned as something of an enemy agent, leaking secret commission materials to the press, publicly urging Nixon to disband the body, and suing the commission to gain more time to prepare his lengthy dissent.[53]

The actions of Commissioners Keating and Hill advanced the issue goals of their groups in three senses. First, the commission's report was rejected out of hand by the government and public. Second, the press coverage they received increased public awareness of both obscenity issues and the groups the men headed. Third, the public and political uproar they helped generate was not lost on Nixon, who would appoint two other members to the Supreme Court before leaving office. Thus, Keating and Hill contributed to the ongoing maintenance of their groups while furthering the goals they were established to advance.

At the operational level, the subject goals of pro-decency groups reflect their issue focus. Common to them all is the desire to enhance the ability of governments, especially at the local level, to define and combat obscenity as they see fit. As such, they intervene politically to promote policies that would allow, among other things, state proscription of the obscene through zoning regulations, "covering" laws, child pornography laws, extension of public nuisance and racketeering laws, regulation of broadcast and cablecast media, and prohibition of "sex toys." MM and CDL have also been active in attempting to force the federal government—the Department of Justice in particular—to prosecute the "adult products" industry more vigorously under existing legislation. Most groups devote the bulk of their attention to a subset of these specific concerns. For example, as noted above, MM concentrates more heavily on cable television and child pornography than on other issues, while CH/IYA focuses almost exclusively on the latter. NLC and NIMLO limit their obscenity concerns to the promotion of local procedural (e.g., zoning) controls over adult emporiums. NLF and FCF activate to protect what they conceive to be religiously defined "pro-family" concerns. CDL stands as the most eclectic of the proscriptionist groups, engaging itself in almost all subject areas touching on obscenity law.

Linking the specific subject goals of all these groups is a need to secure strong constitutional support for obscenity regulation per se. Here, the need is for courts to adopt doctrinal postures on all legal questions relating to obscenity that are consistent with a broadly proscriptionist reading of *Roth*, *Miller*, and the First Amendment. This development would allow the groups, and the government, to plug the loopholes in the current law that plague efforts to enforce existing and prospective obscenity statutes.

The need to develop and nurture constitutional doctrine consistent with the goal of proscribing obscenity is made manifest in the approach pro-decency groups take toward litigation. As is true of the other groups involved in this issue arena, the proscriptionists developed a layered goal structure to guide their litigation. The preeminent litigation goal of these organizations is buttressing and furthering the *Roth/Miller* approach. This effort is directed toward providing national, state, and local governments the tools to attack obscenity without undue concern for the technical and procedural niceties of complex constitutional doctrine. To this end, both CDL and MM continue to press on the courts a "variable" conception of pornography, one that allows wide latitude for successful application. To move incrementally toward this end, these groups pursue secondary litigation goals that are as many and varied as the legal issues that arise in obscenity litigation.

Because of its broad perspective on obscenity questions, and because it is the most active pro-decency litigator, CDL has developed an extensive set of litigation goals. In the past, these included allowing trial courts to make nearly final decisions on the obscenity of litigated materials,[54] keeping the Court from adopting a "consenting adults" approach to permissible regulation,[55] allowing states to use a nuisance abatement approach in dealing with obscenity,[56] avoiding judicial rulings that prior adversary hearings are constitutionally required for the issuance of search warrants and the conduct of criminal prosecutions,[57] denying that the three-pronged *Memoirs* approach has any force of law,[58] arguing that prosecutions under civil laws are not subject to the *Miller* test for obscenity,[59] contending that the padlocking of theaters convicted as public nuisances for showing obscene films is constitutionally permissible,[60] urging the Court to extend the abstention doctrine so that federal courts will have little authority over state obscenity cases,[61] and getting the Court to declare child pornography *malum in se* (bad in itself).[62] Currently, the group is looking for cases that pointedly raise a range of issues: whether obscene films can be copyrighted; the legitimacy of using 42 U.S.C. § 1983 (the Civil Rights Act) to grant court costs, fees, and punitive damages to defendants successful in arguing that the government is harassing them through arbitrary application of obscenity laws;[63] the use of public nuisance statutes to attack "adult" stores, to padlock them for a set period of time, and to force them to turn their profits over to the government; the ability of cities to zone out "adult" businesses; the permissibility of requiring store owners to cover the fronts of sexually explicit magazines and books; and the further extension of the abstention doctrine to keep federal courts from interfering with state enforcement of obscenity laws. It is through these litigation goals that proscriptionist organizations present their more general political goals to the judiciary.

The judicial strategy used by these groups to attain their goals is twofold. First, CDL and MM seek to assist prosecutors directly by providing them with information and expertise. One problem faced by local prosecutors handling obscenity cases is that defense counsel is often experienced in this type of litigation and they are not. This means not only that defense counsel have a better chance to get the client off with no sentence or a minimal one, but also that prosecutors—who have other demands on their resources—will have little further incentive to push these kinds of cases before the courts. Thus, obscenity laws already on the books will often go unenforced. It is to counter the expertise developed by the "obscenity bar"—those lawyers (many of whom are affiliated with the FALA's information clearinghouse or the AFAA) and groups that regularly litigate these issues on the libertarian side—that CDL and MM assist prosecutors.

MM's NOLC was founded to act as a source for specialized information on obscenity issues and has two attorneys on staff, Paul J. McGeady and James Alleva. These men convey relevant information on obscenity law to the NOLC's subscribers. MM *never* sponsors litigation, nor does it attempt to take control of cases already before the judiciary. According to group officials there are three reasons for this. First, MM's function is to provide assistance to *all* governmental authorities, not to get bogged down in any particular branch. Second, the group does not have the resources—in counsel, funds, or time—to involve itself deeply in litigation. Finally, and perhaps most important, CDL has long been active in trials.[64] Thus, something of a de facto division of labor has evolved between these groups. NOLC subscribers, however, include prosecutors, and these officials have access to the legal information the group collects and the *Obscenity Law Bulletin* it regularly publishes.[65] Its counsel also provide the prosecutors with whom they deal advice on the handling of their cases.[66]

CDL is more actively involved in the actual prosecution of obscenity cases. While it disseminates information to prosecutors, it also provides them with staff assistance to prepare and execute their litigation. To this end, CDL has assembled a legal staff of three full-time attorneys (all of whom have previous prosecutory experience), and it maintains other counsel on part-time retainers. These resources enable it to pursue a strategy to project itself directly into the litigation fray. This kind of deep involvement in trial court litigation allows the group to extend its expertise into the courtroom. This provides an opportunity to develop the law in ways favorable to the group's goals and, perhaps as important, to educate local prosecutors on successful prosecutory techniques. Bruce Taylor, CDL's general counsel, sees it as his responsibility to tutor local prosecutors in the elements of successful prosecution of their more experienced foes. He shows them how to use "dirty tricks" (e.g., how to discredit expert witnesses by tying them to pornographers, hot tubs in their sex institutes, and participation in AFAA-sponsored conventions), how to anticipate and counter commonly used defense arguments (e.g., consenting adults can do whatever they wish, material must be "utterly without redeeming social value" to be obscene, and the general availability of materials similar to those on trial means that they are within "contemporary community standards"), and how to mobilize the public to impress on the court the seriousness of the situation. MC's general counsel, Michael Bamberger, details one such CDL tactic: "A whole bunch of mothers came to the trial with their babies to demonstrate to the judge their concern for their children. To have fifteen to twenty little babies in a courtroom is somewhat bizarre" (interview with the author).

These local activities allow CDL to advance many of its goals. They provide it an opportunity to shape the law while at the same time educating local prosecutors and showing them that they *can* win these cases over the defense's experienced "hired guns." To the extent that CDL is able to penetrate the trial courts, it believes that it will be able to match the libertarian obscenity bar with a pro-decency counterpart. Thus, more libertarian attorneys and groups will have the same experience as MC's Bamberger and the obscenity counsel Robert Smith, who, on seeing Taylor seated at the prosecution's table at the beginning of a trial, approached and asked him what he was doing. "Watching you" was Taylor's reply. Active participation in obscenity trials also serves to raise the organization's public profile. This can aid organizational maintenance by giving potential and actual members a sense of a group that is actually doing something to attack the obscenity problem. This can lead to greater donations, which might otherwise go unmade or, given the availability of MM and other similarly inclined groups, go elsewhere. Indeed, group officials see this as a very important maintenance technique; one noted that "people like paying a champion."

The second judicial strategy employed by these groups is somewhat less direct in its effect on the prosecution of obscenity offenses—filing amicus curiae briefs before appellate courts. Although the influence of these briefs may be indirect, if the groups' arguments are adopted by the court—as they seemed to be in *Ginzburg* v. *U.S.* (1966)[67]—their impact can be far greater than a success in a discrete trial. Amicus briefs also are well suited to the litigating posture of proscriptionist groups. Since obscenity is largely a matter of criminal law, these groups are not really in a position to sponsor litigation. CDL attorneys are occasionally asked by local prosecutors to take over and argue cases, but this is not a common occurrence. Moreover, amicus participation is cheap and requires only that the group hear about the case before formal filing deadlines. As such, groups can prepare briefs on issues of concern and submit them to appellate courts with little expenditure of organizational resources. Finally, these briefs can be disseminated to interested others. This allows the groups to get their arguments "out" to local prosecutors and, if these officials use them in the conduct of their litigation, before the courts. Significantly, this is one of the clearinghouse services provided by both CDL and MM's NOLC. Also of utility, at least for CDL, is the publicity it can generate by filing these briefs; its *National Decency Reporter* informs supporters that the group is a constant litigator before the Supreme Court. This may enhance its image with its donors and members, both potential and actual, and promote their largess by giving them a heightened sense of political efficacy.

As with their legal activity more generally, proscriptionist participation as amici curiae is heavily skewered toward CDL. MM joined a handful (7%) of the cases formally decided by the Supreme Court and occasionally files in support of the proscriptionist position in lower federal courts.[68] Although the group is active in these judicial fora—particularly in cases that touch on its specific interests in children and the media—it has yet to emerge as a consistent litigator of general obscenity issues. The amicus participation of the remaining pro-decency groups is far less substantial. CDL, although the frequency of its amicus participation decreased after Taylor became its general counsel in 1981, uses this mode of judicial participation more than all other proscriptionist groups combined.[69] The group, or attorneys affiliated with it, filed amicus briefs in 28 cases decided by the Supreme Court since 1957. One of its retained counsel, James Clancy, argued one case, *Huffman* v. *Pursue* (1975). Further, Taylor was the counsel in one case, *Flynt* v. *Ohio* (1981), which was dismissed, after argument, as improvidently granted. CDL has also filed briefs supporting governmental regulation of obscene and "indecent" materials in lower federal courts.[70] In addition, the group submitted amicus briefs in 27 cases not decided by the Supreme Court.[71] CDL's activity, in conjunction with that undertaken by the other pro-decency organizations, represents a substantial judicial presence and the beginnings of a proscriptionist bar.

The case selection strategy of the pro-decency groups varies with the range of their interests and goals. The occasional participants in obscenity litigation will file as amicus in cases that directly touch on the relatively narrow interests of their members. Thus, for example, it is not surprising to see NLC and NIMLO involved only in the *Renton* (1985) case, a case involving local authority to confine emporiums specializing in sexual materials through zoning regulations. Likewise, CH/IYA intervenes only in instances involving the involvement of youth in the production or distribution of sexually explicit materials. MM's approach is somewhat broader. Its counsel look for cases that frame issues dealing with the regulation of broadcast media and the nexus between youth and sexual materials. On the former, it seeks to extend the Court's ruling in *FCC* v. *Pacifica Foundation* (1978)—allowing FCC regulation and, in some instances, proscription of "indecent" speech from public airwaves—to include a broader category of speech and to encompass cablecast (as well as broadcast) television. It likewise seeks to join cases involving child pornography to facilitate the expansion of the logic of the Court's *Ferber* decision. Although it does not directly involve group action, MM's counsel—through NOLC—will occasionally urge states to appeal important cases on their own.

CDL's litigation strategy is to push the courts, especially the Supreme Court, to accept the logical conclusion of *Miller*: obscenity is a variable concept, unprotected by the First Amendment, that can be proscribed under local standards. Its legal counsel survey the litigation field—drawing information from local decency organizations, media reports, and individuals and attorneys who share its concerns—and join cases that stand to promote this end.[72] CDL officials think that proscriptionists stand today where the libertarians stood after *Redrup*: the Supreme Court is denying review to lower court obscenity convictions, but it must be pressed to make a clear and final pronouncement on lingering questions. Without such a clarification—without a clear and strong rejection of the arguments used successfully by libertarians—the law will remain ambiguous and its enforcement will be problematic. Thus, CDL seeks to participate in cases that could generate new doctrine applicable to the production, distribution, and sale of sexually oriented material, doctrine to buttress and extend the local focus it sees inherent in *Miller* and its progeny. This, in part, explains its (or its affiliated attorneys') presence in cases such as *Brockett* (1985)—involving the use of a "moral nuisance" statute against an "adult" bookstore; *Arcara* (1986)—treating the closing of a bookstore on the grounds that solicitation of prostitution and lewdness occurred on its premises against a state statute making such acts a public health nuisance; and *Pope* (1987)—defining the relevant decisional referent of *Miller*'s "serious . . . value" prong. The successful pursuit of this litigation strategy, group officials believe, will enable proscriptionists to realize the full promise of *Miller*.

Newcomers: Feminist Anti-Pornography Movements

The proscriptionist field cannot be left without giving brief attention to the feminist groups that have gained recent prominence in the obscenity debate. Essentially, the feminist critique of pornography is very simple: pornography, largely produced by and for men, "objectifies" women by presenting them solely as instruments for gratification of male desires, and this objectification denies women the status of equal beings possessed of dignity and rights. The psychological consequences of pornography are not isolated; the consumption of this material leads men to act violently toward women. As such, pornography perpetuates gender-based political and social imbalances in power and status. Beyond this core, the elements of the feminist critique grow more diverse, with distinctions made, for example, between *erotica*—works that, though explicit and graphic, portray women as sexual beings equal to men—and *pornography*, with the former protected by the First Amendment. However, many feminists differ over the substantive content of these categories. These differences aside, the general perspective of this approach is well summarized by Robin Morgan: "Pornography is the theory and rape the practice."[73]

The dramatic growth in feminist theory in the early 1970s was the genesis for this critique of obscenity. It—in conjunction with the increasing availability, graphicness, and violence of sexually oriented material—stimulated the organization of a variety of groups, for example, Women Against Violence Against Women (Los Angeles), Women Against Pornography (New York), and Women Against Violence In Pornography (San Francisco). These groups oppose pornography as exploiting and degrading women in the name of commercial profit, although they make the distinction between erotica and pornography. Their goal is to educate the public on the destructiveness of pornography, and to this end they urge mass letter writing to politicians, conduct tours through the "combat zones" of their cities, organize pickets and boycotts of establishments that disseminate this material, and present slide shows depicting a link between pornography and violence against women. Although active in this arena, however, these groups have not engaged in litigation. The most prominent national feminist organization, the National Organization for Women, has litigated issues of perceived importance to women, but its "participation in this area [obscenity] has been negligible."[74] The legal void left by these groups was, to an extent, filled by the feminist scholars Andrea Dworkin and Catherine MacKinnon.

Dworkin and MacKinnon are primary proponents of a distinctly different legal approach to obscenity, one premised on the idea that those dealing in pornography (defined in feminist terms) can be made the subject of civil action by women "harmed" by it. To this end, they wrote a "feminist antipornography" statute and sought its adoption in a few cities. The first city to consider this approach was Minneapolis, Minnesota. There, in December 1983 and January 1984, the proposed ordinance passed the city council by a vote of 7–6 but was vetoed by Mayor Donald Fraser.[75] Interestingly, the impetus for this ordinance came not from any national group but from the confluence of local factors: the concerns of two neighborhoods that had, for years, sought the removal of "adult" bookstores and theaters from their vicinity, the personal experiences of a number of very vocal women who believed their sexual abuse was "caused" by pornography, a University of Minnesota Law School seminar on pornography taught by MacKinnon and Dworkin, and the perceived ineffectiveness of traditional criminal and zoning restrictions to control obscenity. "Neither the Moral Majority nor other Right wing organizations were among the supporters of the ordinance. The only exception was the president of Morality in Media of Minnesota, Inc., who testified that his group was '100 percent in favor' of the ordinance. He later retracted his statement, saying that the existing obscenity laws should be enforced instead."[76]

Although Mayor Fraser's veto of the proposed ordinance in Minneapolis killed the reform effort there, a similar city ordinance was passed in Indianapolis, Indiana. This ordinance, however, was struck down on constitutional grounds by a federal district court in *American Booksellers Association, et al.* v. *Hudnut* (1984) when the Media Coalition (MC) sued to enjoin its enforcement.[77] This case, unlike the Minneapolis example, saw significant group interest. Filing as amicus on behalf of the city were Andrea Dworkin, the Minneapolis Neighborhood Task Force, some women's shelters, a few chapters of NOW, Linda ("Lovelace") Marchiano, La Raza Centro Legal, and Catherine MacKinnon. Filing in support of MC were the ACLU, the Indiana CLU, the Indiana Library Association, the Feminist Anti-Censorship Task Force (a group formed to oppose the MacKinnon/Dworkin ordinance), and the feminist attorneys Sylvia Law and Nan Hunter.[78] Efforts to secure adoption of similar ordinances in other cities failed (Brest and Vandenberg, 1987, p. 657).

Conspicuously absent from these battles are the pro-decency groups noted at length in this chapter. MM's Minnesota chapter made a brief appearance on the Minneapolis stage but soon took refuge in the more comfortable arena of criminal, as opposed to civil, approaches to this litigation. Why would this seemingly natural issue alliance not form, especially in light of CDL's interest in civil regulation of obscenity and the breadth of application of the feminist statute? The answer is largely organizational, philosophical, and ideological.

The pro-decency organizations traditionally active in this arena are politically conservative, what has, in recent times, been termed "pro-family." The leaders of, for example, CDL and MM are uniformly Catholic in their religious beliefs and social perspective,[79] and as previously noted, the FCF and NLF are tied to the Christian Broadcasting Network of evangelist Pat Robertson. Their political concerns are informed and guided by a conservative Christian vision of the public good. This vision is, put in the popular tongue, akin to the world of June and Ward Cleaver—a return to middle-class, Christian bourgeois values. This is the orientation shared by their donors and members, those who make their activities possible. As purposive organizations, their political actions must stay within the bounds of their supporters' zone of acceptability.

The orientation of the political world of the feminist anti-pornography groups could not be more different. These groups are dominated by people whose social vision is characterized by a dislike of traditional political, social, and moral structures; indeed, these groups hold these structures to be oppressive. Much of what they want is tied to undermining the existing order, and obscenity is merely a symptom of the larger structural ills they see as subordinating women, ills traceable to traditional Judeo-Christian cultural norms. For example, many feminists active in this area espouse "alternative lifestyles" (e.g., lesbianism) as appropriate and liberating. Where pro-decency groups see the family unit as the savior of society, many feminists believe it to be another tool of subordination and domination of women. As a result, many leaders and members of these feminist groups have a palpable contempt for the values and vision that undergird the pro-decency perspective.[80]

This hostility—of both camps toward the other—makes political cooperation difficult, if not impossible. Add to this hostility the need, if these groups do attempt to cooperate in this area of common concern, for group officials to explain this alliance to members. As one pro-decency official told me: "How can I explain to my members being on television panel discussions with people who, while they 'support' our concern about pornography, are hairy legged, unkempt, advocate lesbianism, are pro-choice, hate men and marriage, and are atheistic? What are they going to think? How can I explain this to good Christian people?" Given the underlying moral dimensions of the obscenity debate, these difficulties are substantial and could pose a threat to organizational maintenance. Yet, the pro-decency groups have something that the feminists need: litigation know-how and experience. Also, both camps share a bottom line: obscenity is awful and must be stopped. It is conceivable that, in the future, left and right will meet and will temporarily put aside their larger differences to fight together in the short term. This, however, has yet to happen.

Summary

Like the libertarian groups they so bitterly oppose, the proscriptionist organizations entered obscenity litigation to advance the interests they represent. These interests, however, unlike those of their libertarian counterparts, did not vary substantially, and the goals pro-decency groups sought were, if not identical, complementary. All of these groups are purposive—they exist to promote desired states of political affairs. Groups such as NIMLO and NLC, though marginal actors in this drama, sought to promote a legal and prosecutory climate consistent with confining "adult" outlets to specific portions of cities. FCF and NLF intervened to protect the "family values"—specifically as they relate to children—which these groups see as their primary charge from further dilution at the hands of those who deal in sexually oriented material. CH/IYA filed as amicus in cases that touched on the use of youth in the production and dissemination of these works. Women's groups (e.g., WAP, WAVAW, and WAVIP) and feminist spokespersons such as Andrea Dworkin and Catherine MacKinnon mobilized to portray most sexually explicit works as a violation of the civil rights of all women.

MM and CDL, the most frequent and prominent proscriptionist litigators, entered a wider range of cases at all levels of the judicial system, raising broader issues central to the development of obscenity law as a whole. Despite the differing foci of these groups, all sought the same end: at the minimum, the delegitimization of materials dealing with explicit sex; at the maximum, the end of obscenity as a commodity of trade with a veneer of legal protection.

For all but the feminists, the primary vehicle for the trek of these proscriptionist groups was established Supreme Court precedents. The *Roth* approach, if read and used in light of pro-decency concerns, would allow local communities the legal means and statutory latitude to fight the growing prevalence of this kind of material in their midst. Proscriptionist groups went to court to foster this development, but the forces in opposition to their goals were strong and organized and were successful, at least initially, in getting the ear of the Supreme Court. The proscriptionist path through the courts was long and bumpy, but it was the only path that could lead to the goals they sought—goals inextricably intertwined with the development of constitutional doctrine. Whereas decisions subsequent to *Roth* had frustrated the achievement of their ends, their perseverance kept them in the battle long enough to reach a time and a Court more sympathetic to their concerns. This alone, however, was not enough to insure their success.

CONCLUSION

From its very beginnings in *Roth*, the politics of obscenity drew a varied field of organized actors into the judicial system. The issue orientation of these groups was dichotomous: groups either favored or opposed the public availability of sexually explicit material. Beyond this categorization, the groups active here differed on dimensions relevant to their political behavior. On the libertarian side, groups with primarily political concerns sought an outright end to obscenity regulation. Others, with more material bases of organization, sought less grand results. Commercial groups simply sought to protect their members in the production, distribution, and sales of their wares. Professional groups shared these essentially economic concerns but further sought to protect political, legal, and constitutional principles central to their conception of their vocational function and integrity. These different interests, which stem from the bases and modes of their organization, led these groups to different postures in their approaches to the courts.

Pro-decency groups did not share either the organizational or issue-concern diversity that characterized their libertarian counterparts. All of these organizations are political and purposive—they exist solely to promote a vision of a "good" society, one free of easy availability of sexually explicit fare. Although their position initially gained judicial support—remember that *Roth* (1957) saw the Supreme Court uphold their obscenity convictions and that, in doing so, the Court pointedly left "obscene" expression outside of First Amendment protection—the 15 years after this decision were not so kind. In the 1960s, the Warren Court proved largely insensitive to proscriptionist concerns, and by 1971, given Court rulings and the President's Commission on Obscenity and Pornography *Report*, the possibility that states would lose the legal ability to enforce their obscenity legislation was very real. Libertarians were clearly winning the legal and, perhaps more important, societal and economic wars.

President Nixon's first-term appointment of four new justices to the Supreme Court, and the Court's decision in *Miller* (1973), changed the climate of obscenity politics. *Miller* gave pro-decency groups—at that time limited to CDL and MM—new hope and life. Libertarians, so long in control of the doctrinal direction of law, were forced into, for the first time since the brief period immediately following *Roth*, an unfavorable legal position. For them, politics (and litigation) as normal was no longer sufficient. The Burger Court had changed the field on which the politics of obscenity would play out. In changing the legal climate in which these groups sought their goals, the Court created a new context for obscenity litigation and altered the group dynamics that characterized this political struggle. The reactions of these groups to this cataclysmic environmental upheaval is the subject of the remainder of this book.

NOTES

1. Initially I termed these groups *suppressionist*, but in speaking with their leaders, I learned that they felt this was a liberal buzzword that deflected attention from their core concern: decency. Hence they are characterized in the text as *pro-decency* or *proscriptionist*.

2. Schauer (1976) provides a compendium of state and federal anti-obscenity laws.

3. At the time of Comstock's death in 1915, he claimed to have destroyed 50 tons of books, 28,425 pounds of printing plates, four million pictures, and 16,900 negatives and was reputed to have driven 15 people to commit suicide. See, generally, Haney (1960), ch. 1, Boyer (1968), Pivar (1973), and Schauer (1976), ch. 1.

4. Indeed, the names on the subscriber list for the New England Society for the Suppression of Vice could be those of the social register: Cabot, Lodge, Lowell, Holmes, Thayer, and Morgan.

5. Haney's (1960) treatment of the activities of the NLD and the NODL is highly critical. A Catholic perspective on the question is provided by Gardiner (1958).

6. The ACLU archives at Mudd Library, Princeton University, contain many letters and press releases from the mid-twentieth century that note and condemn the use of these materials by various police departments. See also Walker (1990), pp. 100, 232.

7. The ACLU had participated in obscenity cases (*Ulysses*, *Wilson*), but it had no coherent obscenity agenda until the 1950s (see Walker, 1990).

8. As in many political arenas, the labels assumed and used by groups, both to

characterize themselves and their opposition, are significant. Although the dual la-
beling used in this sentence will not be maintained throughout the book, it is employed here to convey the competing perceptions involved in this debate.

9. *Newsweek*, 18 March 1985, p. 62. Note that this figure does not include the
profit from the sales of cassettes, books, magazines, arcade videos, etc. It also merits
mention that other, "legitimate" commercial outlets (e.g., major motion pictures,
national magazines) have also benefited from the legal liberalization of obscenity
standards and that the revenues of those outlets are not included in the $500-million
figure.

10. The VLA filed an amicus brief in *Pope* v. *Illinois* (1987), a case that involved
the scope of the community relevant to the determination of materials possessing
"serious literary, artistic, political, or scientific value" under the *Miller* test. Interestingly, Irwin Karp, the legal counsel for the Authors League of America (AL), a
prominent material-professional group considerably more active in obscenity litigation
than the VLA, wrote this brief. The AL is discussed in more detail below.

11. It needs to be noted that, as Michael Dukasis found out, despite Reitman's
claim—and this is the claim of other ACLU officials as well (see Neier, 1979)—this
neutrality is subject to debate. See, for example, Bishop (1971), McIlhany (1975),
Lukas (1978), and Mann (1978). For one response to these critics, see Walker (1990),
parts 6 and 7.

12. On Black's absolutism, see his dissents in *Dennis* v. *U.S.* (1951) and *Barenblatt*
v. *U.S.* (1959). For the most renowned statement of Brandeis's variant of the clear
and present danger test, see his concurrence in *Whitney* v. *California* (1927).

13. Its previous involvement was sporadic and largely dealt with cases treating
what were arguably "classics" or serious literature. See *U.S.* v. *Dennett* (1930), *U.S.*
v. *Ulysses* (1934), and *Winters* v. *New York* (1948), and, more generally, Murphy (1975),
pp. 33–35.

14. Minutes of the Censorship Committee meeting of 14 April 1960, ACLU archives. In the ACLU amicus brief in *Roth*, Emanuel Redfield stressed the clear and
present danger prong of this statement in arguing against Roth's conviction.

15. ACLU press release of 28 May 1962, ACLU archives. The chairperson of this
committee was the dramatist Elmer Rice. Staff members included Lawrence Speiser,
Alan Reitman, and Melvin Wulf. Other participants included the ACLU's Ephraim
London, Harriet Pilpel, and Emanual Redfield and two legal counsel from the Association of American Publishers (AAP), Dan Lacy and Horace Manges.

16. Noted in interviews with group officials. Also see the ACLU amicus briefs in
Jacobellis (1964), *Ginzburg* (1966), and *Aday* (1967).

17. This strategy was first discussed by the Censorship Committee immediately
after *Roth* was handed down, was a part of the Southern California CLU's amicus
brief in *Smith* v. *California* (1963), and provided the underpinning for the group's
amicus argument in *Ginzburg* as it moved through the federal courts.

18. On the latter point see the *Ginzburg* amicus brief to the Supreme Court and
Wulf's letter of 3 January 1964 to the Philadelphia CLU accepting an offer to join
their amicus brief at the district court level.

19. Cases summarily reversed are not granted oral argument. Because of this, third
parties seldom have a chance to participate in the litigation. Thus, summary reversals
are not counted as cases in which groups could have participated. It should be noted
that counting participation in this way does not count the involvement of the ACLU

in three cases—*Times-Film* (1957), *Sunshine Books* (1957), and *Aday* (1967)—and that of the AAP in one—*Aday* (1967)—because, although these groups filed amicus briefs in these cases, the Court decided them without hearing arguments. The percentages cited here are drawn from data presented in tables 1.2 and 2.2.

20. In interviews with the author, group officials noted only three areas in which the ACLU actively looked to develop a series of cases to lead the courts to the group's ultimate goals: church-state relations, women's rights, and defendant's rights.

21. Proposed statement of policy with respect to obscenity, 13 April 1960, ACLU archives.

22. See, for example, the arguments it tendered in *Grove Press* v. *Gerstein* (1964) and *Jacobellis* v. *Ohio* (1964).

23. See, for example, its arguments in *Dyson* v. *Stein* (1971) (argued by General Counsel Melvin Wulf) and its amicus briefs in *Byrne* v. *Karalexis* (1971) and *Miller* (1973).

24. See the dissenting statements of Commissioners Morton A. Hill, S. J. (the president of Morality in Media) and Charles H. Keating, Jr. (the president of Citizens for Decency through Law). See also Berns (1971), Bickel (1971), and Clor (1971).

25. See, for example, its amicus briefs in *Hamling* v. *U.S.* (1974), *Young* v. *American Mini Theatres* (1976), *FCC* v. *Pacifica* (1978), *New York* v. *Ferber* (1982), and *Virginia* v. *American Booksellers Association, Inc., et al.* (1988).

26. The DGA filed an amicus brief in *Jenkins* v. *Georgia* (1974), the ASJA in *Virginia* v. *American Booksellers Association, Inc., et al.* (1988).

27. This information is drawn from *The Encyclopedia of Associations* and from the AAP's publication "An Introduction to the American Association of Publishers."

28. This information is drawn from *The Encyclopedia of Organizations*, various amicus briefs, and a letter from General Counsel Irwin Karp to me (16 March 1983).

29. Information drawn from *The Encyclopedia of Associations*, an interview with Bob Doyle, the assistant to the director of the ALA, and various organizational publications.

30. See the "Memorandum" of the Office of Intellectual Freedom of the ALA, January-February 1983, and the "Freedom to Read Foundation News," vol. 11, no. 4.

31. The first obscenity case in which the AL filed an amicus brief was *Phillips* v. *McCaffrey*, 208 Misc. 267, 143 M.Y.S.2d 138 (Sup. Ct. 1955) (Karp, 1977, p. 3).

32. See the amicus briefs of these groups in, for example, *Jenkins* v. *Georgia* (1974) and *Hamling* v. *U.S.* (1974).

33. See the AL briefs in *Bantam Books* (1963), *Ginzburg* (1966), *Interstate Circuit* (1968), *Ginsberg* (1968), and Karp's testimony before the House Judiciary Committee, 17 November 1970.

34. Letter from Karp to author, 16 March 1983. Karp's recollection here is, in part, in error: the MPAA did file an amicus brief in *FCC* v. *Pacifica* (1978). The explanation for the MPAA's involvement here is in its interest in the rules governing dissemination of material through the electronic media. Put simply, its concern was with the application of any rule regarding "indecency" to movies televised over cable television.

35. In *Jenkins* (1974), the Court, with Justice Rehnquist writing for the majority, unanimously struck down the determination of Georgia courts that the movie *Carnal Knowledge* was obscene.

36. In *American Mini Theatres* (1976), the Court, by a vote of 5–4, upheld a Detroit ordinance that used zoning regulations to confine "adult" theaters to certain sections of the city.

37. This information is drawn from various sources: interviews with the author, testimony before congressional committees, organizational literature, and amicus curiae briefs.

38. Although this potential for ambiguity is most obvious in commercial organizations, it is common in material groups more generally. For example, the ALA is constantly torn between the minimalist goal of protecting the activities of librarians and the goal of advancing its more general First Amendment interests. This tension has been heightened since it took the lead in creating the Freedom to Read Foundation, a group dedicated to its broader position on expression issues. The problem for the group is not abstract; it implicates, among other things, the allocation of scarce organizational resources. This being said, it is also the case that professional groups are not affected by this tension in the same way as are commercial groups because their vocational interests, though occupational and sectoral, are broader; they are not demarcated along media lines.

39. One of the strange consequences of the *Miller* decision is that it did not set loose a consistent and broad-based effort to enforce obscenity laws (see the findings of the Obscenity Law Project, 1976). Thus, although some AFAA counsel and leaders wanted to establish a general fund to support the litigation of members as well as that of the group itself, the members have never supported a more organized group effort to mold the law to the group's formal obscenity goal.

40. Vagueness and overbreadth are related legal concepts. The former is used to strike laws that rest on definitions that are imprecise and, hence, do not give those to whom they apply sufficient notice of what is legally permissible. In obscenity litigation, libertarians often claim that statutes are too vague to allow businesses a clear understanding of what is prohibited. Overbreadth refers to legislation that, though defining a category of proscription, defines that category so broadly as to allow prosecution of expression protected by the First Amendment.

41. Common procedural requirements sought by libertarians include requiring a civil hearing on the "obscenity" of challenged material prior to criminal prosecutions, disallowing prior restraints on potentially obscene materials, and avoiding statutory or administrative restrictions on the circulation or exhibition of materials treating sexual themes.

42. Since *Miller* allows the proscription of materials at variance with community standards, libertarian groups have sought to establish a conception of community that is as broad as possible to support the greatest scope of tolerance and, hence, availability of expressive materials.

43. MC also challenged similar statutes in Colorado, Pennsylvania, and Virginia. The Virginia case, *Virginia* v. *American Booksellers Association, Inc.* (1988) made its way to the Supreme Court of the United States only to be returned to the Virginia State Supreme Court for an authoritative construction of the statute in question. In addition to the "back room" technique, states have also required such materials to be covered, in plastic or by some other blocking device, to prevent public perusal in a store.

44. *Reader's Digest* gave a great deal of ink to the obscenity problem in the mid-

1960s and was very supportive of CDL's activities and goals. See articles in its November 1965, September 1966, February 1967, and January 1971 editions.

45. Interviews with group officials.

46. *Operation Yorkville Newsletter*, February 1965.

47. The evolution of MM and CDL into national organizations runs contrary to the argument of Zurcher and Kirkpatrick (1973, 1976). These scholars suggest that local groups will disband after a self-defined triumph. Whatever the utility of this approach for other groups, it fails to explain the development of CDL and MM.

48. This is not to suggest that these other incentives are unimportant to these organizations. In fact, group leaders attempt to manipulate purposive and solidary incentives to maintain local chapters and membership. This is especially important in an area like obscenity where the life of a local chapter or membership can be exceedingly tenuous (Zurcher and Kirkpatrick, 1973, 1976). The problem group leaders face is one of maintaining interest and involvement, both in terms of activities and monetary support: the momentum developed by the factors that stimulated the formation of a local affiliate is difficult to maintain over time. If the group is successful and the obscenity threat is removed, then its raison d'être is likewise removed. If the affiliate is unsuccessful, members may become disheartened and lose the desire to continue the battle. By constantly stressing the successes of other chapters, the pervasiveness of the problem, and the importance of perseverance, the national office can try to manipulate incentives to keep member and chapter morale high and engaged, mitigating dangers of organizational decay. Solidary incentives specific to a local chapter further facilitate these attempts at organizational maintenance.

49. In May 1989, after the CDL founder Keating became enmeshed in the political controversy surrounding the savings and loan crisis, CDL reconstituted itself as the "Children's Legal Foundation." This new organization, which claims no ties to Keating, maintains the former group's central focus and has extended its activities to include explicit rock-and-roll lyrics and Satanism (Corn, 1990), p. 16. The effect of this change on its litigation strategy is, as of yet, unclear.

50. MM publication "Turn the Tide on Pornography."

51. *National Decency Reporter*, 15 September 1963.

52. For example, the zoning statute at issue in *Renton* (1986) prohibited locating an "adult motion picture theater" within 1,000 feet of "any residential zone, single- or multiple-family dwelling, church, or park, and within one mile of any school."

53. For an extended discussion of Keating's role as a commissioner, see the *NYT* (6 August, 6 September, 1 October 1970), the *Nation* (11 May 1970), and his own analysis in *Reader's Digest* (January 1971). On Hill's activities on the commission, see the *NYT* (6 September, 6 October 1970). He also filed a dissent to the commission's "progress report" and testified against it before House (16 March 1970) and Senate (23 September 1970) committee hearings.

54. See the CDL amicus curiae brief in *Jacobellis* (1964).

55. See the CDL amicus curiae brief in *Paris Adult Theatre* (1973).

56. See the CDL amicus curiae brief in *"Vixen"* (1973).

57. See the CDL amicus curiae brief in *Roaden* (1973).

58. See the CDL amicus curiae brief in *Aday* (1967).

59. See the CDL amicus curiae brief in *Jenkins* (1974).

60. See the CDL amicus curiae brief in *U.S. Marketing* (1982).

61. See the CDL amicus curiae brief in *Huffman* (1975).

62. "Evil in itself" and prosecutable without concern with First Amendment values or doctrine. See the CDL amicus curiae brief in *Ferber* (1982).

63. One device obscenity defendants have recently begun to use is § 1983—which allows someone harassed in the exercise of their civil rights (here, free speech) to sue for costs and damages. Defendants who pursue this strategy successfully not only receive a tidy sum of cash but also create a strong disincentive for future prosecution by financially strapped governments.

64. Both Father Hill and General Counsel McGeady think that CDL is very effective in its provision of counsel to assist prosecutors, the former telling me: "I am happy they exist. I wish we had a dozen more like them."

65. The NOLC, in fact, grew out of a recommendation in Father Hill's minority report to the President's Commission on Obscenity and Pornography.

66. For example, McGeady regularly counsels prosecutors to keep their cases in state courts and, if the defendants bring actions against obscenity laws in the federal courts, to make abstention arguments in an effort to get them dismissed. McGeady, like his counterparts in CDL, believes that state courts are more favorably inclined to obscenity prosecution.

67. CDL, in its amicus brief in *Ginzburg* (1966), urged the Supreme Court to embrace a variable conception of obscenity that would, in this case, include "pandering"—hawking the material in question on its titillating properties—as a component of the offense. The Court did exactly this and, moreover, extended this approach in its decisions in *Mishkin* v. *New York* (1966) and *Ginsberg* v. *New York* (1968).

68. For example, it recently filed as amicus in three cases in the lower federal courts: *Carlin Communications, Inc.* v. *FCC* (1984)—supporting federal regulation of "dial-a-porn" services; *Jones, et al.* v. *Wilkinson, Attorney General of Utah* (1985, 1986)—upholding state efforts to regulate cablecasts of movies with sexual content; and *Action for the Children's Television* v. *FCC* (1988)—supporting FCC efforts to broaden its definition of "indecent material" and ban such from radio broadcast except for the midnight to 6:00 A.M. time slot. Significantly, its brief in the *Action for the Children's Television* case was prepared by, and filed in association with, Taylor and CDL.

69. Taylor, though not discounting the usefulness of strategically filed amicus curiae briefs, has placed more importance on using CDL resources to directly assist local prosecutors in obscenity cases. This may be a result of his previous experience as a prosecutor in Ohio; Keating, the founder of the group, had no such experience and may have seen amicus participation as both inexpensive and publicity producing.

70. Note its briefs in *FW/PBS* v. *City of Dallas* (1986, 1988)—urging the affirmance of a Dallas licensing and zoning ordinance—and *Action for the Children's Television* (1988) with MM.

71. These cases were denied certiorari, dismissed as improvidently granted, or rejected for want of a substantial federal question. (See appendix B for a full listing of these cases.)

72. This method of discovering cases relevant to CDL concerns is far from fail safe, as it allows potentially significant cases to slip through the system unnoticed by group officials. If information on a case is not received, at the latest, before the Supreme Court grants certiorari, the group will miss an opportunity to influence legal development. This information gap explains why CDL did not file an amicus brief in *FCC* v. *Pacifica* (1978), a case of substantial import to its concerns.

73. Quoted in "The War Against Pornography," *Newsweek*, 18 March 1985, p. 60. In 1970, Ms. Morgan led a sit-in at the New York offices of Grove Press to protest the firm's profiting from "the basic theme of humiliating, degrading, and dehumanizing women through sadomasochistic literature, pornographic films, and oppressive and exploitative practices against its own female employees" (Brest and Vandenberg, 1987, p. 611). For some general background on some of the splits in the feminist camp on the issue of obscenity, see Brest and Vandenberg (1987) and West (1987).

74. Information about these groups was drawn from their newsletters and organizational literature. The quote is from a letter from Bernice Hoffman, NOW Legal Defense and Education Fund, to this author.

75. Newspaper accounts of the Minneapolis ordinance can be found in the *Minneapolis Star-Tribune*, 31 December 1983 to 7 January 1984.

76. The quote is from a very good general review of the Minneapolis activity, Brest and Vandenberg (1987), p. 633. While Mayor Fraser was contemplating his veto, officials from his office were quoted in the *Minneapolis Star-Tribune* as saying "no organized groups are lobbying" (5 January 1984). A good general discussion of the Dworkin-MacKinnon approach to pornography regulation can be found in Downs (1989).

77. The district court decision was upheld by the U.S. Court of Appeals for the Seventh Circuit in *ABA, et al.* v. *Hudnut* (1985) and was summarily affirmed by the Supreme Court, 106 S.Ct 1172, 106 S.Ct 1664 (1986).

78. These groups were identified through the *Federal Supplement* and Brest and Vandenberg (1987), p. 654.

79. The religious homogeneity here is striking: the top officials of CDL (Keating, Taylor, James Clancy, Carol Clancy, Paul McCommon), MM (Hill and McGeady), and CH/IYA (Father Bruce Ritter) are all Catholic.

80. For a good discussion of the difficulty of fitting the pro-decency and feminist perspectives into a coherent framework, see West (1987).

3

Organizational Adaptation: Exit

The true scope of civil liberties can be as broad as the Bill of Rights.
—Melvin Wulf, 1970

As a general rule, why bring cases you know you are going to lose?
—Alan Reitman, 1983

One response to a drastic change in a legal or political context is to abandon or de-emphasize litigation that the courts will treat with little favor. This was essentially the reaction of the ACLU to the post-*Miller* environment. Among libertarian actors involved in this area of litigation, the ACLU's response—initial de-emphasis and near abandonment of obscenity litigation—to the legal shift fostered by *Miller* was anomalous. Although the 1980s saw something of a reawakening of the group's participation in obscenity litigation, its nearly decade-long de-emphasis left it outside of the newly emergent group forces that currently direct libertarian litigation of these questions. The ACLU has gone from a dominant to a subordinate status in the organizational pursuit of libertarian obscenity goals.

Before assessing the demise of the ACLU's dominance, we should review in brief its general interest in obscenity politics. Although the group's interest in obscenity is long-standing, it was not of central organizational concern until the Supreme Court handed down its decision in *Roth* (1957).[1] After extensive and sometimes acrimonious internal debate, ACLU leaders decided to develop, and press in the courts, the argument that the First Amendment protects obscene speech.[2] Although it ultimately sought a reversal of the *Roth* approach, the ACLU developed a layered goal structure to facilitate bringing the courts to this position. Its strategy entailed forcing the courts, primarily the Supreme Court, to expand the libertarian dicta of *Roth* while simultaneously curtailing its illiberal aspects. This strategy required considerable organizational presence in obscenity litigation, a presence it was able to project because of its size, resources, and affiliates. From 1957 to 1973, the ACLU was the dominant organizational actor of a libertarian tenor in the obscenity cases decided by the Supreme Court (see appendix C).

Given its goal of abolishing obscenity as an unprotected category of speech, the decade of the 1960s was good to the ACLU. With the Warren Court reversing convictions and deciding in favor of the libertarian position in 84 percent of its obscenity decisions, the group's goal of undermining *Roth* was close to being realized. Indeed, pro-decency groups feared that this was happening. In CDL's amicus curiae brief in *Memoirs* v. *Massachusetts* (1966), its attorneys argued that local prosecutors "lose heart when they see all losses and no victories." If localities were less inclined to prosecute obscenity violations because of the Court's seeming dislike of proscription, the ACLU position would become de facto public policy.

The 1960s saw not only decisional results going the ACLU's way but also, by the end of the decade, doctrinal rumblings from the Court that were even more favorable to the group's goals. *Redrup* v. *New York* (1967) prompted a spate of conviction reversals and suggested that a majority of the justices were adopting a least common denominator approach; without exposure to minors or unwilling adults, and absent pandering, no obscenity conviction was constitutionally permissible. This nascent approach seemed to be furthered by decisions in *Ginsberg* v. *New York* (1968) and *Stanley* v. *Georgia* (1969). *Ginsberg* upheld a conviction for selling to minors such "girlie" magazines as would not be obscene if sold to adults, and it appeared to reinforce the least common denominator understanding of *Redrup*.[3] *Stanley* extended constitutional protection to privately held obscene material and suggested a rejection of the two-level speech distinction that lay at the doctrinal heart of *Roth*. Taken together, these decisions seemed to point to the end of the *Roth* approach.[4] The triumph of the ACLU strategy appeared inevitable.

Despite the favorable development in results and doctrine, a few obstacles remained before the ACLU in its effort to attain its goals. First, the Court was hesitant to extend the "consenting adults" logic that seemed to spring from *Redrup*, *Ginsberg*, *Stanley*, *Rowan* v. *Post Office* (1970).[5] It had the chance to take this step in *U.S.* v. *Reidel* (1971) and *U.S.* v. *37 Photographs* (1971),[6] but it did not act to do so. Second, Richard Nixon appointed four new justices during his first term as president. Throughout his campaign for the presidency, Nixon had been an outspoken critic of the Warren Court, repeatedly pointing to its treatment of obscenity. Further, his experience as

Eisenhower's vice president had taught him the importance of careful and strategic judicial selection. As president, Nixon selected justices who would support his values.[7]

Once the Burger Court was in place, it aborted its predecessor's doctrinal and decisional development in obscenity law. The formal shift came in a series of cases, led by *Miller* v. *California*, handed down in June 1973. *Miller's* test afforded governments more latitude in the determination of obscenity, was reinforced by the decision in *Hamling* v. *U.S.* (1974),[8] and was further buttressed by subsequent decisions and appointments to the Court.[9] Indeed, of the 34 obscenity cases handled by the Burger Court in which its decision can be classified as libertarian or proscriptionist, this Court decided 71 percent in favor of the proscriptionist position.[10]

The advent of the Burger Court's posture on obscenity issues, epitomized by its decision in *Miller*, radically altered the environment in which this litigation occurred. This environmental change moved legal development away from the goals sought by the ACLU. The June 1973 decisions destroyed the group's strategy to end legal proscription of sexually oriented material. No longer were the arguments it proffered given credence by a majority of the Court; no longer was obscenity law moving toward formal extinction. Facing a new and inhospitable legal environment, what would the organization's response be? How would it adapt?

Nearly alone among all of the organizations active in obscenity litigation, the ACLU adapted to the post-*Miller* environment by de-emphasizing obscenity litigation.[11] Although it has occasionally involved itself in cases treating issues related to obscenity, after *Miller* the group curtailed its judicial pursuit of its obscenity goals. Initially, its judicial disinterest in this issue brought it close to abandonment. Only with the rise in social conservatism in the 1980s did the ACLU reenter the field. Its reemergence, however, was neither as strategically developed nor as central to the libertarian cause as its earlier efforts. The reasons for this mode of adaptation to the post-*Miller* environment are complex and include factors both internal and external to the organization. This chapter will examine these factors in an attempt to explain the exit of the ACLU from a position of control over the libertarian litigation of obscenity issues.

ORGANIZATIONAL RESPONSE TO *MILLER*

We can examine the response of the ACLU to *Miller* on a couple of dimensions. One dimension is its verbal or rhetorical response—what its leaders and court briefs said about the decision and the litigation environment it created. A second dimension is behavioral—how the group actually adapted to the new legal context. Although these dimensions are related, they are not interdependent; harsh rhetoric may mask organizational disinterest.

The *Miller* decision was a blow to the progress the organization had made during the 1960s in undermining obscenity law. In essence, the Burger Court had thrown out all of the levers that the ACLU was pulling to pry obscenity from unprotected status. In addition to limiting *Stanley* and rejecting *Redrup*, the Court pointedly discarded the portion of the *Jacobellis/Memoirs* test that made successful obscenity prosecution difficult. In repudiating the "utterly without redeeming social value" prong of the earlier test, the Burger majority took away the avenue of expanding that category to include almost all expression as "of value." Moreover, in reasserting the essential correctness of *Roth*, *Miller* left no doubt that the end of obscenity proscription was not in the offing. With this, the argumentational tacks used by the ACLU during the 1960s were dismissed as irrelevant by the June 1973 decisions.

Hamling v. *U.S.* (1974) provided the ACLU with an institutional path of rhetorical response. In its amicus curiae brief, the group attacked the Court for rejecting the logical extension of *Redrup* and *Stanley* and for reasserting the two-level speech approach of *Roth*. It noted the increased harassment of magazines such as *Playboy* and of major motion pictures such as *Carnal Knowledge* and *Last Tango in Paris*, asserting, "In the months following this Court's 1973 ruling a wave of censorship has swept across this nation, encompassing material admittedly with a sexual content but which in no way could be characterized as 'hard-core' pornography" (ACLU amicus curiae brief in *Hamling*). The basic contention of the brief was that *Miller* gave localities a "green light" to censor: thus, materials that clearly deserved constitutional protection were being prosecuted. The dangers of this were clear to the ACLU. Because of the legal uncertainty unleashed by *Miller*, protected expression would be "chilled"—authors and distributors would be disinclined to produce and circulate materials that could land them in the courts. This "chill" would extend beyond arguably obscene material to works of obvious value. Emboldened by their success, local prosecutors would eventually move against "undesirable" expression more generally. Thus, the ACLU argued that *Miller* created a slippery slope that endangered all expression. It asked the Court to reverse its decision of the previous term.[12]

Despite the ACLU's plea, the Court reinforced its *Miller* approach in *Hamling*. For the first time since the ACLU began making concerted attempts to liberalize obscenity law, its arguments seemed to be falling on deaf ears. Although it joined other cases related to obscenity after *Hamling*, it was not strident in its call for the reversal of the two-level speech approach. ACLU officials stress that they remain committed to *Miller*'s reversal, but the group does not use many occasions to make this point. Its goals in obscenity matters have not changed, but its ability to persuade the Court of their correctness has.[13] Because of this, the group's post-*Miller* strategy softened to the limitation, not abolition, of proscription.

The ACLU's rhetorical response to *Miller* was one of hostility; its behavioral response was clearer and sharper. The organization still formally opposes the proscription of sex-oriented material, but it no longer engages in ob-

Table 3.1
ACLU Participation before the Supreme Court, Pre- and Post-*Miller*

	Involvement*	Involvement Not Counting Summary Reversals
Pre-Miller (#/% of n)	21/23.9% (n=88)	18/39.1% ** (n=46)
Post-Miller (#/% of n)	9/29.0% (n=31)	9/29.0% (n=31)

* Counts amicus curiae and sponsorship participation.
** Does not include participation in Times-Film (1957), Sunshine Books (1957), or Aday (1967)-- all cases summarily reversed.

scenity litigation with its former frequency. Table 3.1 demonstrates its altered litigation posture before the Supreme Court. A close perusal of this table demonstrates one aspect of the ACLU's post-*Miller* shift. Of the 30 obscenity cases in which it participated between 1957 and 1987, 21 came prior to the end of the 1972 term of the Court. Of the nine post-*Miller* cases in which it appeared, three—*FCC* v. *Pacifica Foundation* (1978), *Board of Education* v. *Pico* (1982), and *Maryland* v. *Macon* (1985)—were not "pure" obscenity cases but involved the FCC's regulation of a radio broadcast containing "indecent" speech, a school board's removal of "offensive" books from a high school library, and the search and seizure of materials in an "adult" bookstore. The group's participation in the remaining cases tells us a good deal about its approach to the post-*Miller* environment.

Of the ACLU's six other post-*Miller* cases, it stressed its primary obscenity goal—the end of this kind of regulation—only in *Hamling*. In *Young* v. *American Mini Theatres* (1976) and *Renton* v. *Playtime Theatres* (1986), it argued that attempts to control red-light districts through zoning were unconstitutionally overbroad. In *Ferber* (1982), it joined with Media Coalition (MC) and the American Library Association's Freedom to Read Foundation (ALA/FRF) to oppose New York State's child pornography law because of its perceived vagueness and overbreadth. It also argued in *Arcara* v. *Cloud Books* (1986) that closing an "adult" bookstore for public health reasons was an impermissible prior restraint. Finally, it again joined an MC case when it urged the Court to reject a state "protective covering" law in *Virginia* v. *American Booksellers Association* (1988). These cases, as well as *FCC* and *Pico*, raised new issues in the general area of censorship but did not require the group to address *Miller*-type questions. In all but the *Pico* case, the Court held against the ACLU's position.[14]

This decline in organizational participation before the Supreme Court does not reflect a concomitant shift to lower court litigation by the national organization. Although the national office and its Indiana affiliate supported MC's successful attack on the Indianapolis feminist anti-pornography statute, there has been no general shift in attention to obscenity matters in lower courts. Neither have ACLU affiliates pushed obscenity litigation before the courts with any regularity. Although affiliates are free to undertake any kind of litigation their officials wish, they have not been very active in obscenity litigation since *Miller*. The reasons for this are many and in some senses parallel those that help to explain the shift of the national organization. First, the law is clear and unfavorable to the group's goals—*Miller* left little room for broad-based libertarian arguments. Second, the national organization is not inclined to assist obscenity litigation undertaken by its affiliates. Since obscenity is a low priority for the national office, this gives affiliates little incentive to take such cases. Third, affiliates often have "pet" projects that consume scarce litigation resources and, hence, lessen their ability to handle questions that, in the current environment, seem less pressing. In short, the falloff of ACLU obscenity litigation is not confined to cases brought before the Supreme Court or by the national association.[15]

Thus, the behavioral response of the ACLU to the post-*Miller* environment did not match its rhetorical response. The latter, though somewhat muted, held *Miller* to be a very dangerous precedent that must be overturned. This remains the formal position of the group. Yet, although the subject goals of the ACLU have not changed, its strategy and involvement in obscenity litigation have. Prior to *Miller*, it participated in 39 percent of the Supreme Court's obscenity decisions, not counting summary reversals; since *Miller* it has dropped to 29 percent, and in many of these cases obscenity was not its central concern. In only one of its post-*Miller* appearances did it make an argument based on its specific goal in the obscenity area, the end of the two-level approach. Why did the ACLU adapt to the post-*Miller* environment by de-emphasizing litigation of traditional obscenity issues? What factors conditioned this exit?

CONDITIONING FACTORS: INTERNAL

Two group-specific factors stand out as conditioning the response of the ACLU to the environment created by *Miller*: leadership and membership. Though distinct concepts, these factors are interrelated. Insofar as members join a group to realize certain benefits, the actions of leaders can affect the membership calculus. Likewise, the needs of the members, as perceived by group leaders, can influence the activities that organizations undertake.

The interaction of leaders and members is especially important in purposive groups, those that exist to provide nonmaterial, or "expressive" (Salisbury, 1969), benefits to their members (Wilson, 1973; Moe, 1980, 1981). If an individual joins an organization because of the goals or political positions it expresses, then the issues seized on by the leadership are important chits in maintaining and increasing the membership and resource base of the organization. If the leaders undertake actions that are unpopular with a portion of the membership, those in the offended segment can choose to "exit"—to leave the group (Hirschman, 1970). If enough members express disfavor with group goals in this way, the continuance of the organization can be threatened.

On the other hand, group leaders can adopt expressive goals in an effort to draw new members to the organization. If this can be accomplished without alienating "old" members to the point of exit, the organization can increase its resource base and, hence, its activities. In this sense, the group's leaders can be seen as exercising something of an entrepreneurial function in providing benefits that they believe to have value in the marketplace.[16] Insofar as they do, consumers (potential and actual members) will be encouraged to buy these benefits by joining the group. In this way, the goals expressed and the issues addressed by the leaders of purposive groups are important tools of organizational development and maintenance. Moreover, this relationship is dynamic: the goals and actions of group leaders can attract *or* repel members and resources.

The ACLU is an expressive or purposive organization. The positions its leaders take undoubtedly influence the size and makeup of its membership and its resource pool (Mann, 1978; Lukas, 1978; Neier, 1979; Gibson and Bingham, 1985; Walker, 1990). An examination of these factors helps to explain the ACLU's withdrawal from, and eventual de-emphasis of, obscenity litigation.

Leadership

Two aspects of the ACLU leadership between 1957 and 1987 are especially relevant to the group's response to *Miller*. First, the leadership of the organization began to change in the mid-1960s. Prior to this time, the group was led by people like Ephraim London, Osmond K. Fraenkel, Emanuel Redfield, Harriet Pilpel, and Morris Ernst—"old school" civil liberties attorneys with a profound attachment to general principles of free expression.[17] These individuals were philosophically interested in censorship questions and were in positions of organizational leadership when obscenity became a hotly contested issue. They were involved in the initial ACLU legal attacks on obscenity and in the reassessment of its official position on the question through its Censorship Committee in the early 1960s.[18] Not only were they committed to this issue because of their connection to the ACLU, but they also were involved in obscenity litigation as defense attorneys. In pursuing obscenity concerns through the group, they were involved with something in which they had considerable interest and expertise. Adopting a high organizational profile on these questions surely did not hurt their marketability as private counsel for those accused of obscenity law violations. Furthermore, ACLU successes in this area helped them win their "private" cases.

The new generation that assumed organizational leadership in the late 1960s did not share the same legal interests as their predecessors. They cut their political teeth on the social activism that characterized the 1960s. Many were very active in the campaign for civil rights.[19] Some had sprung out of the New Left movement.[20] Still others, such as the legal director, Melvin Wulf, were active in the organization in the late 1950s but were able to advance *their* goals only once the "old guard" began to dwindle.[21] Indeed, Samuel Walker has argued that the emergence of these leaders "marked the advent of the 'new' ACLU" (1990, p. 314). This leadership shift played an important role in the activities the ACLU undertook.

Leadership change alone does not necessarily cause the reorientation of a purposive organization's political positions.[22] However, the new leaders of the ACLU did move the group into new areas of concern. This shift in orientation did not occur without dissent from some in the organization. Joseph Bishop termed this shift a battle between "traditionalists" and "activists." His characterization of these two camps is illuminating.

[Activists] believe the Union's mission is to crusade for such political causes as find favor in their eyes. [Traditionalists] have an aggravating habit of pointing out that the Union's own Constitution provides that its objects "shall be to maintain and advance civil liberties, including the freedoms of association, press, religion, and speech, and the rights to the franchise, to due process of law, and to equal protection of the laws wholly without political partisanship." Those of the activists who bother to debate the question reply that the Constitution . . . mandates Good and prohibits Evil. (Bishop, 1971, p. 51)

Bishop noted that the new leaders of the organization did "tolerate" the more traditional activities of the ACLU, but he also contended that they "plainly" found them "about as exciting as Civic Virtue" (1971, p. 52). Bishop considers himself a traditionalist, and this may explain a portion of the venom directed at the agenda of the new leadership. There is, however, no question that the leadership change brought a concomitant shift in the group's interests.[23]

Animated by the political concerns of the late 1960s and early 1970s, the new leadership pushed the ACLU into new issue areas. In general, its concern was for the entire range of American "political" life, a concept it defined broadly. The perceived dragons with which the group had traditionally tilted seemed small in comparison to the present realities. In one of its recruiting brochures the group stated, "The Nixon/Agnew/Mitchell Administration is engaged in a concerted attack on American liberties" (Goldstein, 1978). This was not an isolated or atypical charge. Legal Director Wulf was quoted in 1969 as saying, "We are not yet a fascist state in general" (Bishop, 1971, p. 50). With threats to individual liberty perceived to be pervasive, the ACLU expanded the scope of its definition of civil liberties (Walker, 1990, chaps. 13, 14). Its broad and flexible issue base became yet broader and more flexible.

In *Democracy in America*, Tocqueville asserted that, in America, all political questions ultimately become legal. This insight can be extended to the ACLU of this period: "hot" political questions were increasingly transformed into civil liberties issues. Wulf believed that the scope of civil liberties was nearly unlimited in a rights-based society, and the ACLU acted on this principle. The manifestations of this broadened perspective were plentiful. For example, the format of the group's *Annual Report* changed with its 1970–71 edition. Gone were traditional headings such as "Freedom of Belief, Expression, and Association." In their place were new section headings ranging from "Migrants' Rights" to "Soldiers' Rights" to "Sexual Privacy." This shift was more than merely editorial in nature. The organization's focus took it into new areas of activity.

The ACLU stayed pretty close to its traditional concerns, closely grounded in the guarantees of the Bill of Rights, through the 1960s. Despite the posture of the national office, some of its affiliates began to plunge into new issues. The Southern California Civil Liberties Union is a prime example. In 1962 it concluded that the death penalty was a civil liberties issue, and in 1968 it took up the Vietnam War. Initially, the national office disagreed with these stances on the ground that they bore no discernible nexus to the Bill of Rights; the connection between capital punishment and civil liberties concerns (the Eighth Amendment) was at least arguable, but the tie between the war and individual rights was somewhat more difficult for its leaders to discern. Yet, with new leaders guiding its affairs, and following the invasion of Cambodia and the killings at Kent State, the ACLU called for the "immediate termination" of the war in 1970 and came out against capital punishment (Lukas, 1978).

The ACLU's position on the Vietnam War is a striking example of the extension of its concerns, but it is not the only one. In 1973, the group called for the impeachment of Richard Nixon (Mann, 1978; Walker, 1990). It got heavily involved in the women's movement, established a "Women's Project" in the early 1970s to mount a litigation campaign to end institutionalized sex discrimination (Cowan, 1976). In December 1977, its board passed a resolution "putting the organization on record in favor of 'economic rights,' on the theory that the failure to solve problems of poverty subjects the poor to violations of their civil liberties" (Mann, 1978, p. 14). This put the group in a position to involve itself further in issues previously not given organizational attention. None of these actions had precedent in past organizational activity. They were clearly the product of an energetic new leadership with a nontraditional agenda.

The ACLU leaders acted as entrepreneurs in modifying the issue goals and expanding the focus of the organization (Salisbury, 1969). Indeed, the group's new goals became crucial instruments of organizational maintenance. The new activism of the ACLU, the "expressive benefits" it offered actual and potential supporters, attracted new members in droves. The organization's membership increased from about 150,000 in 1969 to approximately 275,000 in 1974.[24] Thus, the new leaders not only reoriented and expanded the range of the ACLU's interests but also increased the group's membership by almost 55 percent. Its new orientation seemed to be "paying off."

The reordering and expansion of the group's issue goals did not come without cost. Although its resources grew with the expansion of its membership, so too did the demands on those resources.[25] The various "projects" established by the organization to cultivate intensively specific areas of the law required considerable financial support—support that came at the expense of other potential areas of organizational concern. What was said in the 1953 *Annual Report* was still true in the 1970s and 1980s: "Our basic administrative problem is as plain as a nose on a face. We are being pressed to do too much with too little." In the early 1970s, the financial needs of the group were so pressing that one commentator noted:

the ACLU had put itself in a position like that of an overextended business concern. In order to support its many activities and large professional staff, the ACLU needed to keep recruiting new members and to keep getting renewals from those members already in the organization. In order to keep pace in its recruitment, the ACLU needed to keep finding issues of great public appeal, issues that would attract members. These no longer had to be civil liberties issues—virtually any sort of issue would do so long as one could devise a "civil liberties rational." (Mann, 1978, p. 14)

Later, I examine the results of this "wholesaling" of organizational concerns. For now it suffices to show that, in spite of the unprecedented influx of members, the ACLU was far from "well-heeled." The massive membership exodus of the late 1970s exacerbated this situation.

Tight organizational resources heighten the importance of prioritizing subject goals and litigation involvement. Since the ACLU cannot litigate all of its concerns simultaneously, it constantly has to choose its spots. In the early 1970s, with the group's broad range of traditional interests widened by its new goals, ACLU leaders had to select those areas of organizational interest most crucial to meeting the dangers of the day and maintaining the organization. These demands did not bode well for continued obscenity litigation.

Although the new ACLU leaders did not jettison the specific goals of the organization (Bishop, 1971), it is clear that the new agenda did not leave them much room. With the onset of fascism perceived to be the political reality of the day, the importance of obscenity paled.[26] Given constrained resources, organizationally attractive issue alternatives, and perceived threats of greater importance in the environment, the leadership was inclined to drop the obscenity issue from organizational focus. The Supreme Court's firm rejection of the ACLU's litigation goals in *Miller* and *Hamling* provided an opportunity for the group to de-emphasize obscenity and to pursue other goals more central to leadership concerns.

If the proscription of obscenity was not seen by the leadership to be a major threat facing civil liberties, neither was it perceived to be of any great importance in facilitating organizational maintenance. Although *Miller* clearly gutted the strategy used by the ACLU to liberalize obscenity law, it is doubtful that this was a sufficient reason for the exit of the organization from its preeminent position in this area of litigation. An example clarifies the point. The ACLU would most likely not drop its defense of abortion rights— or women's rights more generally—after adverse Supreme Court decisions. Such an action might cause a membership exodus, especially if other organizations were providing the same expressive benefit. The maintenance of a high profile on such a prominent and important issue would arguably aid organizational support regardless of legal "success."

It is difficult to see obscenity in this light. It is, at best, something about which most feel some unease. Where a cry of "Women, the Supreme Court is trying to take away your reproductive freedom" might attract new supporters and retain current members, it is probably true that a similar charge about the Court and one's right to view explicit sexual images would not have the same maintenance utility. ACLU officials deny that the group's policy decisions are influenced by such considerations, but a primary function of this group, as for all groups, is survival.[27] Purposive groups use policy positions as their chits for survival. Tending to a losing cause—in this case, obscenity—would make *organizational* sense only if a developed constituency within the group held it to be an issue central to their membership. Evidence—the lack of a post-de-emphasis exit—suggests that this was not the case for obscenity. The defense of obscenity was simply not as important to as large a segment of the ACLU membership as were its other activities, especially given the influx of new members drawn by the issue and subject goals the group had recently adopted.

Thus, the internal situation of the ACLU allowed its leaders the latitude to abandon protracted obscenity litigation. Given the apparent low salience of obscenity, the perceived importance of other issues, the constraints imposed on the group's activities by its resource base, and the minimal threat posed by obscenity proscription, the leaders of the ACLU were free to reallocate organizational attention to other areas.

Membership

As noted above, the members of a purposive group can, if they choose, exercise some control over the political positions the group adopts. Had obscenity been an issue of importance to ACLU members, the group's leaders might not have de-emphasized it after the *Miller* decision. Although the research for this study did not include interviews with ACLU members, because of the mass exodus it suffered between 1977 and 1979, the group's membership problems received much attention from the national media and scholars. It is primarily from these sources that I draw inferences about the relationship between the group and its members during this period. These sources, combined with the lack of a membership exit after the ACLU's de-emphasis of obscenity, suggest that members had no pointed interest in this issue and did not constrain group officials from following their personal preferences in this area.

The individual calculus in joining an organization hinges on the perceived benefits membership will generate (Salisbury, 1969; Wilson, 1973; and Moe, 1980, 1981). Groups that do not provide their members with material benefits rely on purposive or expressive incentives to draw support. A goal-oriented, purposive group like the ACLU uses the political positions it adopts as expressive benefits in which its members can share. The leadership brokers these positions in an attempt to enhance the maintenance of the organization. The marketplace of present and potential members determines the success of these machinations. The successful manipulation of these benefits results in organizational maintenance and possibly growth; failure can mean stagnation or exit. The new positions assumed by the ACLU in the late 1960s and early 1970s were successful in the sense that organizational membership increased by about 55 percent in less than five years. The success, however, came at a substantial cost—depreciation of the traditional concerns of the group.

ACLU officials, and those who have examined the organization's boom and bust in the 1970s, believe that the group's rapid membership growth was attributable to the new political positions it adopted.[28] Jim Mann provides this annotated chronology:

By 1970, after the invasion of Cambodia, the ACLU issued a public statement calling for an "immediate termination of the Indochina war." . . . This stance did not hurt the ACLU's steady expansion. . . . In 1970, the year it came out against the war, the organization recruited 10,227 new members. (In 1950, by contrast, the ACLU had a total of about 9000 members.) Richard Nixon was responsible for the most rapid expansion in the ACLU's history. . . . ACLU mass mailings urged individuals to join the organization in order to fight "the Nixon/Agnew/Mitchell administration." It was rewarded with a deluge of new members and money. In 1973 alone, the ACLU attracted 50,545 new memberships—far more than in any other year before or since. In fact, the correlation between Richard Nixon and ACLU recruitment was so strong that... there was a sudden drop-off in membership renewals in August 1974 after Nixon resigned, and then an upswing again a month later, after President Ford pardoned Nixon. (Mann, 1978, p. 13)[29]

Group leaders came to discover that the members attracted during the heyday of its social and political activism were more interested in these specific political causes than in the ACLU's traditional commitment to civil liberties concerns (Neier, 1979; Walker, 1990).

ACLU leaders soon learned of the value commitments (or lack thereof) of their new members as a result of their reaction to three groups' actions. The first incident was the group's defense of the right of Ku Klux Klan members to meet to express their political beliefs. The KKK members in question were marines at Camp Pendleton in California whose meeting was in danger of disruption by some black marines. This controversy split local CLU groups, with the Southern California affiliate defending the blacks and the San Diego chapter taking the side of the Klan. A second event involved the defense of a Saturday demonstration against school desegregation planned by the Mississippi branch of the KKK. The Mississippi CLU voted to accept the Klan's request for legal support, causing the resignation of all seven black members of the affiliate's board. The third, and most noted, occasion came in 1977 when the ACLU supported the right of Nazis to march through Chicago's predominantly Jewish suburb of Skokie. None of these instances of organizational activity were "hard" cases, given the ACLU's traditional commitment to the specific guarantees of the Bill of Rights.[30] However, members' responses to these actions tell a great deal about *their* values, concerns, and goals.

After increasing at an astounding rate for the previous eight years, ACLU membership suddenly declined in 1977. Group leaders largely attribute this decline to its defense of the expression rights in California, Mississippi, and Skokie.[31] The ACLU traditionally prided itself on defending principles of civil liberties and not the causes that gave rise to their need for protection— indeed, the groups *had* defended Nazis before (Neier, 1979; Walker, 1990)— but many members were strongly ideological and had no desire to tolerate fascist and racist expression. Indeed, some group leaders felt the same way: Wulf and Charles Morgan, two of those involved in the reorientation of the organization, left the ACLU at this time because of what they perceived as its growing conservativism. Wulf went so far as to send a letter to all members of the group's board of directors warning that the group was too accommo-dating of forces "hostile to individual liberty."[32] Because political positions provide the incentives to join and remain in a purposive group like the ACLU, membership exit can occur when those positions are perceived to be wrong. This explains a large part of its membership decline. In 1974 it had 275,000 members; by the end of 1977 it had slightly less than 170,000.[33]

The lessons of this exodus were not lost on ACLU leaders. Many now recognize that the group's phenomenal membership increase "was somewhat artificial, built on people who were less interested in civil liberties than in fighting the war or Mr. Nixon" (Lukas, 1978). Executive Director Neier admitted that the organization had probably tried to expand too rapidly, opening itself to overly stretched resources and to members who did not share its core commitment to civil liberties. In retrospect, he believes that the group failed to educate new members to the ACLU's traditional neutrality (Neier, 1979, p. 78). Others see the exodus as a net plus. Bruce J. Ennis, Wulf's successor as legal director, saw the Skokie involvement to be "a good thing, because it weeded out the people who don't really believe in civil liberties" (Lukas, 1978). Although this statement is obviously a post hoc rationalization, it is the case that the group did not back away from its Skokie stand in an effort to preserve the membership of those who found it offensive; an emergency fund-raising appeal sent out to members in March 1978 prominently featured the group's Skokie litigation (Walker, 1990, p. 329).[34] In the aftermath of the exodus, although not cutting back on projects already begun, group officials decided not to push the ACLU into any new issue areas in the immediate future (Lukas, 1978).

The organizational exodus and financial drain that ACLU leaders attribute to the group's involvement with Nazis and the KKK did not occur when it largely abandoned its obscenity litigation. A number of explanations are conceivable. Insofar as new members came to dominate the group, obscenity litigation may have been perceived as insignificant, given the greater threats facing the nation. This being the case, there was no reason for them to exit— the group was merely acting in concert with their concerns. If members believed that obscenity law had been settled by *Miller*, they may have supported switching the resources formerly committed to it to other areas of concern. This could have been the case regardless of the depth of their commitment to the organization's stated goals for obscenity law. It is also possible that many members were not aware the group had been involved in this litigation or had left it; ignorance of organizational activities may explain a lack of response to them. It is also conceivable that members did not understand the relationship of the group's obscenity goals to its other issue goals; the nuances of this area of law are reasonably complex. Finally, it is possible that members were pleased with the decision to de-emphasize obscenity. They may not have believed that "hard-core" pornography was constitutionally protected, or they could have objected to it on other grounds—its "objectification" and "exploitation" of women.

The evidence on the effect of feminist perspectives within the ACLU is sketchy, but it is possible that they influenced the initial decision to withdraw the group from obscenity litigation and the decision to de-emphasize it once the activist leadership left the organization. Officials of some other libertarian groups contend that this is indeed the case, that the ACLU is intimidated, by its feminist members, from pursuing litigation in this area.[35] ACLU officials steadfastly deny this, but it is undeniable that feminist concerns are appreciated within the organization. It established the "Women's Project" to ferret out sex discrimination in the law in the early 1970s. Furthermore, it is more active in the litigation of women's rights than the National Organization of Women, and almost as active as Planned Parenthood in abortion litigation. Indeed, in 1977, it established as its primary priority the campaign to guarantee the right of a woman to an abortion, and about 20 percent of its 1978 budget for special projects went to advancing this goal. Additionally, the women's caucus on the board of directors is the only caucus in the organization.[36] Clearly feminist concerns are prominent in the group and have affected its allocation of resources. If feminists within the organization share (or are sympathetic to) the feminist position on pornography, this may affect the litigation priorities and actions of the organizational leadership.

In a purposive organization, the relationship between membership and leadership is extremely close. The activities of one may affect the activities of the other. The internal dynamics of the ACLU conditioned its response in the post-*Miller* litigation environment. In a sense, *Miller* orphaned the ACLU's obscenity campaign. Once the Court shifted, the lack of a vocal constituency within the group—either in its leadership or its membership—consigned this specific goal to a lower priority than it had previously enjoyed. However, although internal dynamics oriented the ACLU toward exit from obscenity litigation, its perceptions of factors external to the group also conditioned this choice.

CONDITIONING FACTORS: EXTERNAL

An analysis of organizational activity cannot focus exclusively on the internal dynamics of group decisions. All organizations exist within a context. Although factors internal to a group help to set its general orientation, the environment in which it acts works to condition the alternatives its leadership can select. Although the new orientation of the ACLU made its leaders less inclined to engage in obscenity litigation, three prominent environmental factors made their decision to de-emphasize this activity a relatively low-cost one: the solidity of the *Miller* majority, the continuing presence of other attorneys and organizations in this litigation, and the perceived ineffectiveness of *Miller*.

Intransigence of the *Miller* Majority

The *Hamling* (1974) decision made it clear that the *Miller* majority was not transient. The ACLU's amicus curiae brief urged the Court to see the dangerous forces *Miller* set loose and reverse course before irreparable damage was done to expression. Citing the suppression by local authorities of such literary works as *Spoon River Anthology*, *A Clockwork Orange*, and *Slaughterhouse*

Five, various "girlie" magazines, and major motion picture releases, the group asked the Court to adopt Justice Brennan's dissenting opinion in *Paris Adult Theatre* (1973) as law. The Court refused and, in fact, tightened the *Miller* approach, making it potentially more restrictive. The ACLU's obscenity goal, once so close to realization, was stymied by a cohesive majority.

The *Miller* majority has held firm. Given the Court's intransigence, ACLU officials saw little point in pursuing its obscenity goals through the judiciary. The specific goals have not changed—the group still professes that there is no such thing as a distinct category of obscene expression—but the chance of getting the Court to reverse itself is presently so slim as to be negligible. Given the hostility of the Court to its obscenity arguments, the small size of its legal staff, its tight resources, and its broad range of interests, the ACLU leadership felt that there was little sense in pushing cases they knew the group would lose even if the Court granted certiorari, something the Burger Court was not often inclined to do.[37] In short, obscenity litigation was no longer an efficient means of pursuing organizational goals.

Since *Hamling*, the ACLU has not framed its obscenity arguments to the Court on its goal in this subject area; it has not pressed the Court to overturn *Miller*. In the obscenity cases in which it has participated since 1974, it has merely sought to check the extension of the *Miller* doctrine and to safeguard sex-oriented materials that are not obscene under *Miller*. This tendency is most clear in the cases it joined through the early 1980s. The national organization joined its Detroit affiliate's brief in *Young* v. *American Mini Theatres* (1976)—an attempt to limit the use of zoning statutes to control "adult establishments." It joined the AAP in *FCC* v. *Pacifica* (1978) to argue that government could not prohibit public broadcast of "indecent" speech, just that speech obscene under *Miller*. It joined MC's brief in *New York* v. *Ferber* (1982) to argue that a state child pornography law was constitutionally overbroad. Only in *Pico* v. *Board* (1982), a case supported by the ACLU from the trial stage on, did it deeply involve itself in litigation. Here, however, the group opposed the removal of books from a school library, and although one of the justifications for the removal was the "indecency" or "obscenity" of the content, obscenity was not the centerpiece of the case.

After *Ferber* and *Pico*, the frequency of the ACLU's involvement in obscenity cases decided by the Supreme Court increased—it filed as *amicus* in four of the eight cases—but the content of its arguments remained consistent with its general post-*Miller* posture as it opposed zoning regulations (*Renton* v. *Playtime Theatres*, 1986), warrantless searches of bookstores (*Maryland* v. *Macon*, 1985), bookstore closings (*Arcara* v. *Cloud Books*, 1986), and protective coverings of printed materials (*Virginia* v. *American Booksellers Association, Inc., et al.*, 1988). This recent increase in participation, however, has not been prompted by a renewed campaign to undermine obscenity regulation. Rather, the group is still working at the margins of *Miller*, attempting to limit its further extension into other areas of law.

With the Supreme Court's steadfast adherence to the *Miller* approach, the ACLU could not have the effect on obscenity law its leaders believed it had had during the Warren Court years. This was influential in their decision to de-emphasize this realm of litigation. However, group officials leave open the possibility that the ACLU might seriously reenter the obscenity fray if they believe that the Court would be more receptive to their goals. If, for example, the Court's membership underwent a significant change, it might renew its frontal assault on obscenity proscription. It is worth noting, however, that it is one thing to say that an organization *might* renew a concerted litigation campaign and quite another to do it. A web of other factors, not the least of them internal to the organization, makes such a decision more than a purely legal one.

Alternative Actors

Another environmental influence on the ACLU's post-*Miller* calculus was the availability of other agents committed to this type of litigation. Two such actors were present in this litigation field at the time the ACLU decided to de-emphasize its involvement. One was the "obscenity bar"—private attorneys who specialize in obscenity law and litigation. Additionally, the material groups that were tangentially involved in obscenity litigation during the 1960s mobilized to protect member interests after *Miller*. Although I will examine these actors in chapter 5, a brief discussion of their relevance to the ACLU's retreat from obscenity litigation will be undertaken here.

The Supreme Court's 1960s liberalization of obscenity doctrine prompted the development of a "sex industry." Under the hazy legitimacy extended by the Court, the outlets for sexually oriented material grew, as did its explicitness. This burgeoning market fed profitable businesses, which in turn sought legal talent to fight prosecutions and protect their commercial interests—a series of successful prosecutions could put them out of business. With the need for skilled advocacy on behalf of those who dealt in sex-oriented material becoming manifest, a number of attorneys began to specialize in this type of litigation. These lawyers—for example, Stanley Fleishman, Samuel Rosenwein, Robert E. Smith, Joseph Rhine, Arthur M. Schwartz, John H. Weston, Joel Hirschhorn, and Ralph J. Schwarz—developed special expertise in this area of litigation.[38] The more cases they won, the greater their demand. With demand for this type of expert advocacy growing, more attorneys developed a specialization in obscenity law; their organizational manifestation, the First Amendment Lawyers Association, now has about 125 members. The development and organization of this expertise in a definable sector of the private bar allows one to speak of an "obscenity bar."

The obscenity bar works independently to further the specific goals of the ACLU. These attorneys make a broad range of arguments in defending their clients, among them the absolutist and consenting adults positions favored by the ACLU.[39] The existence of a competent group of private attorneys making broad First Amendment arguments assured ACLU leaders that positions consistent with their obscenity goals would be presented to the courts even in the organization's absence. ACLU officials contend that involvement in a case the group knows will be well handled from its point of view wastes resources that could be expended in other areas of organizational interest; there is little utility in participating in litigation merely to say "me too."[40] The presence of the obscenity bar assured ACLU leaders that the group's de-emphasis of obscenity would not leave a legal void, and this eased their exit decision.

The presence of other organizations interested in obscenity litigation further insured a post-*Miller* presentation of libertarian arguments to the courts. Shortly after *Miller*, ACLU officials invited these groups to join an informal ad hoc committee on obscenity. Representatives for both commercial (for example, the American Booksellers Association, the Council for Periodical Distributors Association, and the Motion Picture Association of America) and professional (for example, the American Library Association, the National Council of Churches, and the American Jewish Congress) groups attended these meetings. Eventually, the commercial groups broke off to devote all of their energies to Media Coalition while the professional organizations joined the ACLU-sponsored "National Coalition Against Censorship." The latter engages only in "educational" activities, but the former was established to participate in obscenity litigation. Because of their involvement in this communication network, the leaders of the ACLU knew that the members of Media Coalition had a commercial incentive to continue their involvement in obscenity litigation and the resources to secure extremely competent counsel. With the obscenity bar and other organizations committed to continued participation in obscenity litigation, the ACLU's absence would not leave a void in the organized opposition to obscenity prosecution. This made its exit decision easier.

The Misjudged Consequences of *Miller*

Initially, the ACLU feared that *Miller* would stimulate a wave of obscenity prosecutions and the suppression of controversial but non-obscene material. It voiced this fear in its amicus curiae brief in *Hamling* and in an article in its *Civil Liberties Review* (Pilpel, 1974). However, despite occasional celebrated obscenity trials, this fear proved unfounded. In the Times Square area of New York City, literally in the ACLU's backyard, there exists a plethora of sexual stimuli—not just one or two inconspicuous outlets with blackened windows and modest signs but extravagant and obtrusive announcements of the variety of wares within.[41] The same type of scene can be seen in almost any other major American city. "Adult" bookstores and theaters are also found in otherwise sleepy small towns. Although the Moral Majority convinced Southland Corporation to remove *Playboy* and *Penthouse* from their 7-11 stores,[42] many other convenience stores openly stock high-gloss sex magazines. Almost two decades after *Miller*, sex-oriented material is still prevalent and broadly available.

The growing body of literature on impact and compliance speaks to what has become common knowledge among students of the courts—judicial decisions are not self-enforcing.[43] Obscenity decisions are no exception. The fact that *Miller* removed most of the legal constraints that frustrated past attempts at obscenity law enforcement did not mean that prosecutions would result. Indeed, *Miller* did not *mandate* anything—it merely facilitated prosecution by sending the obscenity judgment back to the local arena. The enforcement of obscenity law is not dependent on judicial action but on the actions of police and prosecutors.

Some studies have assessed the effect of judicial rulings on the availability of obscenity. In a pre-*Miller* study, James P. Levine examined the effect of court-pronounced obscenity doctrine on the inventory decisions of bookstore operators (Levine, 1968). He concluded that the stocking decisions of booksellers are influenced more by their own values, and those of the community, than by judicial decisions. Eight years later, the Obscenity Law Project of the New York University Law School measured *Miller*'s impact. Comparing data from before and after *Miller*, it found that the number of jurisdictions prosecuting obscenity law violations actually *declined* after *Miller*. The number of prosecutions per year also declined nationally. The study further presented data that showed that governmental officials perceived sexual material to be more explicit after the decision. Only in the South was there an exception to this general pattern.

The Project suggested a variety of reasons why *Miller* was not a springboard to increased obscenity prosecution. The resources available for such prosecutions are not great. A city attorney in Los Angeles noted that the expense incurred for a typical obscenity case is between $10,000 and $25,000. Trials also consume valuable attorney time—time that could be spent on other problems that prosecutors, police, and the community believe to be more important. This resource problem is compounded by the increased importance of the trial court in the post-*Miller* environment. After *Miller*, appellate court reversals declined from 18 percent of all obscenity convictions to 8 percent. Because the trial is now the crucial battleground for the defense, trial preparation and strategies have geared up accordingly. This increases the cost of the trials and further discourages governments from bringing cases to court. When cases are tried and convictions are secured, the penalties are so minimal as to act as no meaningful deterrent. Moreover, those convicted are merely operatives, not owners. The day after the trial, the bookstore or theater, if it was ever closed down, is back in business. Another reason for the non-enforcement of obscenity law is a lack of police or prosecutorial sympathy for these prosecutions.

Societal factors also conspire to limit obscenity prosecutions. Enforcement officials perceive that the public has come to accept the ready availability of sex-oriented material. The complaints about it are few and seldom sustained. The pervasiveness of sex in contemporary society seems to have acclimated people to its explicit presentation. Without sustained public outcry, already overburdened police and prosecutors have little incentive to pursue obscenity litigation.

The worst fears of the ACLU were not realized; *Miller* did not stimulate massive and wide-ranging suppression. In fact, group officials see the *Paris* dissent position of Justice Brennan to have become the de facto reality of obscenity law enforcement. Although this situation is informal (not codified in law) and could change over time, at present consenting adults are largely free to view or purchase whatever sex-oriented materials they wish. Although not ideal from the perspective of the goals of the organization, the situation is not troublesome enough to warrant concerted organizational attention. Although the ACLU will join litigation raising new issues with potential impact on its general and issue goals—for example, *Pico* (1982), *Hudnut* (1985), *Renton* (1986), and *Virginia* (1987)—its obscenity goals are no longer of paramount organizational interest.

CONCLUSION

The ACLU adapted to the new legal environment created by the *Miller* decision by lessening its emphasis on obscenity litigation. A variety of factors internal and external to the organization conditioned this adaptive response.

The effect of the internal dynamics of the organization on the exit decision can best be understood when the ACLU is conceived of as a purposive or expressive organization (Salisbury, 1969; Wilson, 1973; and Moe, 1980, 1981). The ACLU maintains its membership by providing members with expressive benefits. These benefits take the form of the general, issue, and subject goals it adopts and pursues. Because it is an organization reliant on membership support for funding, its leaders must be sensitive to the political concerns of its members. If they are not, membership exit is a possible threat to the continuance of the organization. This does not mean that the leadership must slavishly cater to the perceived desires of the membership, for they can shape the political values of the members. The firmly held values and positions of the membership, however, do constrain the goals adopted and the actions taken by the group. The interaction between leaders and members conditions the activities undertaken by a purposive organization, constrained only by the goals that group leaders feel to be inflexible and the external environment in which the organization acts.

New leaders moved into control of the ACLU in the late 1960s and early 1970s, and they brought the group a new agenda. They moved beyond the organization's traditional civil liberties concerns by shifting its focus to new issues with tangential ties to them. In light of this new agenda, obscenity—one traditional concern—was not given much weight in the new ordering of the ACLU's goals; the new leaders felt it to be either trivial or of little significance, given other problems. The one thing that might have kept them from de-emphasizing obscenity was not present—the issue had no vocal constituency within the organization.

In purposive organizations, more than in material groups, the membership can influence political decisions of the group. However, a membership un-interested in an issue exerts little influence on leaders deciding its organizational fate. This was the case with the ACLU and obscenity. Many of the group's new members had little concern for traditional civil liberties goals. This seemed to extend to obscenity questions. For some, obscenity merited no protection. Note the comparison of Nazism and obscenity by a member hostile to both:

Many people in [Skokie] claimed that the Nazi march represented an "obscene" event surely as much as the open sale of pornographic material. If the courts are going to leave the latter up to community standards, why not the former? I find the distinction made by the court here very difficult to comprehend. Perhaps other aspects of the case colored the case so unfortunately as to preclude a clearer interpretation of obscenity. (Gibson and Bingham, 1985, p. 79)

For others, obscenity was probably seen as an issue of minor importance. With neither leaders nor members exhibiting much interest in obscenity matters, the way for organizational exit from this issue area was cleared.

Various factors in the organization's environment facilitated the easy execution of the leaders' inclination to de-emphasize obscenity and move on to other issues. The firmness of the *Miller* majority, the presence of other like-minded individual and organizational actors, and the failure of the Court's shift to stimulate wide-scale proscription all gave group officials the latitude to remove the ACLU from its dominant posture in obscenity litigation. What little importance obscenity had would be well tended to by other actors and by the gradual erosion of "outmoded" sexual mores. Thus, the exit of the ACLU from obscenity litigation would be a wash—it would have little effect on the state of obscenity law.

The confluence of these internal and external factors allowed the ACLU to turn its attention to other matters its leadership considered more important than obscenity. This demonstrates the wide range of choice that leaders of purposive organizations have when they address issues of relative unim-portance to the bulk of their group's membership. Obscenity could be abandoned without alienating many members. A similar decision in another area of organizational concern may not have entailed such minimal cost. The decisions to defend the expression rights of Nazis and the Klan are examples of the latter. Intriguingly, these latter decisions *were* made, and the organization bore their considerable cost. This suggests that the ACLU, and perhaps other purposive organizations, have core goals that leaders will not disregard, even in the face of massive membership exit. Thus, the ACLU's goals are not so malleable that they will be shaped into whatever configuration best suits the desires of its members. It does "stand" for something beyond self-maintenance at any cost; the Skokie case makes clear that its leaders are not just membership mongers.[44] However, obscenity, though clearly expression, raised a *different kind* of question from that presented by Skokie. It did not strike as deeply into inflexible organizational values; nor did it inflame the passions of ACLU members. Because of this, the group's leaders had considerable flexibility in dealing with this issue.

Insofar as the leaders of purposive organizations are entrepreneurs, their task is to shape organizational goals in an effort to influence public policy and maintain their group. The latter involves discerning the cleavage lines within the membership. Group goals and actions can alienate as well as attract. Thus, leaders must take care to adopt and discard only those goals that will not alienate a significant segment of their membership. To fail to do so is to flirt with the possible destruction of the organization. Obscenity was not a cleavage issue within the ACLU. Given the wide range of issues on which it attracts and holds members and the low general salience of its obscenity activities in its members' membership calculus, its de-emphasis of this area did not threaten its existence.

Although the ACLU is a purposive group with a broad range of interests, other purposive organizations active in this realm of litigation are not. The pro-decency organizations Citizens for Decency through Law and Morality in Media focus their organizational attention solely on obscenity. Given their normative orientation to the obscenity problem and the narrow range of their interests, their reaction to *Miller* was likely to differ from that of the ACLU. It is to an examination of their adaptive response that we now turn.

NOTES

1. Its early involvements in obscenity litigation usually involved arguable classics by recognized authors. For example, note its participation in *U.S.* v. *Dennett* (1930), *Ulysses* (1933, 1934), *Winters* v. *New York* (1948), *U.S.* v. *Two Obscene Books* (1951), and *Burstyn* v. *Wilson* (1952). See generally Walker (1990).

2. See the general treatment given the ACLU in chapter 2.

3. For one contemporary analysis of the Court's obscenity machinations, which supports this interpretation, see Krislov (1968).

4. This interpretation of the case law was adopted by the legal panel of the President's Commission on Obscenity and Pornography (1970). It was also the dom-

inant gloss offered by contemporary law journals. For example, see Engdahl (1969), Katz (1969), and Vanderbilt Note (1969–70).

5. *Rowan* (1970) upheld a law allowing postal patrons unwilling to receive sexual material through the mails to have it returned to the mailer at the latter's cost.

6. In *Reidel* and *37 Photographs*, the Supreme Court, by votes of 7–2 and 6–3 respectively, declined to extend the emerging "consenting adults" logic to the mail receipt and importation of "obscene" materials by willing buyers.

7. Presidents frequently attempt to appoint "their kind of people" to judicial vacancies. On Nixon's appointments, see Woodward and Armstrong (1980).

8. In *Hamling*, a case involving a mailed advertising brochure for an illustrated version of the Report of the President's Commission on Obscenity and Pornography, the Court, by the same 5–4 margin that decided *Miller*, held that the standards relevant to determining a material's obscenity are those of the vicinage from which the jury is drawn.

9. Of the four dissenters in *Miller*, only Marshall remains on the Court. Of the newer Justices, Stevens clearly rejects criminal penalties for obscenity (see his dissent, for example, in *U.S.* v. *Marks*, 1977), though he has little problem with civil or zoning approaches to obscenity regulation, and Scalia has hinted that he is troubled by the *Miller* approach (see his recent concurrence in *Fort Wayne Books*, 1989). O'Connor and Kennedy seem to have no problems with *Miller*. Thus, there remain at least five votes in support of *Miller* on the present Court.

10. See table 1.2, chapter 1, and appendix A.

11. Although a few other organizations (for example, the DGA, MPAA, and NATO) also eventually withdrew themselves from active involvement in obscenity litigation, the initial reaction of these organizations to *Miller* was to mobilize to protect the material interests of their members.

12. The ACLU made similar kinds of arguments in various other public statements; for example, Pilpel (1974).

13. ACLU amicus curiae briefs in *Young* (1976), *FCC* (1978), and *Ferber* (1982) and its argument in *Pico* (1982) stressed the need only to limit *Miller*, not to reverse it.

14. Because the Court certified the question of the statute's construction to the State Supreme Court in *Virginia* v. *American Booksellers Association, Inc.*, *et al.* (1988), it failed to resolve the issue itself. Thus, neither the ACLU or any of the other groups involved in this case won or lost.

15. Walker's (1990) recent treatment of the ACLU underscores the group's de-emphasis of obscenity litigation. It discusses the ACLU victories of the 1960s but pays scant attention to the post-*Miller* obscenity landscape. In fact, the only cases noted in the post-1973 period are *Pico* (1982)—involving the removal of books from a school library—and the lower court *Hudnut* (1985) cases—striking the feminist anti-pornography statute passed in Indianapolis.

16. Salisbury (1969) limits the entrepreneurial concept to one individual (organizer or leader), but there is no reason why the concept cannot also include a collective leadership acting as entrepreneur.

17. Ernst's crusade against obscenity law was a long one. See his *The Censor Marches On* (1940) and *Censorship: The Search for the Obscene* (1964).

18. London, Redfield, and Fraenkel all participated on the Censorship Committee

when it revised the ACLU's position on obscenity. See files entitled "Censorship" in the ACLU archives.

19. Charles Morgan, Jr., the head of the ACLU's Washington Office in the early 1970s, rose to prominence as the Atlanta CLU director who used his affiliate to battle for the rights of blacks in the 1960s. See Lukas (1978) and Walker (1990), esp. ch. 14.

20. Aryeh Neier was elected to be the executive director of the ACLU in 1970 as "the candidate of the left" (Lukas, 1978) and Walker (1990), esp. ch. 14.

21. Wulf was assistant legal director throughout the 1960s. For a portrait of him, see Bishop (1971), Mann (1978), Lukas (1978), and Walker (1990).

22. The change in the leadership of CDL, for example, did not fundamentally alter that organization's goals or array of interests. See chapters 2 and 4.

23. This has been amply documented in the press. See Lukas (1978), Mann (1978), and the *NYT*, especially during the period 1977–79. See also Walker (1990).

24. Figures drawn from ACLU *Annual Reports* of 1968–69 and 1973–74. Although organizations may overstate their membership strength, these figures are supported by Lukas (1978), Mann (1978), and Walker (1990).

25. Contributions from the membership increased by more than 25 percent between 1969 and 1974, from less than $3 million to about $4 million. Figures from ACLU *Annual Reports*.

26. Wulf told me that obscenity litigation was of very little importance to him as legal director (telephone conversation, 2 December 1982). Indeed, he could not remember any specific obscenity litigation in which he was involved during his time as legal director, despite the fact that he argued two such cases before the Supreme Court and signed onto nine amicus briefs presented there.

27. ACLU Associate Director Alan Reitman argues that such considerations as the popularity of a cause are irrelevant to the decision to take it on for organizational support: "The Bill of Rights is our client." (Interview with author.)

28. On this general point, see Lukas (1978), Mann (1978), Goldstein (1978), Neier (1979), Walker (1990), and the *NYT* from 1977 to 1979.

29. Mann's membership figures are lower than ACLU figures. The latter multiplies its membership by 40 percent to capture its joint husband-and-wife memberships.

30. For example, the ACLU defended Nazi leader George Lincoln Rockwell in 1960. This action caused no significant membership exit. See Lukas (1978) and Walker (1990). For an "insider" account, see Neier (1979).

31. Although officials of the organization largely attribute the exodus to these actions, other reasons are also cited: the decline of social activism, competition from other organizations, inflation, and the disarray in the liberal community on crucial issues like affirmative action and busing.

32. Quoted in the *NYT*, 20 February 1977.

33. These figures are from *The Encyclopedia of Associations*, ACLU *Annual Reports*, and Mann (1978). Neier (1979), p. 79, contends that the ACLU lost about 15 percent (30,000) of its membership over Skokie. It is worthy to note that Gibson and Bingham (1985) found that the ACLU grossly exaggerated its membership loss from its defense of the Nazis and that the loss that did occur did not come disproportionately from its newer members. However, they do not have the data to assess the loss of income the group felt as a result of this action. Neier (1979), p. 78, and Walker (1990), p. 327, put this total at about $500,000.

34. This demonstrates that leaders of purposive organizations are not *wholly* concerned with maintaining or increasing membership. An organization's goal structure may be elastic in some senses, but inelastic in others. Goals are more than instruments, they can also be constraints.

35. Officials of the Adult Film Association of America feel this way. Interviews with Friedman and Weston.

36. Information used in this paragraph is drawn from the articles by Mann (1978) and Lukas (1978).

37. Interviews with group officials who passed on the judgment of Legal Director Burt Newborne. The Burger Court has declined to review most lower court obscenity decisions by denying certiorari or by dismissing them on jurisdictional grounds or for want of a substantial federal question.

38. These men specialize in the legal defense of those charged with obscenity law violations. They are, or have been, active in groups such as the AFAA and the FALA.

39. Indeed, many attorneys active in obscenity litigation got into it because of their general interest in First Amendment principles and litigation. Interviews with Schwarz, Weston, London, Fraenkel, and Fleishman.

40. London interview; see also the comments of former Legal Director Bruce J. Ennis in *Office for Intellectual Freedom* (1983).

41. In the last decade, the number of sex-oriented shops in Times Square has dropped by almost half. This, however, is more the result of economic forces and home videotape recorders than legal prosecution. See *Newsweek*, 18 March 1985, p. 61.

42. Southland's April 1986 decision to drop these magazines from its stores came during the crest of the Reagan administration's attention to obscenity and pornography. Indeed, Attorney General Meese's Commission on Pornography sent a letter to "numerous U.S. companies that owned stores distributing or selling the magazines" (Blodgett, 1986, p. 28).

43. For a general survey of the literature on impact and compliance and the difficult methodological questions such studies face, see Levine (1970).

44. Group interaction theories that draw on microeconomic analysis tend to either overlook or neglect this point. Salisbury's (1969) exchange theory is an example of this tendency. Especially with purposive organizations, strong substantive values can often underlie and condition the actions they take.

4

Organizational Adaptation: Continuance

The root of this nation's [obscenity] problem is the United States Supreme Court.

—James J. Clancy, 1968

The Supreme Court should speak out against the type of hard-core pornography herein under consideration [*Behind the Green Door*] to the fullest extent possible within the framework of this appeal. . . . Contrary to what the majority of this Court must have intended, the *Miller*, et al., decisions have not provided the spark which would ignite law enforcement efforts and bring about a curtailment of this nation's obscenity problems.

—CDL amicus curiae brief, *Ballew* v. *Georgia* (1978)

Like the ACLU, the pro-decency groups active in obscenity litigation are purposive organizations; they exist to promote political positions that, if achieved, will provide a public good (Olson, 1965). There, however, is where the similarity ends. Whereas the ACLU treats a broad and elastic range of issues, Citizens for Decency through Law (CDL) and Morality in Media (MM), the two most active proscriptionist groups, confine their focus to matters of obscenity and public morality. Whereas the ACLU seeks the abolition of obscenity laws, CDL and MM work for their passage and enforcement. Whereas the ACLU is distinctly liberal in outlook, CDL and MM are conservative in the Catholic tradition.[1] Whereas the ACLU was founded in the early twentieth century in a response to perceived civil liberties violations during World War I, CDL and MM are products of the mid-twentieth century and were created to discourage the dissemination of sex-oriented material. The other proscriptionist groups involved in this litigation—Covenant House/Institute for Youth Advocacy (CH/IYA), Freedom Council Foundation (FCF), and National Legal Foundation (NLF)—share the generally conservative, "pro-family" perspective of CDL and MM. Similar to the ACLU in purpose and in membership incentives, the pro-decency groups are otherwise very different from the ACLU.[2]

Proscriptionist organizations have had a rocky relationship with the courts. After *Roth*, they thought that the Supreme Court had affirmed what few had ever formally questioned—that obscenity could be proscribed by government.[3] Understood in this light, *Roth* supported their specific goals: it established a variable standard whereby communities could apply *their own* standards to adjudge obscenity. Legally, thus, obscenity was "primarily a matter of fact to be tried by a jury."[4] When the Court began overturning obscenity convictions and laws in the early 1960s, these groups initially read it to be acting on procedural grounds. However, in its amicus curiae brief in *Memoirs* v. *Massachusetts* (1966), CDL commented on the frustration these decisions were creating at the local level. "The prosecutors are claiming that they have no remedy [for obscenity law violations] and that the Supreme Court stands too eager to overturn their successes when they occur. *Amici* do not picture this to be the true situation" (CDL amicus curiae brief in *Memoirs*, p. 26).

The group went on to note that the Court had denied certiorari to 21 criminal convictions since *Roth*. CDL's briefs in the 1966 cases—*Memoirs*, *Ginzburg* v. *U.S.*, and *Mishkin* v. *New York*—called on the Court to clarify its position and reaffirm the permissibility of proscription. The group felt vindicated by the *Ginzburg* and *Mishkin* decisions;[5] the Court was perceived to have once again come down foursquare on the side of decency interests.[6]

After *Roth* the rumor was widespread that this Court was tolerating obscenity, when in reality it was developing harsh procedural restraints where previous restraint controls were used. . . . *Ginzburg* and *Mishkin* . . . have provided the signal which was needed to release the prosecutive forces in a renewed effort to slow down the momentum which has been building up in the obscenity trade since 1957. (CDL amicus curiae brief in *Austin* v. *Kentucky*, 1967, p. 60).

Redrup v. *New York* (1967), and the summary reversals that followed it, burst this bubble of optimism. Although the Court did not agree on a single rationale to cover its per curiam reversals of 35 obscenity convictions between 1967 and 1971, it was clear that a majority of justices were hostile to decency arguments (Schauer, 1976). Despite the lack of a clear legal definition of obscenity, the "least common denominator" approach of *Redrup* led many legal analysts to believe that the Court had adopted, de facto, the tripartite definition suggested by Justice Brennan in his *Memoirs* opinion. In practice, this was interpreted to reduce to a "hard-core" test—only hard-core pornography could be proscribed.[7] In petitioning the Court for a rehearing on *Redrup*, CDL attorneys voiced their outrage at this development.

Until *Austin* and *Redrup*, we had thought this Court's decisions . . . to have recognized the special public policy favoring the obscenity laws and to have been in support of criminal prosecution by the states of those dealing in obscenity. . . . With this Court's opinion in *Redrup/Austin/Gent*, our convictions have suffered. . . . In our reappraisal we are forced to conclude that this Court does not have a clear understanding of the practical effect of its multi-faceted, esoteric opinions on the rulings of trial judges, the prosecutors' efforts under the law and the continuing struggle of the communities to halt the moral erosion and sagging standards of sexual morality within the community. (CDL petition for rehearing, *Austin*, 1967, p. 17).

The *Ginsberg* v. *New York* (1968) and *Stanley* v. *Georgia* (1969) decisions loomed even more ominous from this perspective. It appeared that the Court was moving to the position that absent exposure to minors or nonconsenting adults, or absent evidence of pandering, obscenity had constitutional protection. An adoption of this position would lay to legal rest the concept of public morality that undergirded the decency position.

It was in this context that Richard Nixon became president, Chief Justice Warren and Justice Fortas resigned, and Justices Black and Harlan died. Just as the Court seemed poised to reverse the *Roth* approach, its membership was radically altered by a longtime foe of its decisions. Nixon appointed four justices to the Court, in the process replacing three of its most liberal members on the obscenity question. The five obscenity cases of its 1972 term gave the new Supreme Court an opportunity to reshape the development of obscenity law. It also gave pro-decency groups a chance to stem what many previously perceived to be an irreversible tide of legal change.

The 1972 term decisions of the Burger Court reversed the liberalization of the Warren Court. *Miller* v. *California* (1973) strongly reaffirmed the basic thrust of the *Roth* approach, and its three-pronged test was intended to lower the barriers to successful prosecutions. The *Hamling* v. *U.S.* decision of the next term seemed to meet the goals of decency groups in permitting the community standards of the vicinage to govern the obscenity determination. Not only did the Burger Court majority reverse the doctrinal drift of its predecessor, but there were actions behind its words. After the Nixon appointees came to the Court, it decided 71 percent of its obscenity cases in favor of pro-decency concerns.[8] After a long period of hostility, the Supreme Court reverted to a conservative approach to obscenity proscription.

The response of pro-decency organizations to the 1972 term decisions differed from that of the other groups active in obscenity litigation. By and large, the proscriptionist groups continued doing what they had done previously, albeit in a legal environment more supportive of their concerns. They continued their amicus curiae participation before the Court, their lobbying for greater enforcement and better laws, and their assistance to local prosecutions of obscenity. The chief change in their behavior after *Miller* was in its intensity—CDL became somewhat more active in its litigation efforts, and MM founded the National Obscenity Law Center (NOLC) to act as a clearinghouse for information on obscenity law. These changes, however, occurred within a context of continued organizational commitment to specific goals. The environmental change fostered by *Miller* did not remove their raison d'être; it merely put them in a stronger legal position. Their post-*Miller* actions, as well as those of the groups that participated, however infrequently, in the more recent litigation period, sum to pressing their newfound legal advantage to achieve their general goals. Because the involvement of CDL and MM was so much more extensive than that of the other groups, my analysis will focus primarily on them.

ORGANIZATIONAL RESPONSE TO *MILLER*

I will examine the response of pro-decency groups on two dimensions: rhetorical and behavioral. Rhetoric is an important tool for a purposive organization. Internally, it acts as a tool of organizational maintenance—a way of retaining current members and funding sources. Externally, it is used to influence political institutions to adopt organizational goals. Although behavior does not necessarily reflect rhetoric, it did for the pro-decency groups active in obscenity litigation.

The pro-decency groups' rhetorical response to *Miller* was interestingly ambiguous. This stemmed from their perception of the Court's disposition of the obscenity issues raised in *Miller* and its companion cases. On the one hand, the *Miller* opinion represented a major victory. It not only signaled the end of the Warren Court's obstructionism but it also indicated that the Court would be more sympathetic to decency concerns in the future. Further, it articulated a doctrine that, though not perfect from these groups' point of view, was something on which they could build. On the other hand, instead of affirming the dozens of obscenity convictions on its docket, the Court vacated and remanded these appeals for further litigation in light of *Miller*. The opinion also seemed to require that state obscenity laws be rewritten to conform to the new doctrine. These actions, from the proscriptionist perspective, left considerable confusion in the law.

Publicly, the proscriptionist reaction was positive. The "Question and Answer" pamphlet that CDL distributes to its supporters has on its back cover a picture of a beaming Charles Keating, CDL's founder, descending the steps of the Supreme Court building after *Miller* was handed down. The message is simple: the Court gave communities the green light to use *their* standards to stop the spread of pornography. Keating relayed this message not only through CDL literature but also by writing articles for national publications such as *Reader's Digest* and by appearing on nationally syndicated television shows such as "The 700 Club" and "The Old-Time Gospel Hour."[9] Although stressing that the fight was not yet over, CDL officials hailed *Miller* as a crucial first step in the pro-decency direction. MM similarly interpreted *Miller* for its members, calling it a "watershed" case that would allow communities to purge obscene materials. In the first issue of its *Obscenity Law Bulletin*, Carl A. Vergari, the district attorney of Westchester County and director of the National District Attorneys Association, wrote: "The stricter standards defined by the Burger Court in *Miller* v. *California* now make it difficult, if not impossible, to justify failure to take appropriate enforcement action in obscenity cases on constitutional grounds."[10] In the next issue, MM's General Counsel Paul J. McGeady wrote, "This standard [*Miller*] expanded criminal liability and considerably eased a prosecutor's burden of proof." MM's organizational literature also informs its supporters that *Miller* gives communities the power to establish and enforce their own standards of decency.[11] Thus, for public consumption, leaders of pro-decency groups point to *Miller* as a decisive blow in the legal battle over pornography.

Despite this public enthusiasm for the *Miller* decision, officials of MM and CDL privately, and in their amicus curiae briefs to the Supreme Court, expressed some dissatisfaction with the new doctrine. Their problems with *Miller* revolve around the complexity of its test. Instead of promulgating a simple variable standard of obscenity—obscenity is that which a jury, subject to the oversight of the judge sitting in the case, finds to appeal to the prurient interest in a patently offensive way—the Court established something of a constant test with three prongs: prurience, patent offensiveness, and "serious" value. All three have to be met to secure a conviction. Proscriptionists see this formulation as playing into the hands of defense attorneys by giving them great latitude in which to maneuver in defense of their clients.[12]

Beyond their difficulties with the *Miller* test, CDL and MM believe that the Court's approach leaves open a vast array of important subsidiary questions of obscenity law. For example, it has not treated the abstention issue involved in the "race to the courthouse." "Pornographers" occasionally can frustrate the local proscription envisaged in *Miller* by challenging, in federal court, local statutes before they have been enforced.[13] The Court has also failed to address directly the propriety of 42 U.S.C.§1983 penalties assessed against governments that lose obscenity cases. Monetary awards not only benefit individuals who deal in sex-oriented material but also discourage enforcement because prosecutors do not want to lose a case that siphons tax dollars from local treasuries.[14] Neither has it confronted the constitutionality of "padlocking"—forced closing for a set period of time—"adult" emporiums convicted of obscenity violations.[15] Decency groups would like to see this

Table 4.1
Pro-Decency Group Participation before the Supreme Court, Pre- and Post-
Miller

	Involvement*	Involvement Not Counting Summary Reversals
Pre-Miller (#/% of n)	18/20.5% (n=88)	16/34.8%** (n=46)
Post-Miller (#/% of n)	16/51.6% (n=31)	16/51.6% (n=31)

* Counts amicus curiae and sponsorship litigation.
** Does not include participation in Aday (1967) and Cain (1970)-- cases summarily
reversed.

practice legally validated because it would provide a strong sanction against
sex-oriented stores, but it raises prior restraint issues and is of unclear constitutionality. Thus, from the perspective of these groups, although *Miller*
re-legitimated obscenity proscription, it did not provide the "knock-out
punch" for which they had hoped.

In the end, officials of decency organizations see *Miller* as a mixed blessing.
However, the decision did provide a badly needed piton from which they
can climb to their ultimate goal—effective proscription of obscenity. Thus,
the decision was a necessary, if not sufficient, movement toward organizational goals. It converted a bad legal situation into one open to improvement.
This is why CDL's national director and general counsel, Bruce A. Taylor,
believes that pro-decency forces stand today where libertarians stood after
Redrup—on the side of the mountain moving up. *Miller* did not put them
on the top, but it did stop their fall. Their post-*Miller* task was twofold:
avoid the doctrinal slippage that had characterized the Court's retreat from
the *Roth* test in the late 1950s and 1960s, and push doctrinal development
further along toward proscriptionist ends.

The rhetorical response of these groups to *Miller* was consistent with their
behavioral response: continued legal activity. This activity was designed to
press the advantage that *Miller* afforded. Table 4.1 presents one measure of
legal activity: organizational appearances before the Supreme Court. The
participation of pro-decency groups increased after *Miller*. Because of the
issues left unresolved by that decision, it was crucial to press the Court to
extend the *Miller* approach to its proscriptionist conclusions. In sum, their
post-*Miller* participation was intended to fill the remaining legal gaps with
proscriptionist logic and promote legal implementation.

The data presented in table 4.1 hide an important aspect of the obscenity
litigation of pro-decency groups—CDL dominates their judicial participa-

tion. MM presented the Court two amicus curiae briefs prior to *Miller* and filed three more after that decision. This is not to say that MM did not increase its legal activity in the post-*Miller* environment. It created and maintains the National Obscenity Law Center (NOLC) to assist the case preparation of interested prosecutors. This type of assistance is indirect and difficult to measure, but it is legal activity aimed at furthering the general goals of the organization. The 1980s also saw five other groups weigh in to the Court on the pro-decency side; three (CH/IYA, FCF, and NLF) are "pro-family," two (NLC and NIMLO) represent local governments. Their litigious efforts have been infrequent, but they show that the proscriptionist environment, like that of the libertarians, is capable of growth. These developments noted, CDL continues to dominate the activities in which it engaged prior to *Miller*—filing amicus curiae briefs before the Supreme Court and assisting local prosecutors in their obscenity litigation. Indeed, it has increased its activity in both of these areas.

The *Miller* approach made the trial stage more important than ever. With appellate court reversals of trial court convictions declining, a victory for the state in the trial is almost always final.[16] This is why MM created its NOLC to channel information to prosecutors and why CDL increased its efforts to assist local obscenity prosecutions. To this end, the latter hired its first full-time general counsel and added two other full-time counsel to complement the five it has on retainer.[17] This enlarged staff enabled CDL to increase its field coverage.[18] With these expanded resources, it can send out experienced former prosecutors to give seminars to law enforcement officials, testify before legislative hearings, and assist in trials.[19] Thus, MM and CDL responded to the heightened importance of trial courts by giving them greater attention.

Although MM was never deeply involved in litigation before the Supreme Court, CDL has participated heavily here. Its leaders perceive the group's prosecutorial work and its amicus curiae briefs to go hand in hand. Increased fieldwork is necessary to win cases, but amicus participation is important to prod the Supreme Court to extend its rulings in ways more favorable to decency concerns.[20] Thus, increased trial work alone is insufficient to secure good obscenity law; amicus curiae participation is also crucial. Since *Miller*, CDL has participated as amicus in 45.2 percent of the Court's obscenity decisions, up from 30.4 percent in the pre–1973 cases.[21] However, this measure does not fully capture the extent of CDL's amicus activity because it ignores the group's forays into other federal courts[22] and fails to include the briefs it filed in cases denied certiorari. Table 4.2 speaks to the latter. Table 4.2 shows that the majority of CDL's attempts to participate in Supreme Court litigation as amicus curiae occurred after *Miller*. Thus, its participation before the Supreme Court has increased not only as a percentage of obscenity cases decided since *Miller* but also in absolute terms as measured by the number of amicus briefs filed.

The rhetorical and behavioral responses of pro-decency organizations to

Table 4.2
CDL Attempts to Participate in Obscenity Litigation before the Supreme
Court, Pre- and Post-*Miller*

	Number of Cases	Percentage of Total CDL Participation
Pre-Miller	22*	38.6%
Post-Miller	35	61.4%

N=65.
* Includes Stanley amicus curiae brief.
Data in table drawn from appendix A.

Miller were consistent. Their leaders saw in *Miller* not a panacea, but a
stepping stone to greater proscription. Their post-*Miller* activities seek to
move courts and legislatures to the full realization of *Miller*'s promise. Thus,
the Court shift did not prompt them to change their goals or general behavior
but simply to intensify the provision of the services they previously rendered.
MM continued its non-litigation activities, its occasional amicus participation,
and its indirect assistance to prosecutors. CDL continued its emphasis on
direct assistance to local governments and on participation before the Supreme Court as amicus curiae.

CONDITIONING FACTORS: INTERNAL

Three factors internal to CDL and MM conditioned their adaptation to
the post-*Miller* environment: their leaders, members, and focus. Both of the
major pro-decency groups are what Wilson termed ideological, purposive
organizations, those "which seek to alter radically the lives of others, rather
than adventist or gnostic movements, which seek to perfect, redeem, or
specially enlighten the lives of their own members" (Wilson, 1973, pp. 46–
47). CDL and MM believe that the availability of explicit sexual material
undermines the moral character of the nation—that which made it great. To
allow this to occur is to allow a once great civilization to decay. This is the
tie that binds members and leaders of these organizations to the single issue
they treat—the proscription of pornography for the good of the whole.

Leadership

There are two striking characteristics shared by the leadership of CDL
and MM: organizational power and Catholicism. Unlike the ACLU, these

groups are extremely centralized in decision-making processes. ACLU leaders must react to the strongly held preferences of their members, but the leaders of the pro-decency groups are largely autonomous. These officials—appointed by and accountable to the founders of the groups—articulate organizational goals and design strategies to achieve them while largely unfettered by concern with members' attitudes. Unaffected by organizational instability and shifting issue goals, another point of difference from ACLU, these officials, through the centralized locus of organizational power, hold unthreatened control over the actions taken by their groups. Without distractions from within the group, these leaders have the luxury of focusing on a single concern—obscenity—and their attention to that concern is unrelenting.

Religious beliefs further unify the perspectives of the leaders of pro-decency groups. This is of more than demographic interest. Prior to the late 1950s, the preeminent pro-decency organizations were the National Legion of Decency and the National Office for Decent Literature. Both of these groups had strong ties to the Catholic church. Except for the secular NLC and NIMLO, the organizational successors of these groups are dominated by sectarian perspectives as well. This continuity in the religious grounding of proscriptionist organizations is not accidental. It suggests that Catholicism and conservative Protestantism foster a worldview that sees immorality in the form of obscenity as a major societal problem. This perception is grounded in a conception of the nature of man. Although man has the potential to be "good," this potential is undermined by a strong tendency to betray this true nature. In short, man is a sinner whose conduct and potential cry out for socially prescribed limits.[23]

The positions taken by pro-decency groups demonstrate their leaders' perception that obscenity is a consequence of man's fall from grace. Obscenity feeds on a particular weakness: lust—sexual passion as appetite, not love. Thus, it turns humans away from their purpose: to be rational and moral agents who treat others as ends in themselves rather than as instruments of selfish sexual gratification.[24] From this perspective, a society that legitimates obscenity will succumb to the "Monster Vice."[25] If this happens, civilization will disintegrate and America will go the way of Rome.[26] Given these stakes, government must proscribe obscenity.

This understanding of human nature shapes the goals of pro-decency groups and informs the actions their leaders undertake. It leads them to a common perception of the obscenity threat and unites the leadership within each group. This fundamental unity is especially important when organizations undergo leadership changes: it helps insure continuity in perspective and goals. A bond between past and present leadership was lacking in the ACLU, and this, in part, explains its adaptive behavior after *Miller*. MM has not undergone a change in its leadership since it was founded, but CDL has. The common vision of its past and present leaders helped it to maintain a stable goal structure and eased occasional strategy disagreements between the two generations.[27]

Because the propensity to sin is constant, leaders of pro-decency groups believe that they must be vigilant in urging the protection of public morality. Thus, their goals were not affected by *Miller*. The continuing presence of sexually explicit materials serves a dual purpose for the leaders. First, they see it as justifying their continuing activity. Second, the persistence also serves as a tool of organizational maintenance; officials use it to request more donations from supporters and to solicit new members and funds.[28]

In the aftermath of *Miller*, the leaders of CDL and MM saw the need to press the advantage it gave them. However, their approaches to this end differed. Although the groups engaged in the same *type* of activities—lobbying, litigating, sponsoring rallies and conferences—their emphases differed. This difference historically stems from the leaders' perceptions of what actions will have the most impact and from the fact that CDL had occupied the litigation field before MM was organized. This led the latter to place more of its emphasis on the popularly elected branches of government. Adding to these differences are those stemming from the different resources of the groups: MM has two attorneys on its staff; CDL has a staff of four full-time counsel and five part-timers at its disposal. Thus, CDL is better equipped to litigate.

After *Miller*, MM's leaders maintained their group's focus on obscenity issues related to children.[29] Two current areas of organizational attention, the exhibition of sex-oriented films on cable television and the radio broadcast of "indecent" material,[30] demonstrate this characteristic focus. Beyond this specific focus, the primary response of MM to the litigation of obscenity was its establishment of the NOLC. Group leaders believe that this service assists prosecuting attorneys in a way that CDL cannot, given its focus on participation in litigation. Although MM officials deny this, the NOLC may have been established to seize the mantle of legal expertise that CDL leaders claim for their group; the NOLC's stated purpose is, "To realize and deserve the reputation of being the most authoritative source for obscenity law matters."[31]

Feeling it to be their greatest strength and the best way to develop *Miller*'s promise, CDL leaders continue to devote most of their resources to broad-ranging participation in litigation. They perceive this to be the only way to clarify the law to promote successful obscenity prosecutions. This became especially clear after the Court's *Jenkins* v. *Georgia* (1974) decision.[32] Had *Jenkins* been decided the other way, it would have been the legal knockout punch for which CDL officials had been waiting. Such a result would have held obscenity prosecution wholly subject to local standards. This would have created, de facto, a variable concept of obscenity.[33] When the Court refused to accept CDL's position, its leaders increased its amicus curiae filings and assistance to local prosecutors. The continued amicus activity was required to change the law incrementally, since the Court failed to do so in a single decision. Because of poor organizational record keeping, it is difficult to determine how much CDL's activities in support of prosecuting attorneys increased after *Miller*, but interviews with its leaders and one independent measure—the number of full-time attorneys employed—suggest that it probably has.[34]

In addition to the difference in how the leaders of CDL and MM allocate the activities of their organizations, a second factor distinguishes them. During the period covered by this study, MM was dominated by Father Hill and its other founders, but CDL underwent a nearly complete transferal of power to a new generation of leaders. Its new officials are tied to the group's former leaders by their common perception of the problem, by their Catholicism, and, in some cases, by family ties.[35] Although they see each other at meetings and speak regularly over the phone, Taylor and Carol Clancy now run the organization founded and nurtured by Charles Keating and James Clancy.[36]

The present CDL leaders developed new strategies to attempt to secure the goals they share with the group's previous officials. It was Taylor, a former prosecutor, who began the expansion of CDL's legal staff to enable the group's presence to extend to a greater number of obscenity prosecutions. The new generation not only brought new blood into the group but also gave new vigor to its operations. An observer's impression is that the mood in CDL's headquarters is far more positive and optimistic than that at MM. This could be a function of the age difference between the leadership— Carol Clancy is in her 30s and Taylor is in his 40s, whereas Hill and McGeady are both over 60. It also could be the result of the relative newness of these battles to Taylor and Clancy. MM's leaders have been fighting this war for over 25 years, and it is possible that time has worn away their optimism. The new CDL leaders are relative newcomers to this battle. Whatever the reasons, the enthusiasm brought to CDL by its second-generation leaders is reflected in its intensified activity and the more buoyant atmosphere at its headquarters.

A number of shared characteristics conditioned the leaders of these groups to orient themselves similarly to the post-*Miller* environment. The centralized locus of decision making enabled them to control completely the response of their groups to the altered legal context. The continuity in leadership and its shared religious perspective led them to see the problem in the same light and react to it in a similar manner. In general, their response was to continue to do those things they had done previously, albeit now more vigorously. Despite the overriding similarity of their response, however, a subtle difference can be seen. After *Miller*, CDL increased the scope, frequency, and intensity of its litigation activities; this was less true of MM. This difference is a result of a change in leadership. Although the issue goals of CDL and MM leaders have remained constant since *Miller*, the prosecutory experience and youth of CDL's new leaders worked to make its response to the new environment somewhat more energetic and innovative than that of its primary pro-decency counterpart.

Membership

In adapting to the new legal environment, officials of proscriptionist groups could be expected to consider the reaction of their members. Membership exit is always a constraint on the positions assumed by the leaders of purposive organizations (Hirschman, 1970; Wilson, 1973; Moe, 1980, 1981). The ACLU was free to de-emphasize its obscenity litigation, in part, because this action was perceived by its leaders to be unlikely to provoke a membership exodus. Like the leaders of the ACLU, the leaders of the pro-decency groups provide expressive benefits to their members (Salisbury, 1969). It is their opposition to, and activity against, obscenity that attracts and maintains organizational support.[37] Unlike members of the ACLU, however, members of these groups seem to have little influence on the types of activities their organizations undertake. Indeed, beyond their dislike of obscenity, CDL and MM leaders know very little about the particular preferences of their members. Moreover, they do not seem to need to know any more than they do. Contributors to CDL and MM do not seem to have the same participatory expectations as those who join the ACLU. Thus, membership factors have little, if anything, to do with the adaptive decisions of the leaders of these groups. Although the research on which this study is based did not include interviews with members of these groups, inferences drawn from other sources suggest an explanation of this phenomenon.

It is far too strong of a statement to say that the leaders of CDL and MM know nothing about their members. Both groups have state and local affiliates, and their leaders visit these affiliates on occasion and correspond with them regularly.[38] The importance of these functions should not be depreciated, because personal attention from leaders is one way to keep members interested in a group's activities. Organizational newsletters also provide this service. Insofar as the funds used to operate CDL and MM are largely drawn from member contributions, these methods of maintaining organizational interest are not negligible.

The *Miller* decision appears to have had some effect on the membership of MM. Its membership jumped from 35,000 in 1972 to 50,000 in 1978; at present it stands at 55,000.[39] Although it is impossible to say with certainty that the 30 percent increase between 1972 and 1978 stemmed from a reaction to *Miller*, it is not inconceivable that this was the case. *Miller* was *the* significant legal development in obscenity matters during this period, and it was exploited by the group to demonstrate the potential effectiveness of its activities.[40] It is reasonable to conclude that the *Miller* decision, in addition to

Hill's well-publicized participation in the 1970 presidential commission, accounts for much of this membership increase.

CDL's records for this period are so poor that it is impossible to tell exactly what effect *Miller* had on its membership. Proxy measures lead to inconsistent conclusions. The number of active local CDL chapters has been declining since the late 1960s. In 1962 it claimed 300 local chapters; in 1982 group leaders put the figure at about 110, and it currently stands at 120.[41] This might suggest that the organization is losing strength. However, officials are quick to point out that the type of work in which CDL specializes—litigation assistance—does not require any active local chapters as long as the group continues to receive individual contributions. Thus, the number of active affiliates may not be a reliable proxy for membership. Indeed, its fund-raising increased by 40 percent since 1976 (Taylor interview), and this could be interpreted to suggest that its membership is increasing. Whatever, this confusion over membership numbers suggests a plausible explanation for the seeming ignorance both CDL and MM officials display toward the makeup and attitudes of their membership: dollars, not bodies, is what most concerns them.

It is possible that the leaders of these groups do not concern themselves with the nature of their membership because it is largely irrelevant to their activities. CDL does not require anything of its supporters other than their contribution. With its organizational focus generally on litigation, a large and active mass membership would be a luxury, not a necessity. In providing assistance to obscenity prosecutions, CDL does not discriminate on the basis of whether a case was forwarded by a member or a nonmember. Its litigation activity does not require a large or active membership base but merely funding and information. Although a larger membership could generate more funding, increase CDL information sources, and bring more pressure to bear on local prosecutors, none of these things is necessary for the group's maintenance or the successful pursuit of its goals.

The above discussion may not be as true for MM. Because its activities are aimed primarily at the popularly elected branches of government and include letter-writing campaigns, the larger its active membership, the more political clout it could possibly generate. However, organizational officials have not invested much effort into attracting new members (McGeady interview). This suggests a couple of things. First, its leaders may perceive the group's formal lobbying efforts to be more important than its mass-based campaigns.[42] Second, its sources of income other than its membership—foundations, a few big givers, special fund-raising efforts—may be sufficient to support its activities. Thus, one possible explanation for these groups' relative inattention to their members may be the unimportance of members to core organizational activities.

A second factor seems to combine with the irrelevance of members to explain the lack of attention given to specific membership concerns: the focus of the group. Unlike the ACLU, a purposive organization that pays some attention to its members' concerns, CDL and MM are largely single-issue groups.[43] This difference suggests a third internal factor that conditioned their response to *Miller*.

Organizational Focus

The raison d'être of pro-decency organizations is obscenity. It is the only issue with which they involve themselves. Because of the focused nature of the organizations' interest their leaders may not feel the need to consult the membership to discern their interests. If one is already a member of the group, it is safe for the leadership to assume that the goals it adopts and the actions it takes to control this agreed-upon ill will be supported. In this sense, leaders of these groups always "know" what their members want. The very fact the members joined the groups tells the leaders that their goals are the goals of the members. For this reason, the detachment of leaders from members is of no great concern to either party. As long as there is a perceived obscenity problem, and as long as leaders can convince members that the group is at least somewhat successful in combating it,[44] the concentrated nature of organizational interest insulates leaders from day-to-day concern with the interests of their membership. It is not that the leaders are ignoring the wishes of the members, it is simply that they know these wishes by virtue of the members' support of the group.

The structure of organizational decision making seems to support this hypothesis. In neither group is any facet of the membership formally involved in decision making. There are no formal channels through which members can express their opinions for consideration by the leadership. In each organization the leadership is a small, fairly cohesive group of people who make all the decisions of relevance. Neither group has suffered an organizational schism. It seems a fact of the existence of CDL and MM that their leaders can stay somewhat aloof from their members without any discernible cost to organizational stability. Indeed, the homogeneous goals of their leaders make these groups the epitome of stability in the presentation of organizational views to the political institutions they seek to affect.

It might be that this type of relationship between the leaders and members of a single-issue group is quite common, especially when the issue stance is as clear-cut as it is here. Only a few things could disrupt the continuance of this type of relationship between the leaders and supporters of CDL and MM. First, if the perceived threat that gives life to the groups was removed, the leaders would either find new issues of interest to their members on which to focus their energies or go out of existence. The threat could be removed by either the disappearance of obscenity or its ultimate acceptance as legitimate, and neither seems likely. Second, if the leaders did something that went against the fundamental purpose of the group as it is understood by its members, then exit could threaten its continued maintenance. This might explain why neither of these organizations has become especially active with their potential allies; close organizational affiliation with feminist groups or strongly fundamentalist Christian political organizations might alienate enough members to threaten their existence as autonomous organizations.[45] Thus, the decision-making flexibility that the single-issue orientation of these groups gives their leaders is not unlimited, but it is considerable. This is a third factor that helps to explain their adaptive response to the post-*Miller* environment.

These three factors—leadership, membership, and organizational focus—conditioned the adaptive response of CDL and MM to the legal environment created by the *Miller* decision. However, like all other organizations, pro-decency groups exist within a larger context. Although these internal factors shaped their response to *Miller*, they interacted with external factors that also affected the way these groups approached obscenity after 1973.

CONDITIONING FACTORS: EXTERNAL

The internal dynamics of the pro-decency organizations oriented them to continuing their obscenity involvement after the 1972 term decisions of the Supreme Court. However, factors external to these groups interacted with this orientation to make certain alternative strategies more attractive than others. I will examine four such factors here: the position of the Supreme Court, the continuing problem of obscenity, the existence of libertarian attorneys and organizations, and the rise of conservativism in the political arena.

The Position of the Supreme Court

CDL and MM saw the Supreme Court's 1972 term decisions to be an acceptable first step toward the development of good obscenity law. Its decision in *Jenkins* (1974) was something of a setback, but those in cases such as *Hamling* v. *U.S.* (1974), *Young* v. *American Mini Theatres* (1976), *FCC* v. *Pacifica* (1978), *New York* v. *Ferber* (1982), *Brockett* v. *Spokane Arcades* (1985) and *Renton* v. *Playtime Theatres* (1986) supported the decency position. Except for the votes of two justices perceived to be the weakest links in the *Miller* chain—Powell and Blackmun—the proscriptionist argument would have won in *Southeastern Promotions* v. *Conrad* (1975) and *Erznoznik* v. *Jacksonville* (1975) as well.[46] The departure and replacement of Douglas (1975), Stewart (1981), and Powell (1986) left the personnel on the Court more favorably disposed toward "decency" goals. Thus, the Court is ripe for the further extension of proscriptionist doctrine. In this environment, leaders of these groups believe that they can press the initial advantage *Miller* presented them to its logical end.

Because the decision in *Jenkins* (1974) denied these organizations the quick knockout punch they desired, they had to adopt a strategy of incremental correction of obscenity doctrine. CDL is the pro-decency group most active in litigation, and it is not surprising that it developed the most coherent legal strategy to effect this end. Since *Miller* it urged the Court, among other things,

- to allow communities to prohibit the performance of plays that contain nudity as *malum in se*—"evil in itself"—*Southeastern* (1975);

- to extend the abstention doctrine to civil proceedings against obscenity, *Huffman* v. *Pursue* (1975);

- to uphold jury instructions based on *Miller* for trials of those arrested prior to that decision, *U.S.* v. *Marks* (1977);

- to permit jurors to apply their own conceptions of community standards in federal trials regardless of legislated state standards, *Smith* v. *U.S.* (1977);

- to reaffirm that evidence of pandering can be used to determine obscenity, *Splawn* v. *California* (1977);

- to allow the use of open-ended warrants as a way of collecting evidence for a criminal prosecution of obscenity, *Lo-Ji Sales* v. *New York* (1979);

- to hold constitutionally permissible the padlocking of "adult" businesses convicted as public nuisances, *U.S. Marketing* v. *Idaho* (1982);

- to exempt child pornography statutes from the restrictions of the *Miller* test and declare it *malum in se*, *Ferber* (1982);

- to sustain the use of moral nuisance statutes against "adult" stores, *Brockett* (1985);

- to uphold, as a public nuisance, the closing of an "adult" bookstore where solicitation occurred, *Arcara* v. *Cloud Books* (1986);

- to accept local definition of the "serious value" prong of *Miller*, *Pope* v. *Illinois* (1987).

MM followed a similar strategy, filing amicus curiae briefs in *Pacifica*, *Ferber*, and *Brockett*. In the first case, for example, it argued for a less strict definition of "indecency" than that applied to obscenity in *Miller*. The structure and approach of the *Miller* opinion forced these groups to engage in this kind of incremental litigation to advance their goals.

Officials of both CDL and MM are grateful that President Reagan served two terms. This is so not only because he shares their values and gave the nod to the Meese Commission but also because he appointed justices who will support pro-decency positions.[47] They hope that Bush's appointees will follow suit. Decency litigators believe these personnel changes—especially should future appointees replace aging *Miller* critics Marshall and Stevens— will assist the further development of favorable obscenity law.

Thus, the Supreme Court is a primary environmental influence on the activities undertaken by proscriptionist organizations. Its decisions create new issues that must be dispatched to enable them to attain their goals. Should the Court ever resolve all of the constitutional questions that linger around the obscenity issue to the satisfaction of these groups, it will also affect their decisions as to future courses of organizational behavior.

The Persistent Prevalence of Obscenity

The leaders of pro-decency organizations do not live in cloistered environments. They are well aware that obscenity is as prevalent, if not more so, now than it was when *Miller* was decided. Although leaders of these groups agree that the *Miller* decision has made it legally easier to prosecute pornographers, they understand that this has not been enough to cure the problem.[48]

Officials of proscriptionist groups give the same reasons for their inability to capitalize fully on *Miller*. First, those who produce, distribute, exhibit, and sell these materials are motivated by profit and will not stop pushing their wares until they are forced to do so. Second, because "pornographers" have a commercial incentive to protect their businesses, they hire skilled attorneys to conduct drawn-out and expensive trials that confuse and mislead jurors and drain prosecuting governments of scarce resources. The length and cost of these trials, as well as the minimal sanctions brought to bear against those who are convicted, further discourage prosecutions. Third, the media, "overly zealous of First Amendment rights," convinced the public that it is impermissible to regulate obscenity. Fourth, many prosecutors are afraid to bring obscenity cases for fear of humiliation at the hands of defense attorneys or because they do not personally support obscenity law and are not forced by other officials and public sentiment to enforce it. Finally, the Court's obscenity opinions have left the law less than crystalline. This leaves room for prosecutors to duck potential cases and for defense attorneys to obfuscate issues at trial. Thus, obscenity persists.

These perceptions are part of the reality with which CDL and MM must deal. In one sense they treat them the same way—as levers to maintain their organizations. Their literature points out that even though the legal questions surrounding obscenity are being resolved in favor of decency concerns, obscenity is as prevalent as ever.[49] Thus, more needs to be done, and it is important to support the group (either CDL or MM) to win this final battle. Beyond this, however, these perceptions condition the behavior of these groups in different ways. The leaders of MM see the problem as requiring sustained pressure on the popularly elected institutions of government, whereas CDL officials see it as calling for concerted judicial attack.[50] These responses are conditioned by what the leaders of the organizations perceive to be their forte.

The continuing prevalence of obscenity reinforces the inadequacies of *Miller* and the need for further organizational activity to realize its promise.

Group officials use this to urge their members to continue supporting the work of the group. Since these leaders have long since determined the best way for their organizations to spend their resources, the persistence of obscenity simply reinforces their prior decisions about how to fight its prevalence.

The Existence of Organized Legal Opposition

Because of their continuing battles with the ACLU, CDL and MM have long been aware that litigators other than "pornographers" are interested in the development of obscenity law. Throughout the 1960s, other groups became active in obscenity litigation—all of them on the libertarian side. The development of the First Amendment Lawyers Association (1970) gave the defense attorneys involved in this litigation an organization in which to develop and share expertise in obscenity law. With these libertarian actors in the field, local prosecutors were overmatched when they went into court to try an obscenity case—the prosecutor may have been dealing with his or her first obscenity case, whereas the defense counsel had the expertise developed by years of specialized practice and conversations with other defense attorneys. In such a setting, the cards were stacked against successful prosecutions. Thus, many prosecutors felt it not worth their time to try obscenity cases.

CDL developed its litigation specialty, in part, to educate local prosecutors in the nuances of obscenity law.[51] Its counsel have long been aware of the obscenity bar, and see their activities as an effective way to counter it. By sending CDL attorneys to assist local obscenity prosecutions, group leaders believe that their legal expertise can offset that of the well-schooled defense counsel. This is considered to increase the chances of favorable trial outcomes. CDL officials believe that this function is even more important in the post-*Miller* environment. "Pornographers" have economic incentives to continue litigation to frustrate the intent of *Miller*. Accordingly, they will continue to hire skilled counsel to protect their interests. This is one reason why General Counsel Taylor added experienced prosecutors to CDL's legal staff—he envisions the group developing a national pro-decency bar to counteract the influence of libertarian attorneys and organizations. To the extent that this occurs, local prosecutors will be trained by experts in obscenity law (CDL attorneys) to cope with the tactics used by the libertarian bar. This knowledge will enable them to win cases and will remove one point of hesitance in the prosecution of obscenity violations.

MM, unlike CDL, was not traditionally involved in lower court obscenity litigation. Prior to *Miller*, its judicial activities were confined to occasional amicus curiae participation before the Supreme Court. However, in his dissent to the report of the Presidential Commission on Obscenity and Pornography, Father Hill recommended the creation of an entity to counteract the emerging obscenity bar. He urged

the establishment, by Federal legislation, of a National Crime Research and Reference Library on the Law of Obscenity. . . . [Its] purpose will be to service prosecutors nationwide to expedite preparation of cases. . . . It will contain everything written on the law of obscenity: statutes, ordinances, decided cases, texts, commentaries, etc. . . . Law enforcement officials believe that the convenience of finding all precedents, statutes, briefs, etc., in one location will save countless hours in case preparation. (President's commission, 1971, pp. 501–2)

The National Legal Data Center (NLDC) was established, although not by federal law, at California Lutheran College in early 1973. It received some support from MM but was primarily funded by a $350,000 grant from the Law Enforcement Assistance Administration (LEAA).[52] Its director justified its existence by arguing that "the defense is already doing what we are doing"[53] and suggested that the NLDC would serve the same function for prosecutors.

Shortly after the *Miller* decision, the NLDC came under fire.[54] The attack was based on three points: the services of the center were not available to the legal profession or the public as a whole; its governmental support violated the separation of church and state; and it interfered with the First Amendment rights of legitimate businesses. The ensuing uproar was sufficient to cause the denial of a pending $100,000 LEAA grant (*New York Times*, 28 December 1974), and the NLDC closed its doors in 1975. However, MM officials felt that the existence of such a clearinghouse was critical to the successful prosecution of obscenity, and resuscitated it in 1976 as the NOLC under the sponsorship of MM. The intent of the NOLC is the same as that of the NLDC—to counter the expertise of the obscenity bar.

The existence of the obscenity bar and the libertarian organizations involved in obscenity was a factor conditioning the post-*Miller* adaptation of proscriptionist organizations. It helped persuade CDL officials to intensify in quantity (numbers of attorneys) and quality (time spent in the field) the traditional services of their group. It also prompted MM leaders to champion, and then house, a national clearinghouse on obscenity law.[55] The creation and resurrection of the NOLC was an innovation for MM. Prior to 1973, it was uninvolved in trial court litigation. Its influence in these actions, although indirect, increased because of the NOLC.

The Rise of the New Right

The growing political conservativism of the mid to late 1970s and 1980s also affected the adaptation of pro-decency organizations to the new legal environment. The depth of this influence is difficult to assess directly, but it affects CDL's leaders more than those of MM. However impressionistic, this effect seems real and is buttressed by some empirical evidence.

I noted above that the mood in CDL offices is strikingly more optimistic and buoyant than that in MM headquarters. Part of the difference lies in personalities and age. Another factor contributing to the enthusiasm of CDL officials is their perception that the new conservativism will ultimately work in favor of their goals. They believe that "decency" values are no longer out of favor, as was the case in the 1960s and early 1970s. This perception is supported by some political events. One is the election of Ronald Reagan. CDL officials argue that this not only put a good—from the group's point of view—man in the White House but also suggested that Americans were beginning to come to grips with the "moral mess" before them. General Counsel Taylor went so far as to say, "Ronald Reagan is the best thing that ever happened to this country." CDL leaders saw him as a charismatic figure who catalyzed and legitimized decency concerns in the eyes of many. Reagan's presidency not only educated the public—note the report of the Meese Commission—but also told the public that it was alright to import Christian principles into the political sphere.[56]

A second factor adding to the enthusiasm of CDL leaders is the rise of the religious Right. Taylor commented that Jerry Falwell succeeded in teaching Christians that "being religious does not disenfranchise people or make their beliefs politically irrelevant"; the same is true of Pat Robertson. CDL officials believe that the general religious revival will generate more support for their group and its goals. This will enable it to pursue its goals more effectively by fostering a political climate that views obscenity proscription as an important goal of public policy. With public opinion perceived to be turning this way,[57] CDL's leaders see their litigation as central to converting this opinion into law. The change in the public mood, combined with the support afforded by the courts, makes the advancement of CDL goals seem ever more possible to these officials.

MM leaders do not seem to be as excited by the rise of the New Right. Since MM and CDL perceive the obscenity problem in the same light, this seems odd. Although MM officials welcome this development, they have not exploited it as actively as has CDL. CDL officials appeared on Falwell's "Old-Time Gospel Hour" and Pat Robertson's "700 Club" television shows and wrote articles for Moral Majority literature. The group was also a member of the Coalition for Better Television. Although MM officials have appeared on the "700 Club,"[58] the relationship between their group and others with similar values is minimal. Whereas the *National Decency Reporter* frequently carries stories about the activities of the Coalition for Better Television, Moral Majority, and Eagle Forum, MM's newsletter seldom mentions other morally conservative groups. The existence of other similarly oriented groups and the rise of political conservativism just do not seem to be of much interest to the leaders of MM.

The reasons for this difference between CDL and MM are difficult to discern. It might be that CDL's leaders are more attuned to the general political climate. It could also be the case that CDL officials see some maintenance utility arising from its connections with these other groups. On one hand, CDL may tell members that there are other people out there who share their values and that, with persistence, those values will prevail. Since none of the other groups engage in obscenity litigation, CDL leaders do not fear that they will lose members to them—their functions and strengths are different. On the other hand, officials may also believe that the high profile created by CDL involvement in these groups may draw new supporters to CDL. MM leaders, lacking CDL's litigation specialization, may fear that highlighting the actions of these other pro-decency groups could drain their membership.

Another plausible explanation for this difference between CDL and MM has to do with the nature of their leaders. For most of MM's organizational life it has existed in a climate largely hostile to its concerns. Until recently, there have not been many other groups supporting its causes. It is possible that, coming to organizational maturity in an environment in which they were largely isolated,[59] MM's leaders do not know how to deal with one more hospitable.[60] The new leaders of CDL, on the other hand, do not have any old habits of organizational behavior to overcome. Their rise roughly coincides with the revival of the political Right. Never having learned to "go it alone," they may have found a loose alignment with other groups less difficult.

For these or other reasons, the new political climate of the late 1970s and 1980s acted like a shot of adrenaline to CDL's leaders. They believe that if they press hard enough on all fronts of their legal battle, their group's nearly 30-year-old goals can finally be realized. This seems to have quickened their resolve to carry on the fight.

CONCLUSION

The *Miller* decision was greeted enthusiastically by pro-decency groups. Although it was not everything they wanted, it did mark the end of the Court's hostility to proscriptionist concerns. The *Jenkins* decision of the next term made it clear that the Court would not accept the full thrust of their variable obscenity position, but *Hamling* (1974) suggested that the Court would seldom reverse obscenity convictions grounded in local standards. Pro-decency groups adapted to this new legal environment by continuing to participate in litigation. This decision was influenced by factors internal and external to the groups.

After *Miller*, the leaders of CDL and MM continued their efforts to further their proscriptionist obscenity goals. Their paths varied, however, in large part because of their different foci and resources. Where CDL's adaptive response stressed litigation, MM's aimed more toward the other branches of government. The latter, however, perceiving a need for information service for prosecutors, founded the NOLC. Thus, the organizational tools these groups plied prior to *Miller* were basically the same ones they used in its wake. Even when faced with a new environment, these groups continued the traditional services their leaders felt they did best.

An important difference between these groups is the nature of their leadership. MM remained under the direction of its first generation of leaders. However, CDL saw the transfer of organizational control to a new generation of officials shortly after *Miller* was decided. This shift corresponds with greater organizational activity. Although the goals and general perspective of the group were maintained, the new leadership brought with it new strategies for promoting organizational ends. They increased the level and intensity of CDL activity and rationalized and professionalized its operations. MM's less dynamic reaction to *Miller* seems, in part, due to the continuance of a leadership whose strategies and tactics were shaped by a previous legal environment.

These pro-decency groups, like all purposive groups, exist to express positions on political questions and draw supporters on this basis. Because of this, one would expect the decisions of their leaders to be constrained by their members. However, the members of CDL and MM had little influence on their groups' adaptation to the post-*Miller* environment. Indeed, their leaders seem unconcerned with members' reactions to their activities. However, this is not to say that the leaders are unconstrained in the political positions they adopt. Although not intimately in touch with their members, these officials feel that they "know" what the members want. This is not the result of some mystical process but of the issue foci of the organizations. They are both "single-issue" groups that draw and maintain supporters because of their obscenity goals. With such a narrow base of organizational concern, the leaders have great latitude in selecting the strategies to be used to pursue these ends. As long as members think that there is an obscenity problem, and that the organizations can do something about it, they will continue to support the groups. Through organizational literature, newsletters, and appearances, these leaders influence the perceptions of their members and hold them to continued support of the groups.

Several external factors also conditioned the adaptation of CDL and MM to the post-*Miller* scene. The Supreme Court, although not as friendly as they would have preferred, was generally hospitable to pro-decency arguments. Thus, participation before it continued to be a major avenue for organizational activity. Though group leaders would rather have focused attention on grass-roots enforcement of obscenity laws, the Court's *Jenkins* (1974) decision forced them to continue to participate in Supreme Court litigation to shape the incremental development of "good" obscenity law.

The continued persistence of obscenity, and the presence of attorneys and organizations working to frustrate the enforcement of laws proscribing it, further influenced the adaptive behavior of these groups. In this environment, trial participation and information sharing was perceived as crucial. Group leaders responded with increased support to local prosecutors and with the NOLC. These factors were also used by leaders to retain current members and attract the support of new ones.

Additionally, the political conservativism of the post-*Miller* period influenced the leaders of CDL. They now believe that with the favorable legal start provided by *Miller*, new appointments to the Court, and broad-based popular support for their position, the goals of the group are closer to being realized. To this end, CDL officials appealed to other organizations and their members to gain further support for their goals.

The leaders of purposive organizations must, in some sense, act as entrepreneurs (Salisbury, 1969); they must take positions that make them attractive to their actual and potential membership. The ACLU could afford to transfer its attention to other issues after the libertarian defeat in *Miller*, but pro-decency groups could not. For one thing, they are single-issue groups whose existence depends on pressing obscenity matters. For another, *Miller* did not finish the job. Obscenity still is out there, and the law regarding it is not uniformly sensitive to proscriptionist concerns. It may be that single-issue purposive organizations have an incentive to pursue their issue until it or they no longer exist. Without the range of alternatives supplied by a broad base of organizational interest, these groups will continue to pursue their narrow goals no matter what the external environment. This is especially true when their opponents mobilize to pursue goals contrary to their own. Although the ACLU de-emphasized its involvement in obscenity litigation, other libertarian groups filled the void left by its de-emphasis. Because of their material interests in obscenity law, these libertarian organizations did not have the exit option used by the ACLU. Chapter 5 examines their response to the post-*Miller* environment.

NOTES

1. It is interesting to note that the leaders of CDL (Charles Keating, James and Carol Clancy, Bruce Taylor, Paul McCommon) and MM (Father Morton Hill, Paul J. McGeady) are religiously Catholic.

2. NLF and FCF differ from CDL and MM in two respects: they are more Protestant in organization and more eclectic in goals. CH/IYA is solely concerned with the link between obscenity and the youth used in its production. See chapter 2.

3. See the dissenting reports filed by Hill and Keating to the majority *Report* of the President's Commission on Obscenity and Pornography (1970).

4. CDL amicus curiae brief in *Jacobellis* v. *Ohio* (1964), p. 38.

5. See the CDL *National Decency Reporter*, June-July 1966: "In *Ginzburg* and

Mishkin, a solid majority of the Court made it impossible for the reluctant prosecutor [to fail to enforce] obscenity laws. No longer can he place the blame upon the Court."

6. See Armstrong (1967a).

7. See discussion of this point in Schauer (1976), Note (1969), Engdahl (1969), Katz (1969), Note (1971b), and the *Report* of the President's Commission on Obscenity and Pornography (1970).

8. The 71 percent figure includes only those Burger/Rehnquist Court decisions that could be coded as libertarian (10) or proscriptionist (24); it does not include those (11) decided on other grounds or not easily categorized as libertarian or proscriptionist.

9. Keating (1974) and interviews with Ray Gauer, the former CDL national director, 19 January 1983, and Bruce A. Taylor, the CDL vice president and general counsel, 22 January 1983.

10. *Obscenity Law Bulletin*, January 1977. The *Bulletin* is a publication of MM's National Obscenity Law Center.

11. MM publication "You Can Help Turn the Tide of Pornography."

12. Interviews with J. Clancy, 11 January 1983; Taylor, 22 January 1984; and McGeady, 6 December 1982.

13. Its use as a strategem by defense counsel is discussed in chapter 2.

14. A similar issue was raised in *Clancy* v. *Jartech* (1978)—Clancy is CDL's James. After the appellate court reversed an award of penalties to the City of Santa Ana, Clancy requested the Supreme Court to issue a writ of certiorari. It denied this request.

15. The Court would have considered the padlocking question in *U.S. Marketing* v. *Idaho* (1982), but it dismissed its certiorari grant when the defendants, at the urging of attorneys for MC and the AFAA, asked it to do so. This infuriated pro-decency groups (Taylor, J. Clancy, and McGeady interviews). A similar issue was presented in *Arcara* v. *Cloud Books* (1986), but this case turned on the presence of on-cite solicitation. In its 1988 term decision *Fort Wayne Books, Inc.* v. *Indiana* (1989), the Court again touched on this question—this time as it relates to racketeering (RICO) prosecutions, but it did not finally decide the issue.

16. Obscenity Law Project (1976) and interview with Stanley Fleishman 1 April 1983. The project found that 18 percent of all obscenity convictions in 1971–72 were reversed by appellate courts, compared with 8 percent of the convictions in 1974–75 (1976, p. 921).

17. Interviews with group officials.

18. The effect of the two newest full-time CDL attorneys is difficult to measure. Taylor said that, prior to their appointment, for every assistance request he could accept he had to turn down "four or five" others. Even if this is exaggerated, the new counsel can pick up some of the overflow.

19. "Summary of Legal Activities of CDL Affiliated Attorneys" (internal CDL document) for 1981 and 1982.

20. Interviews with group officials.

21. The 30.4 percent does not include cases summarily treated by the Court. Including these cases lowers the group's pre-*Miller* participation to 20.5 percent (see appendix A).

22. Note its amicus participation in *Action for the Children's Television* v. *FCC* (1988) and *FW/PBS* v. *City of Dallas* (1988).

23. For a discussion of the Catholic position on obscenity, see Gardiner (1958).

24. Note the parallels here with the feminist perspective on pornography. See Dworkin (1981, 1987) and MacKinnon (1984, 1985), but note the analysis of West (1987).

25. Early CDL amicus curiae briefs were quite philosophical in their treatment of obscenity. They spoke of the nature of man and how obscenity perverted it, and quoted Alexander Pope's poem "The Monster Vice" to show that obscenity, if tolerated, would destroy civilization.

26. Hill, Taylor, J. Clancy, and Gauer interviews. See also CDL's early amicus curiae briefs—for example, *Jacobellis*, *Memoirs*, and *Redrup*—and those of MM—for example, *Rabe* v. *Washington* (1972) and *FCC* v. *Pacifica* (1978).

27. One such disagreement has arisen over the utility of public nuisance approaches to obscenity control. Clancy believes they are the best way to attack the problem, but Taylor believes in an approach that stresses both civil and criminal prosecutions.

28. The newsletters of these organizations are an important tool for this type of organizational maintenance. They report on the groups' activities. This not only keeps members informed but also tells them that the group's activities are helping.

29. Its post-1973 amicus curiae briefs stressed the dangers obscenity poses to youth. See its briefs in *Pacifica* (1978), *New York* v. *Ferber* (1982), and *Brockett* v. *Spokane Arcades* (1985).

30. Note its amicus participation in the federal appellate cases *Jones, et al.* v. *Wilkinson, Attorney General of Utah* (1986) and *Action for the Children's Television* v. *FCC* (1988).

31. First edition of the NOLC's *Obscenity Law Bulletin*, January 1977. MM officials argue that the NOLC is meant to complement, not compete with, CDL's activities.

32. In *Jenkins* (1974), the Court, with Justice Rehnquist writing for the majority, unanimously struck down the determination of Georgia courts that the movie *Carnal Knowledge* was obscene.

33. See the CDL amicus curiae brief in *Jenkins* (1974).

34. Taylor contends that these activities have increased. CDL did not keep detailed records of its attorneys' activities until 1981. This corresponds with the group's professionalization that began with the addition of Taylor and a full-time staff after its move to Phoenix. Indeed, Taylor, Carol Clancy, and the other two staff attorneys are the first full-time counsel the group has retained.

35. Carol Clancy is James Clancy's daughter. The former president of CDL, Gary Hall, though not a full-time staffer, is married to one of Keating's daughters.

36. Since Keating's savings and loan problems, these lines of communication have, according to group officials, been closed down (Corn, 1990, p. 16).

37. Both of these organizations provide their members with organizational literature, membership cards, and newsletters, but these are not likely to be a strong material incentives to join. The groups are purposive and political organizations, and the incentives for membership reflect that.

38. This is the function of the CDL national director. Father Hill fulfilled this role as the president of Morality in Media.

39. Statistics drawn from its amicus curiae briefs in *Rabe* (1972) and *Pacifica* (1978), and *The Encyclopedia of Associations*.

40. See the MM newsletter covering the last four months of 1973. The organization's literature also prominently features *Miller* to demonstrate that citizens can

legally fight against pornography without violating expression rights guaranteed by the Constitution ("Turn the Tide of Pornography").

41. C. Clancy and Taylor interviews, amicus curiae briefs, and *The Encyclopedia of Associations*. These numbers get a bit tricky. Because they were self-reported during a time of poor organizational record keeping, the numbers for the early 1960s are very questionable. This is, however, all with which we have to work.

42. Hill met with President Reagan a couple of times to urge increased prosecution of federal obscenity laws. See *Minneapolis Tribune*, 29 March 1983 and 25 May 1983. This goal was given at least lip service in the *Final Report* of the Attorney General's Commission on Pornography (1986).

43. This may change for CDL, given its evolution into the Children's Legal Foundation (Corn, 1990, p. 16).

44. These are perceptions that leaders can manipulate and shape through organizational literature, newsletters, and public appearances.

45. Taylor and J. Clancy raised this possibility as a constraint on leadership attempts to work more closely with Eagle Forum or Moral Majority. The fear is that a significant number of CDL supporters would balk at such a relationship because of their perceptions of what those groups stand for. The same holds for an alliance with feminist anti-pornography groups (see chapter 2).

46. Taylor interview. In *Erznoznik* (1975) and *Southeastern Promotions* (1975), the Court, by a vote of 5–4, struck governmental efforts to prohibit the exhibition of films containing nudity at outdoor theaters and to deny permission for a traveling production of the play *Hair* in a city-leased theater. Taylor believes that Brennan has captured Blackmun on obscenity questions. Although he does not think Blackmun will renege on his *Miller* position, he does not look for him to support further pro-decency advances.

47. Of President Reagan's Supreme Court appointments, only Justice Scalia seems to harbor significant concern about the *Miller* approach (see his concurring opinion in *Fort Wayne Books*, 1989), but he does not seem to be in any hurry to drastically modify *Miller*, and even if he was, the opinion still has the support of a majority of the justices.

48. McGeady, Taylor, and McCommon interviews. Taylor, during one of our interviews, made reference to the Obscenity Law Project of the New York University School of Law.

49. See MM's "Turn the Tide of Pornography" and CDL's "Question and Answer" publications.

50. This is not to suggest that either organization applies itself exclusively to one type of activity. Both groups engage in a wide range of activities that overlap. However, each tends to focus its resources in one area of activity with greater intensity.

51. See the first issue of the *National Decency Reporter*, 15 September 1963.

52. For information on the NLDC, see *Washington Post*, 29 August 1973; *NYT*, 28 December 1974; papers in the 1973 files of the ACLU archives; and the March and September 1975 and June 1976 issues of the National Committee Against Censorship's newsletter.

53. Comments of Philip Cohen, the NLDC director, quoted in the *Washington Post*, 29 August 1973.

54. Some of its accusers were the attorney Stanley Fleishman, the American As-

sociation of University Professors, the ACLU, the AAP, and some of the faculty at California Lutheran College. *NYT*, 28 December 1974.

55. CDL officials believe that they have done an adequate job of doing this throughout the group's existence. Apparently, either MM leaders did not think this the case or they wanted to move in on CDL's nearly exclusive hold on the legal aspects of obscenity.

56. Taylor met with Reagan at the White House. The July-August 1983 *National Decency Reporter* includes on its front page an autographed picture of the president shaking hands with Taylor.

57. This perceived change does not show up in public opinion polls. A Gallup poll, reported in *Newsweek*, 18 March 1985, shows little change in public attitudes on obscenity between 1977 and 1985. The movement that has occurred concerns "violent" obscenity, with between 63 percent and 73 percent favoring its ban.

58. The "700 Club" did a series of shows on pornography. This is why CDL and MM officials have been on the show.

59. Interestingly, the relations between MM and CDL have traditionally been chilly. Part of this is attributable to the tensions between their founders, Hill and Keating. This tension stems from a couple of sources, primary among them the competitiveness engendered by running groups doing very similar things and a personal dislike growing from their joint participation on the President's Commission on Obscenity and Pornography (1970). One group official put it to me this way: "They are like two parents managing rival little league teams." As these individuals recede from organizational dominance—Keating turned things over to Taylor in 1979, and Hill "retired" in 1987—the groups may cooperate more than in the past. Indeed, Taylor's amicus brief in *Action for the Children's Television* (1988) was joined by MM.

60. The MM position may also reflect the traditional Catholic fear of fundamentalist Protestantism and its "anti-popery."

5

Organizational Adaptation:
Mobilization

The members of CPDA are vitally interested in the outcome of this
appeal . . . because the New York [statute], and comparable statutes in
other states, which make it a crime to distribute to minors certain vaguely
defined classes of non-obscene literature, will (a) deter the sale of constitutionally protected literature to adults, and (b) make it extremely
difficult (and in some cases virtually impossible) for minors to purchase
any work which refers to sex. This will obviously hurt the businesses of
responsible wholesalers and retailers of publications. More importantly,
it will erode First Amendment freedoms.
> —CPDA amicus curiae brief, *Redrup* v. *New York* (1967)

The interest of *amicus curiae* is frankly commercial.
> —CPDA amicus curiae brief, *Jenkins* v. *Georgia* (1974)

Writing on political decision making in another context, Graham Allison
noted, "Where you stand depends upon where you sit" (Allison, 1971).
Despite differences in goals, the ACLU and pro-decency groups engage in
obscenity litigation for reasons that are eminently political. They are purposive organizations devoted to furthering visions of a good society, and they
pursue these visions through the channels of government. Their participation
is motivated by the philosophical and societal importance their leaders and
supporters attach to the issue at hand. The great majority of groups active

in obscenity litigation, however, are not primarily or preeminently political in nature. The vantage point from which they survey the obscenity scene is the vocation of their members, and this strongly conditions their interest in this area of litigation.

The differences between the bulk of the organizational litigators active in obscenity and the purposive organizations discussed in chapters 3 and 4 are profound. The members of the first groups, unlike those of the ACLU, Citizens for Decency through Law (CDL), and Morality in Media (MM), are primarily corporate or professional.[1] They represent subsets of the general population involved in the creation and dissemination of expressive materials: publishers, producers, distributors, sellers, exhibitors, and loaners. The primary incentives they use to attract and retain members are material and include the provision of information important to a particular vocation or business, certification for employment or operation, specialized training, and access to exclusive benefits such as low-cost insurance and car rentals. Although they may be politically active on occasion, such is not their raison d'être. Their interest in obscenity is perked less by a concern for the "public good" than by the proximity of the issue to the daily business of their members. In short, they are preeminently "material" organizations (Olson, 1965; Salisbury, 1969; Wilson, 1973; Moe, 1980, 1981).

Their material basis of association gives these groups a different perspective on the problems entailed in obscenity regulation. Whereas the ACLU's obscenity participation is grounded in its understanding of political principles related to expression, the interests of material groups are somewhat more tangible and less philosophical. Their paramount goal is the protection of something specific—the occupation of their members—and not an abstract idea of a "good" society.[2] Thus, the reasons they engage in obscenity litigation differ from those of purposive groups. The threats posed to them by the 1973 decisions are not philosophical, but commercial and professional: the potential for local obscenity regulation occasioned by *Miller* threatened their profitability. Obscenity proscription could drag them into protracted litigation, cause local retail outlets to turn away their products out of a fear of prosecution, and disrupt national distribution patterns of sex-oriented materials. *Miller* also posed a threat to the integrity and function of their members. These interests, tangible and particular to their members, place them on a different plane of concern than that occupied by other obscenity litigators. This difference in associational nature conditioned their response to the legal environment ushered in by *Miller*.

Despite differences in associational nature and perspective, the material organizations involved in obscenity litigation, like the ACLU, are generally libertarian in orientation. They oppose obscenity laws, at least insofar as they are applied to their members. They also, at least in part, use the First Amendment to justify their position. These similarities sometimes obscure their primarily material orientation to this issue. Narrow, basically private concerns can be framed to look less so by the use of principled First Amendment argumentation; such argumentation can be used to place a political veneer over what is essentially a material concern. An example of this can be seen in the Adult Film Association of America's (AFAA) amicus curiae brief in *Jenkins* (1974): "The Association is opposed to censorship, believing it to be the sworn enemy of freedom and liberty . . . [and] is deeply committed to the principles of freedom of speech and press upon which our country was built and prospered" (p. 20). This argument is probably more compelling than something along the lines of, "We oppose proscription because it impinges upon our ability to make money by producing and distributing images of copulation." In this way, the First Amendment allows these groups, in effect, to move between markets: an argument for free enterprise is converted to one for free expression of ideas. Even though the First Amendment lends itself to this kind of argumentation, this should not hide the primary incentive that draws the AFAA and other material groups to this litigation.

Although material organizations are a subset of the libertarian type, they do differ among themselves on dimensions relevant to participation in obscenity litigation. Some of these groups are concerned solely with obscenity matters, whereas others have interests that extend to a broader range of concerns. The membership of some of them is made up of corporations, whereas that of others is composed of individuals in particular vocations. The nature of their interest in obscenity can also differ. These groups are drawn to this issue because of material concerns, but not all material concerns are the same. A group may have professional interests underlying its obscenity involvement. It may seek to limit the application of these laws not because of regard for profitability but because of concern for the integrity of a particular occupation or activity. Concern for profitability suggests a more commercial interest. Professional and commercial interests can be conceived of as poles on a continuum of material interests, suggesting that some groups may be moved by a combination of these interests. Thus, although material organizations are distinguishable from their purposive counterparts, they are not uniform in the precise nature of their specific goals and litigation incentives. These differing goals and incentives affect their approach to litigation.

The characteristics that distinguish material from purposive groups, as well as from one another, can be expected to condition different organizational responses to *Miller*. Their different perspectives and goals suggest that their adaptive response will differ from that of purposive groups. Whereas the ACLU had the flexibility to de-emphasize its obscenity goals, material groups could not do so unless they were satisfied that the new legal environment posed them no danger, or unless they decided to sacrifice their interests to possible prosecutions. The different directions of organizational concerns—libertarian and proscriptionist—suggest that the adaptation of material groups would differ from that of pro-decency groups. However, both had strong incentives to continue in obscenity litigation—the former material, the latter political. The differences among material organizations could also be expected to generate a range of similar yet varied specific responses to *Miller*. These could include the degree of their litigation response, the cases in which they involved themselves, and the arguments they presented to the courts.

The conceptual distinction between material and purposive groups is borne out by their response to *Miller*: after the decision, material groups became the preeminent libertarian obscenity litigators. The gradual liberalization of the Warren Court allowed these organizations to act as "free riders" on the victories of others during the 1960s; the altered legal environment sparked them to mobilize, at least initially, to meet the threats it presented. Their involvement in trial and appellate litigation increased dramatically and broadened to include sponsorship as well as amicus curiae participation. A new organization, Media Coalition (MC), was created to contend with the new legal environment, and one group that had been largely dormant during the Warren Court years, the American Library Association (ALA), increased the frequency and intensity of its participation in obscenity cases. In general, these groups, because it was from their material vantage point that the threat of *Miller* seemed greatest, filled the libertarian void left by the ACLU's abdication of litigation leadership.

ORGANIZATIONAL RESPONSE TO *MILLER*

Previous chapters demonstrated that the rhetorical and behavioral reactions of groups to *Miller* were not necessarily consistent. Although the behavioral reaction of pro-decency organizations mirrored their rhetorical response, that of the ACLU did not. The latter voiced great concern with the new state of affairs but took the occasion to de-emphasize its obscenity litigation. The response of material groups to *Miller* was different from that exhibited by other organizational actors. Their rhetorical responses diverged: some accepted its approach to obscenity, others rejected it. However, common to these groups was a desire to limit *Miller*'s effects. As a result, they coalesced around a "least common denominator"—living with *Miller* but confining its scope. Their behavioral response was consistent with this point of limited consensus: mobilization.

Those material groups that rhetorically supported the 1973 decisions held that they were correctly decided but were not applicable to the wares of their members. The organizations making this argument were the American Booksellers Association (ABA), the Authors League of America (AL),[3] the Council for Periodical Distributors Association (CPDA), the Directors Guild of America (DGA), the Media Coalition (MC), the Motion Picture Association of America (MPAA), and the National Association of Theatre Owners (NATO). At core, their rhetorical concern was that obscenity proscription, although a valid governmental function, endangered the livelihood of their members.[4] They feared that overzealous local enforcement of obscenity laws would pose practical problems for their members. Prosecution would needlessly concern producers of serious literature and movies with legal attacks[5] and would "chill" sex-oriented expression not obscene under *Miller*. It would also "chill" constitutionally protected expression by making distributors, exhibitors and sellers chary of handling works with sexual themes.[6] Since sexual themes were quite popular in film and literature, proscriptionist prosecution would restrict a wide range of materials. These fears were heightened by a number of prosecutions that occurred immediately after *Miller* was handed down.[7] These groups sought judicial action to clarify *Miller* and protect the specific interests of their members. First Amendment principles, though supporting their essentially material arguments, were not portrayed as their central concern.

Other material groups loudly rejected the approach taken by the 1973 decisions. These organizations—for example, the Adult Film Association of America (AFAA), the American Library Association (ALA) and its litigation arm the Freedom to Read Foundation (FRF), the Association of American Publishers (AAP), and the First Amendment Lawyers Association (FALA)— argued that the *Miller* approach failed to protect First Amendment rights, ignored legal development since *Roth*, was inherently vague and overbroad, and institutionalized the subjectivity of judgments about obscenity.[8] The arguments of these groups are more pointedly grounded in First Amendment concerns than are those of the material groups that accepted *Miller*. Their formal position on obscenity is akin to that urged by Brennan in *Paris*— consenting adults should be allowed access to whatever material they desire. However, their obscenity goals, like those of the other material groups, turn more on the specific concerns of their members than on general First Amendment considerations. Their amicus curiae briefs always note the impact of obscenity regulation on their members' professions or businesses. The AFAA amicus in *Jenkins* illustrates this point: "[Because of *Miller*,] members of the Association, all of whom are law abiding citizens, face the possibility of criminal prosecution under standards which are essentially meaningless" (p. 2). The organizations of librarians and publishers are no less blunt about their motivating interest in obscenity litigation; their more general contentions are self-consciously made from their material perspective.[9] Although their First Amendment commitments may be held deeply, it is the relationship of the law to their members that leads these groups to involve themselves in this issue.

The rhetorical positions of these two categories of material organizations are different, but the realities of the post-*Miller* environment created a point of common agreement. This commonality is a function of their shared material orientation. In a legal environment inhospitable to their concerns, the ALA/FRF, the AAP, and the FALA had to lower their legal expectations.

Table 5.1
Participation of Material Groups before the Supreme Court, Pre- and Post-
Miller

	Involvement*	Involvement Not Counting Summary Reversals
Pre-Miller	21/23.9%	20/43.5%**
(#/% of n)	(n=88)	(n=46)
Post-Miller	19/61.3%	19/61.3%
(#/% of n)	(n=31)	(n=31)

* Counts amicus curiae and sponsorship participation.
** Does not include Aday (1967) -- reversed summarily.

This lowering brought them into line with the material groups that chose
not to challenge *Miller*. In essence, the more libertarian material organizations
had to make the best of a bad legal situation. Their long-run goal remains
the establishment of a consenting adults test, but in the short run they must
protect the specific interests of their members as best they can.[10] Thus, the
new legal context made these groups strategically backtrack. This led them
to adopt the rhetorical goals of their less libertarian material counterparts.
Living with *Miller* and checking its extension is the "least common denominator" that unites these groups in their present approach to obscenity issues.

The behavioral response of material organizations was consistent with this
"least common denominator" position: they mobilized to protect the interests of their members from the enforcement of obscenity laws. This mobilization occurred primarily through the courts. Although some of these groups
had long been active in obscenity litigation, the frequency and intensity of
their involvement increased after *Miller*. One measure of this increased participation is presented in table 5.1.

Although table 5.1 demonstrates an increase in the Supreme Court participation of material groups, it does not reflect the change in the intensity
of that involvement. One way to measure this is found in raw form in
appendix C. Examining the data presented there shows that, with the exception of the Direct Mail Advertising Association (DMAA) and the FALA,
the frequency of participation before the Court increased for all material
groups in the post-*Miller* period.[11] Also consider table 5.2, which averages
the number of appearances of material groups before the Court against the
number of obscenity cases it handled. These data more readily show the
increased intensity of the groups' involvement. Clearly, *Miller* stimulated
more frequent and intense material group litigation.

Three other aspects of the behavioral response of these organizations are
unique. First, the high-water point of their interest in obscenity issues came

Table 5.2

Incidence of Participation of Material Groups before the Supreme Court, Pre- and Post-*Miller*

	Incidence*	Summary Reversals
Pre-Miller	.477	.891**
	(n=46)	(n=88)
Post-Miller	2.645	2.645
	(n=31)	(n=31)

---

* Incidence = summation of individual participation by material organizations divided by
   the number of obscenity cases treated by the Supreme Court.
**Does not include AAP participation in Aday (1968)-- reversed summarily.
Data drawn from appendix A.

the year after *Miller* in *Jenkins*. All material groups, with the exception of the DMAA and the FALA, participated in this case. The reason for this is clear. The greatest potential threat from *Miller* was manifest in the attempt to proscribe a major motion picture, *Carnal Knowledge*. If the Court had opted for the variable approach in its entirety, the operations of the members of these groups would have been in great peril. When the *Jenkins* decision abated this threat, the interest of a couple of groups in obscenity litigation— DGA and NATO—immediately dissolved as their specific goals were secured. With the scope of *Miller* somewhat confined by *Jenkins* and a few subsequent decisions, the incentives for other organizations to litigate also decreased.[12] This response to *Jenkins* shows that the specific material interests—and the subject goals that spin off from them—that drive this type of group to the courts are not uniform. When threats to material interests are broad, a wide range of groups will mobilize to protect the position of their members. This was the case in *Jenkins*. The breadth of the threat stimulated the most extensive response of material groups in the post-*Miller* period. When the scope of the prosecutory threat narrowed, those groups associated with the threatened sector assumed the costs of protecting it alone. The nature of a group's interest conditioned its perception of the threat posed by obscenity laws and thus its participation in obscenity litigation.

A second consequence of the new legal environment was a shift in the arguments that material groups presented to the courts. Although the ACLU and the pro-decency groups altered the pitch of their arguments after *Miller*, arguments of material groups changed tone: they shifted from a constitutional to a more pragmatic plane as they stressed the practical effects of obscenity proscription on their business or profession. Prior to 1973 they tended to stress grand First Amendment principles. After *Miller*, these principles took a backseat to pragmatic and narrow concerns related to legal application in concrete instances. The shift in argument stemmed from a shift in goals.

This shift in goals—living with proscription instead of trying to undo it—is manifest in the emergent "least common denominator" consensus. The leaders of these groups believed that this kind of argument would be more persuasive to courts less sympathetic to broad First Amendment contentions.[13]

A final peculiarity of the response of material organizations is the focused nature of their judicial participation. The ACLU and pro-decency groups did not confine themselves to any particular aspect of obscenity litigation. Their interest in the subject was general, not particular. The litigation of material groups demonstrates a more focused interest.

The general pattern evident in table 5.3 is one of concentrated litigation effort: these groups tend to limit their participation to cases relevant to *their* specific material concerns. For example, NATO and the AFAA participated solely in cases raising the obscenity issue in the context of films. A similar concentration of effort is seen with the ABA, CPDA, DMAA, DGA, and MC. However, some material groups participated in a broader range of cases. Although most of the MPAA's participation was confined to cases with a nexus to films, the group did engage in cases raising other issues. However, its participation in *Pacifica* (1978) was explicitly premised on commercial grounds,[14] and its involvement in *McKinney* (1976) was through MC and not independently undertaken.[15] Narrow commercial interests seem to account for the focused nature of the obscenity litigation of these groups.

The participation of the AAP, ALA, and AL ranges more widely than that of the other material groups. The commercial connections that explain the MPAA's extended range of interest are not as apparent for these groups. The breadth of their participation is a result of a couple of factors. First, the commercial interests of their members lead them to join a wider range of cases. For example, authors have commercial interests that span media types. This causes the AL to enter a wide variety of obscenity cases. Second, these groups have a different perspective on the obscenity issue than do the other organizations. The professional interests of their leaders and members lead them to see the issue in broad relief. As a result, they perceive the development of one area of obscenity law to be related to that with which they are most closely associated. This broader vision, one with more clearly principled First Amendment overtones, orients these groups to a broader-ranging participation in obscenity litigation. Their stance as publishers, authors, and librarians conditions their preceptions of the problem posed by obscenity regulation. In this way, their interests in this area of law, though still material, are less commercial and more professional[16] than those of the other material groups involved in this litigation.[17]

The discussion above focuses on the litigation of material groups before the Supreme Court. Prior to *Miller*, this is where most of their litigation activity was aimed.[18] Yet, *Miller*'s localization of obscenity law made the trial stakes higher than was previously the case. Stanley Fleishman, the preem-

Table 5.3
Distribution of Participation of Material Groups in Obscenity Cases Decided by the Supreme Court, 1957–1987

Range of Issues Treated by the Court*

Group	Print	Movie	Radio	Theater	Schools	Total**
AFAA	0	4	0	0	0	4
ABA	8	3	0	0	0	11
ALA	10	3	0	1	1	15
ASJA	1	0	0	0	0	1
AAP	19	4	1	0	1	25
AL	8	4	1	1	1	15
CPDA	12	3	0	0	0	15
DMAA	1	0	0	0	0	1
DGA	0	1	0	0	0	1
FALA	1	2	0	0	0	3
MC	8	3	0	0	0	11
MPAA	2	7	1	0	0	10
NATO	0	3	0	0	0	3
OAA	0	1	0	0	0	1
VSDA	0	1	0	0	0	1

* The figures in these columns represent the number of cases in each
  category litigated by a particular group.
** Figures represent involvement (in number of cases) of a group in
  obscenity litigation before the Supreme Court.
Data drawn from Appendix A.

inent attorney active in obscenity litigation throughout most of the period under study here,[19] put in this way: "[Appellate courts] obviously have been rejecting [arguments to reverse obscenity convictions] right and left, so *Miller* certainly had that effect. If you don't win in the trial court you're in a lot of trouble" (interview with author). The data assembled by the New York University School of Law's Obscenity Law Project support this assessment (Obscenity Law Project, 1976). With fewer appellate court reversals of obscenity convictions, the decisions of trial courts became crucial. In reaction, some material groups became active at the trial level.

The trial court activities undertaken by material organizations are not uniform. Some groups have not directly engaged in much of this activity. For example, NATO undertook no trial litigation to protect the interests of its members.[20] The trial court impact of the FALA, although significant, is indirect.[21] The AL participates only as amicus.[22] The AFAA occasionally brings cases in its own name,[23] but its primary influence on obscenity trials is indirect—the advice its legal staff provides the counsel of members. However, other organizations became increasingly active in lower court litigation. The ALA/FRF sponsored a case in its name, and it supplies monetary grants to individuals and groups involved in obscenity litigation.[24] Through MC, the AAP, ABA, CPDA, MPAA, and Magazine Publishers Association (MPA) all participated in obscenity trials. Although MC was founded after *Miller* to help protect the commercial interests of its members and was not initially charged with engaging in lower court litigation, its responsibilities evolved to include such activities; direct participation in obscenity litigation is now a primary tool to protect the interests of its members. Using this strategy, MC has taken the offensive against state obscenity statutes it perceives to especially threaten the commercial interests of its members.[25] Thus, in an attempt to protect the interests of their members more effectively, some material groups shifted a portion of their litigation efforts to direct participation in trials.

To summarize, the litigation activity of material groups increased in quantity, frequency, and intensity after *Miller*. With the withdrawal of the ACLU from libertarian domination of obscenity litigation, material groups became the preeminent libertarian actors in this issue area. A new organization, MC, formed specifically to protect the commercial interests of some of these groups. Organizations that existed prior to 1973 also increased their obscenity litigation. As the post-*Miller* period wore on, some of these groups turned to the sponsorship of litigation testing the constitutionality, under *Miller*, of obscenity statutes. Their particular vantage point—that of commercial and professional interests—changed the tenor of obscenity litigation. Instead of the broad rights-based theory of the ACLU, courts were now confronted with the pragmatic concerns of representatives of American institutions— publishers, filmmakers, distributors, sellers, and librarians. Given this mobilization and the shift in the locus of organizational litigation, the question becomes "Why?" What factors conditioned this response to the legal environment created by the Burger Court?

CONDITIONING FACTORS: INTERNAL

Three factors internal to material organizations seem to account for their adaptive response to *Miller*: leadership, membership, and clarity of goals.

Unlike the ACLU and the pro-decency groups examined previously, material organizations do not maintain themselves, as a rule, by providing expressive benefits to their members (Salisbury, 1969; Wilson, 1973; Moe 1980, 1981). This makes the relationship of their leaders and members somewhat different from that of those groups that are expressly purposive. Members join these organizations to attain specialized or exclusive benefits that they could not realize on their own. The range of organizational activity includes nonpolitical concerns—indeed, these material interests tend to predominate within the organization. The political goals and actions of these groups are largely a by-product of their material concerns (Olson, 1965). These factors condition the response of these groups to the public context in which they operate.

Leadership

The leaders of material groups provide their members with exclusive benefits. They can be considered entrepreneurs because they offer benefits in a market setting to attract and maintain their membership (Salisbury, 1969). Rational potential members will commit themselves to join the group only if they receive goods that are otherwise unattainable. Leaders affect this calculus by offering selective benefits (for example, low-cost insurance, "insider information," pensions, job security) they believe will attract and hold the most members. If the costs of membership are perceived to exceed its benefits, then the group will lose members and endanger its continued existence. Thus, the potential for membership exit can constrain the activities of leaders (Olson, 1965; Hirschman, 1970; Wilson, 1973).

The posture of material organizations active in obscenity politics is consistent with that outlined above. With one exception, their existence and maintenance does not depend on obscenity litigation, and the exception (MC) was not created exclusively to litigate.[26] To engage in this litigation, the leaders must either provide the membership with benefits so desirable that the added cost of supporting litigation becomes irrelevant or convince them that organizational participation in such litigation—although it provides a "public good"—is sufficiently important to merit the costs necessary to provide it. Although leaders cannot control membership decisions, they can influence them through the provision of information and persuasion.

The leaders of the material groups maintained their organizations while expending their resources on obscenity litigation. Although group actions to protect sex-oriented material provide a public good, two factors aided their attempts to pursue this litigation. First, the magnitude of *Miller*'s perceived threat was sufficient to outweigh the costs of mobilizing to protect their material interests. In a context where works such as *Carnal Knowledge*, *Deliverance*, *A Clockwork Orange*, and *Slaughterhouse Five* were targets of proscription, the material interests of the members of groups as different as the AFAA and the ALA were perceived to be threatened. To not fight back would be potentially to will the demise of a significant portion of their professional autonomy and commercial profits. Insofar as leaders were able to show members that group litigation protected their interests,[27] they could make a strong (and materially based) case for judicial participation. Second, the start-up costs to engage in extensive litigation were low. All of these groups except MC existed prior to 1973, as did the groups that founded this exception. Moreover, most engaged in some obscenity litigation prior to *Miller*. Thus, the price of mobilization was cheap compared with that associated with starting anew—especially in light of the threat posed to their material well-being.

A good example of leadership moving to meet the threat posed by *Miller* and then working to gain the offensive is MC. MC was founded by representatives of the AAP, CPDA, MPA, MPAA, and the International Periodicals Distributors Association (IPDA) the Sunday after the *Miller* decision was handed down. The representatives of these organizations knew each other through their participation in the ACLU's ad hoc Committee on Censorship and had left that committee when it became clear that the legal environment created by the Burger Court required new strategies to protect their particular interests.[28] MC's leaders eventually decided that its work load was too much for one layperson to handle and hired Michael Bamberger as MC's first general counsel in 1977. Bamberger's presence made MC more autonomous than it had been previously, when its member groups had lent it their attorneys. Given this autonomy, the group developed a litigation strategy designed to enter this area of law aggressively. Thus, MC began to directly challenge obscenity legislation believed to threaten the material interests of its members. This new strategy, relying on vagueness and overbreadth arguments, produced a number of legal victories and served two purposes for the group.[29] First, it helped to protect its members' commercial interests. Second, it aided organizational maintenance: the group was able to point to its concrete judicial victories and keep its members constantly aware of the threats present in the environment. Not only does MC use its litigation efforts to maintain its membership base, but it also uses them in an attempt to attract new members.[30] In this way, MC's leaders turned the new legal environment somewhat to their advantage.

Where MC's leaders took steps to adapt to the legal environment created by *Miller*, the lack of strong leadership stymied a similar response by the AFAA. This seems odd because the AFAA would seem to have at least as great an incentive to engage in protective litigation in the post-*Miller* context as any other material organization. Its members produce 35-millimeter "adult" films that flirt with the legally obscene as defined by *Miller*. However, its reaction to *Miller* has been tepid. This laxity is not for want of trying to mobilize. Its leaders tried to gird it for a sustained attack on obscenity laws. They urged members to authorize a "litigation war chest" to fund direct support of litigation and extensive amicus curiae participation, and they

sought funds to create an information clearinghouse on obscenity developments to enhance the group's ability to monitor and shape developments in
the law. The members voted to establish these programs, but the AFAA's
leaders have been unable to persuade them to fund them.

Compounding the difficulties posed by the weakness of the AFAA's leadership is its maintenance of co-counsel. The co-counsel arrangement resulted
from a compromise between the AFAA's leaders and influential members who
wanted their attorneys to be counsel to the organization.[31] The arrangement
generates tensions revolving around ego difficulties, differences in opinion
on proper legal strategy, concern with private practices rather than organizational interests, and the perceived incompetence of some counsel by other
counsel. The squabbles among the co-counsel keep them from presenting
a unified front to the group and limits their ability to forge a coherent litigation
strategy. Insofar as the leaders of the group are responsible for staffing its
counsel, they share the blame for its ineffectiveness. It is in part because
of this that the AFAA has been unable to mobilize to face the post-*Miller*
environment in the manner desired by some of its officials.

Organizational leadership is one internal factor conditioning the post-*Miller*
adaptation of material groups. When that leadership was strong and persuasive, groups mobilized to protect the particular interests of their members.
When strong leadership was absent—and the AFAA is the only example of
this—the organization was unable to exercise much direct influence on the
development of obscenity law.[32]

Membership

The members of a material group do not join it to support the political
positions it may have occasion to take (Olson, 1965; Wilson, 1973; Moe,
1980, 1981). As long as the group provides exclusive benefits that the members perceive to be worth the cost of membership, it has a great deal of
flexibility in the political positions it can assume. However, exit is a possibility
if members do not perceive the benefits the group provides to be worth the
cost or if the political positions it takes are so odious that, despite the benefits
received, membership is no longer sustainable.

The members of most of the material organizations with obscenity concerns either acquiesced in or supported the post-*Miller* mobilization. This is
largely the result of a commonality of interest—grounded in a shared and
narrow perspective defined by material concerns—between leaders and
members. The economic interests of the members of commercial groups—
their concern with their continuing markets and profitability—are consonant
with the "least common denominator" approach adopted by their leaders.
Thus, mobilization in the face of a threat to these interests is consistent with
the commercial concerns that led members to the organization. The creation
and maintenance of MC is a prime example of this.[33] In those groups with

broader-ranging professional concerns, members see this participation as a way of protecting their vocation as well as making a statement about the role of expression in a liberal society. The legal arguments of the AAP, ALA, and AL are premised on this duality. Indeed, the AAP and the ALA manifest this concern in their organizations; they have standing committees on the "freedom to read" and worked together to found the FRF.[34] The material incentives that bind these groups individually and collectively and the absence of membership exit in light of their stepped-up activities suggest that the members generally supported mobilization as an appropriate response to the perceived threat posed by *Miller*.

Although inferences of member support for the post-*Miller* mobilization can be drawn from sketchy data, two examples demonstrate that the members of material organizations can affect group response to a changed litigation environment. The MPAA and the MPA, founding members of MC, withdrew from that organization in 1977. The reason was simple: their leaders decided that the legal context it created was not as chilly as had initially been feared. Their departure diminished MC's resource base and caused it to recruit new members. It also shifted the litigation interests of the group. After their exit, MC refocused its attention on issues of importance to those who deal with printed material. Not coincidentally, its current membership is made up exclusively of groups involved with the printed medium.[35]

Where the withdrawal of the MPAA narrowed the range of MC's activities, AFAA members kept their group from becoming deeply involved in obscenity litigation. Its members are corporations involved in the "adult" film industry. They see themselves as "rugged individualists" doing battle with the state in an effort to pursue the profits their businesses generate. This individualist orientation extends to their litigation decisions. Participation in litigation, even as amicus, is expensive, and past involvements by the AFAA have been controversial among the membership. One official told me that, although the AFAA "has helped to fund particularly significant battles, partisan battles, fought by its members on a couple of occasions, those situations created great rancor because people were asked to contribute to their competitors." Many members object to funding the litigation (no matter how significant) of nonmembers. They are even leery of supporting the litigation of fellow members, believing that each member corporation should secure counsel and fight its legal battles (which are, after all, part of the business) on its own. There are many examples of the effects of this orientation. Group members failed to fund the AFAA's information clearinghouse and litigation war chest. They also rejected the decision of their leaders to contribute $5,000 to the plaintiff's appeal in *Red Bluff Drive-In* v. *Vance* (1981). Only through the insistent urgings of the leadership was $3,500 of the promised amount finally delivered to the plaintiff (interview with author). The AFAA members, though affiliated through the group, are basically competitors, and they do not want to assist their competition any more than they believe absolutely necessary. The AFAA's general counsel are available for consultation by the attorneys of members, but seldom does organizational assistance extend beyond this.

In sum, members of most material groups went along with their post-*Miller* mobilization, but those of a few decided not to bear the cost of this mobilization. The MPAA and the MPA decided to leave MC after they determined that their commercial interests were unlikely to be endangered by obscenity prosecutions. The members of the AFAA preferred to bear the occasional cost of litigation individually rather than to subsidize the litigation of fellow members and competitors. Thus, although the members of material groups usually acquiesce in the litigation decisions of their leaders, they can also constrain and shape those decisions under certain circumstances.

Clarity of Goals

It is surprising that the range of interests common to material organizations do not correlate with a particular adaptive behavior. One might hypothesize that those groups with narrow and intense obscenity interests would mobilize more vigorously than those with broader and more diffuse interests, but this relationship does not hold. The AFAA has an exceedingly narrow range of interests, and yet it failed to mobilize to protect them after *Miller*. MC was created to treat obscenity concerns by groups with broad-ranging interests, and it became one of the most active group litigators in the period after *Miller*. Groups that count obscenity as one of their many interests also did not respond to *Miller* uniformly. Some (AAP, CPDA, MPAA) created MC, others (ALA, AL) accelerated their participation in obscenity litigation, while still others (DMAA, DGA, NATO) touched a toe to the obscenity pool and quickly withdrew. Thus, it is clear that neither narrowness or breadth of organizational interest is a characteristic that meaningfully separates the type of adaptive behaviors present in the post-*Miller* environment.

Although the range of interest fails to provide insight into the specific adaptive responses of material groups, something closely akin to it does: the clarity of organizational goals. The shared goals of material organizations are clear—to protect the material interests of their members. However, not all material interests are the same—some tend to be professional in nature, others are more commercial. Commercial interests, moreover, are not unidimensional. Different types of groups protect different types of interests: publishers, distributors, and sellers are concerned with printed media, whereas movie producers, distributors, and exhibitors are concerned with film and electronic media. Thus, their obscenity goals differ, and this conditions varying adaptive responses.

The goal common to material organizations is to protect their members. In the post-*Miller* context this entailed insuring that their activities were not unduly fettered by prosecution attempts. Given a Court hostile to general libertarian claims, this was the best they could do in the short term. This reality conditioned the development of the "least common denominator" approach. MC is a prime example of organizational action on this principle. It formally accepts *Miller*, and its goal is to make sure that no materials produced by its members are subject to prosecution under *Miller*. Its goals are kept simple and noncontroversial to maintain its coalition. Although some members would like to see a "consenting adults" position adopted in the stead of the *Miller* test (AAP, for example), others accept the current test and merely wish to confine it to materials other than their own.[36] Accordingly, MC adopted a litigation strategy that stresses the pernicious effect of overbroad and vague obscenity laws on the commercial interests of "legitimate" companies and does not seek the reversal of *Miller*. Its clear and narrow subject goals serve two functions. They minimize the potential for disagreement and divisiveness in the organization. This aids organizational maintenance. They also allow MC to project itself decisively into litigation to protect its members.

The MPAA was a founding member of MC but left in 1977. In part, this exit resulted from the clarity of the MPAA's specific goals—goals that, for a time, overlapped with those of MC. Like NATO and DGA, the MPAA is a commercial organization solely concerned with the material well-being of its members. *Miller* created a potential threat to these interests: a threat that was made clear with the legal prosecution of *Carnal Knowledge* and *Last Tango in Paris*. Facing such threats, the MPAA led in the establishment of MC. However, the *Jenkins* (1974) and *Erznoznik* (1975) decisions made it clear that the Supreme Court would not countenance obscenity prosecutions of major motion pictures. This result secured MPAA's goals, and it decided to leave MC shortly thereafter.[37] This left MC's membership composed entirely of groups with a nexus to printed media—a commercial area afforded less protection by the Court. NATO and DGA, not having the sunk costs of being a founding member of MC, left this litigious realm after the *Jenkins* decision. The narrowness and clarity of the goals of these organizations, combined with other demands on their resources, led them to abandon obscenity litigation.

The goals of some of the other material groups involved in obscenity litigation are not as clear and unidimensional as those noted above, and this affected their adaptation to *Miller*. The AL has long been involved in a wide range of obscenity cases (see table 5.3). Because of the breadth of its member authors' activities, and the philosophic commitment of its general counsel to this area of law, it maintained its frequency and distribution of involvement in the post-*Miller* era. The ambiguity in the goals of the ALA/FRF—the tension between its commitment to the library community and to expression rights more generally construed—led it to react to *Miller* by considerably increasing its litigation. The ambiguity and resulting breadth of its obscenity goals drew it into litigation over a broad range of issues. Like the AL, and to a lesser extent the AAP,[38] the ALA/FRF, because of the breadth of its goals, will most likely be committed to this type of litigation well into the future. The broad and ill-focused goals of these groups, in tandem with their materially grounded interest in the subject, made their adaptive response to *Miller* multi-faceted and vigorous.

Lack of clarity in goals does not always lead groups to litigate broadly in their defense. For example, the formal subject goal of the AFAA is clear: consenting adults should be allowed access to whatever entertainment they wish. This goal is consistent with its commercial interest in sex-oriented productions. Yet, the seeming clarity of this goal is illusory. It hides an ambiguity that works against the efforts of its leaders to develop a coherent litigation strategy; the economic realities that seem to give rise to the formal goal subvert action based on it. One AFAA official noted, "Generally, the AFAA wants to see a continued gray area in obscenity law black enough so that Universal Pictures and other big production companies won't be competing with its members, but light enough so that legal and governmental pressure is not such that their productions will be endangered or that they will have to pay exorbitant fees to their attorneys" (interview with author). Viewed in this way, the murky legal context enhances the profitability of the AFAA's members. Because profit is the general goal of the group, this situation minimizes its incentive to attain its formal obscenity goals. This further depresses the development of a litigation strategy and inclines the group to enter only that litigation raising issues of concern to the narrow, commercial interests of its members.

Thus, clarity of group goals is a factor that orients an organization's response to a shift in a relevant legal context. Clear goals generally provide a focus that allows a group to target a specific threat and mobilize to meet it. This is especially the case when the goals are held deeply by group officials and members. An ambiguous goal structure can condition a couple of responses. If it works to increase organizational awareness of the breadth of a threat, it can lead a group to participate in a wide range of obscenity issues and cases. If it works to obscure the reasons for litigation involvement, it can constrain a group's attainment of its specific goals.

CONDITIONING FACTORS: EXTERNAL

The material nature of the groups that mobilized in the wake of *Miller* suggests that the environment was of paramount importance in conditioning their adaptive response. More so than for purposive organizations, which are internally geared to engage in litigation to achieve their philosophical goals and which maintain themselves by expressing membership concerns, the specific nature of their environment causes material groups occasionally to undertake uncharacteristic political activities. In the area of obscenity, *Miller* threatened their material interests and acted as a catalyst for their mobilization. Three environmental factors conditioned the reaction of these groups to the new legal context: the intransigence of the Supreme Court, the relationship between the threat and their interests, and the general political climate from which those threats emanated.

Intransigence of the Supreme Court

General agreement exists among the leaders of material groups that the *Miller* majority is still solid. The doctrine promulgated in that decision is likewise still "good law" in the sense that it is binding on all American courts. This perception is supported by the Burger Court's general hospitality to obscenity proscription (see table 1.1) and its decisions in cases such as *Hamling* (1974), *Young* (1976), *Ferber* (1982), *Renton* (1986), and *Pope* (1987). The liberalization of obscenity doctrine by the Warren Court is a thing of the past. The legitimacy of laws proscribing obscenity is unquestioned by the Burger, and now the Rehnquist, Court majority.

The post-*Miller* environment presented material groups with two realities: a majority of justices unsympathetic to libertarian arguments; and material interests that need protection from the threat of prosecution. Since the groups cannot get the whole pie and have obscenity laws struck down as unconstitutional, the question before them is how to protect their share of that pie. It is in this context that the "least common denominator" approach was developed. With *Miller* standing as good law and with the Court not inclined to move away from it, these groups were forced to litigate in its margins to protect the interests of their members as best as possible. This suggested two modes of adaptation: confining the Supreme Court's expansion of the *Miller* doctrine and winning cases in trial courts.

Given the intransigence of the *Miller* majority, material groups adopted a simple goal for their post-1973 litigation: keep the Court from developing the *Miller* doctrine in a way that further endangered the material interests of group members. This was the intention on which MC was founded, and the obscenity litigation of other material groups was premised on the same idea.[39] This goal fostered the development of two strategies. One strategy required these organizations to stress constitutional arguments such as vagueness and overbreadth to attain judicial reversals of obscenity convictions. These reversals could then be used as precedents in future cases against laws perceived to threaten the material interests of group members. A second strategy was to litigate obscenity cases in trial courts.

An examination of the types of arguments made by these organizations in their Supreme Court participation before and after the *Miller* decision demonstrates the first strategy. Prior to *Miller*, organizations like the AAP, AFAA, ALA, AL, and FALA always questioned the constitutional permissibility of the *Roth* approach, in addition to making more narrow, technical, and procedural arguments to protect the particular interests of their members.[40] After

Table 5.4
Success of Material Groups in Obscenity Cases Decided by the Supreme Court, 1973–1987

	Libertarian Outcomes	Proscriptionist Outcomes	Other
Material Organizations	6	9	4
Media Coalition (MC)	3	5	3
Overall Burger Court	7	15	9

Data drawn from appendix A.

Miller, with the exception of the AFAA, AAP, ABA, and DGA amicus curiae briefs in *Jenkins*, no material organization called for its reversal. In the new environment, these groups asked the Court to require civil determination of obscenity prior to criminal prosecution for its dissemination,[41] limit the *Miller* test to "hard-core" material,[42] expand the category of "serious value,"[43] void zoning attempts to break up "adult" areas on overbreadth grounds,[44] hold localities to community standards articulated by their states,[45] disallow mass searches and seizures without carefully drawn warrants,[46] prohibit school boards from removing "offensive" books from school libraries,[47] deal cautiously with the definition of what constitutes child pornography,[48] and articulate a national standard to determine the value, in *Miller*'s sense, of prosecuted materials.[49] Conspicuously absent from the post-*Miller* arguments of these groups is a call for the end of obscenity regulation.

There is some evidence that this strategy was somewhat successful in checking the judicial extension of *Miller*. Table 5.4 shows the success of material organizations before the Burger and Rehnquist Courts. Of the 15 cases in which they have participated since *Miller*, and which can be coded as libertarian or proscriptionist,[50] they won six (40 percent). MC's winning percentage is 44 percent. The relative success of this strategy is clear when the results of these cases are compared with the Court's disposition of all post-*Miller* obscenity cases, only 29 percent of which favored libertarian concerns. This success convinced group officials that their strategy, although not a panacea, makes the best of a bad situation.[51] The Supreme Court is generally hostile to libertarian claims, but it seems to be somewhat more responsive to the specific concerns raised by material groups.

The Supreme Court's intransigence also stimulated material groups to develop a second, and somewhat more novel, litigation strategy: winning cases in trial courts. The Court's treatment of obscenity issues led it to stress proscription based on local standards. This effective decentralization of obscenity law, and the Court's disinclination to revert to its "Redrupping" role, led to the increased importance of winning obscenity trials.[52] If groups could win at this level, they could protect their interests and, perhaps, dissuade prosecutors from bringing more of these cases to the courts. For example, MC brought cases to trial in the name of its members, with its most prominent victory coming in the feminist anti-pornography cases (*Hudnut*, 1984, 1985).[53] The ALA brought a case in its name in California state and federal courts and helps fund the litigation efforts of MC and other sympathetic parties. Less directly the FALA, and to a lesser extent the AFAA, train their members in trial techniques proven useful in winning cases. The post-*Miller* context places a premium on this sort of activity insofar as it facilitates the protection of the material interests of those involved in occupations that open them to prosecution. A trial victory makes the Court's commitment to *Miller* irrelevant.

The Supreme Court's adherence to *Miller* conditioned the response of material organizations to the legal environment the decision created. They mobilized to meet its potential dangers by litigating more frequently and vigorously, changing the types of arguments they presented the courts, and broadening their activities to include lower court proceedings. Because the Court set the rules for the post-*Miller* game, and material groups have little choice but to play in that game, they accommodated their strategies and tactics.

Relationship between Interest and Threat

The immediate stimulus for the mobilization of material groups was the legal context created by *Miller*. The creation of MC the Sunday after the decision was handed down is symbolic of the immediacy of their concern with the potential threat it created. The threat perceived by these groups differed from that perceived by their purposive counterparts. For the latter, the threat was to a conception of the proper order of a "good" society—the infringement of an idea. For material organizations the threat was more tangible: the survival of their members. This threat was commercial (profits), professional (vocational integrity), or some combination of both. A wave of obscenity prosecutions, even if unsuccessful, would create considerable hassle, legal expense, and perhaps a "chill" that would restrict the quantity and type of material permitted distribution.[54] It was the tangible nature of this threat that propelled these groups into obscenity litigation.

Since the presence of this material threat was the instigating factor in the mobilization of these groups, it is not surprising that its diminution led some of them to withdraw from litigation. The uncertainty of the potential effects of *Miller* led to an immediate mobilization of all material groups. This situation clarified as subsequent litigation set *Miller*'s general parameters, de facto establishing a "hard-core" test for pornography[55] and changing the nature of the threat these groups perceived *Miller* to pose. Material groups adapted to the clarified threat in three discernible ways.

Although the Supreme Court adhered to and extended the doctrine enunciated in *Miller*, its decisions in *Jenkins* (1974) and *Erznoznik* (1975) made it clear that major motion pictures were not considered to be within its reach. This development explains the MPAA's decision to leave MC and drop out of intense involvement in obscenity litigation. These decisions convinced the MPAA's leaders that governments would not be successful in prosecuting the films of its members (interview with author). With *Miller*'s threat diminished, there was no material-based need for the MPAA to continue in litigation. Although the group will occasionally involve itself in obscenity litigation, it intervenes only to protect its previously unsecured commercial interests. It has reverted to being an occasional lone litigator. The cessation of DGA and NATO involvement in obscenity litigation is attributable to the same factor.

The weak enforcement of obscenity laws worked to lessen the interest of other groups in this litigation.[56] The AFAA is a prime example. *Miller* gave local police and prosecutors a "green light," but it did not mandate that they prosecute obscenity. Yet, the diffusion of the prosecutory threat was initially an added cause for libertarian fears after *Miller*—multiple prosecutions in many states would be a nightmare for the members of material organizations. However, this fear went largely unrealized. With the threat of a wave of prosecutions minimized, the AFAA's leaders could not prod their members to support increased efforts to shape the development of the law. Even those localities where obscenity prosecution was undertaken with vigor after *Miller* caused members little concern: if the legal heat got too hot they could move operations to less "confining" locales.[57] In confluence with the AFAA's ambiguous goals and the disposition of its membership, this environmental reality constrained the group's formal response to *Miller*.

The threat posed by *Miller* continued to be felt by members of other material organizations. Unlike those noted above, these groups continued their increased involvement in obscenity litigation throughout the post-*Miller* period. Most of these groups were members of MC. As is evidenced by MC's participation in litigation voiding minors' access statutes, plastic wrapping laws, arguably overbroad statutes, special taxes on sex-oriented magazines, feminist anti-pornography statutes, and standards for determining "serious value," MC has become the preeminent organizational litigator of libertarian concerns. All of its present members are involved in the production and distribution of printed material. This suggests that it is this media sector that faces the greatest threat from obscenity prosecution.[58] This inference draws further support from the continuing presence of the AL and the ALA in obscenity litigation: the members of both of these groups deal with the printed word. The FALA also perceives an ongoing threat (interview with author). This is not surprising, given its members' clientele. Underlying the continued mobilization of these groups is their nexus to the printed medium and the tangible threat *Miller* still poses to it.[59]

The threat perceived by these organizations is a major factor conditioning their adaptation to the post-*Miller* context. It initially caused them to turn to the Supreme Court in an effort to protect their material interests (*Jenkins*, 1974). Once the precise nature of the threat was clarified, those groups most affected remained intensely active in obscenity litigation, while those that felt less vulnerable largely withdrew from persistent judicial participation. Central to these different adaptive responses was the specific material interests that occasioned the organization of these groups.

General Political Context

The intransigence of the Supreme Court and the threat perceived by material groups are the chief external factors conditioning the groups' adaptive behavior, but a third factor deserves some note. The 1970s and 1980s saw a resurgence of political conservativism. The sexual revolution was a dominant theme of the liberalizing 1960s, but that movement, as an organized political force, petered out as the decade receded. A new climate of opinion—perhaps captured in the feminist statutes and the Meese Commission Report—shaped the obscenity debate in the post-*Miller* period. This had an effect, albeit one difficult to measure, on the behavior of groups active in this field. The general political context of the 1970s and 1980s gave heart to pro-decency litigators and increased the anxiety felt by some libertarian material organizations.

One political factor conditioning the response of material groups to *Miller* was the end of the ACLU's dominance of obscenity litigation. The ACLU was not the sole libertarian litigator prior to *Miller*, but it was the preeminent one. Its exit left a considerable void in expertise and strategy. Without the ACLU to carry the litigation ball, and given the nature of their interests, material groups were forced to assume a more active judicial profile.

Another political factor conditioned organizational response to the new environment: the rise of the New Right and the increased political activism of some fundamentalist Christian groups. The 1980, 1984, and 1988 elections heightened the awareness of material groups to the political power of the new conservativism. First, it could fundamentally alter the composition and orientation of the federal courts—especially the Supreme Court. Indeed, the first returns on President Reagan's appointments suggest that this has happened (Gottschall, 1986; Rowland, Songer, and Carp, 1988). Second, it could give new impetus to the prosecution of "victimless" morals crimes. Insofar as groups like Eagle Forum, Moral Majority, and Pat Robertson's Christian network—groups concerned with obscenity[60]—activated their followers to pressure governmental officials, they could force government to treat their concerns more seriously. One manifestation of this kind of threat was the successful effort to persuade Southland Corporation to pull *Playboy* and *Pent-house* magazines from its 7-11 stores.[61] Officials of MC, ALA/FRF, and ACLU worried about the potential "popularization" of obscenity issues—and the concomitant legal enforcement—that these groups could stimulate, and these fears spurred on their litigation and lobbying efforts.[62] In fact, the recent upswing in the ACLU's involvement in this issue, though by no means returning the group to the dominance it had enjoyed in the 1960s and early 1970s, may be attributable to this new political environment.

Feminist anti-pornography efforts are a final political threat to the interests of material organizations. These groups have yet to involve themselves formally in obscenity litigation, but they pose two threats to the interests of material libertarians. First, it is possible that Left could meet Right—these groups could ally with more traditional pro-decency groups—and make the anti-obscenity movement a stronger political force.[63] Second, some feminists have succeeded in passing local anti-pornography statutes.[64] These ordinances allow women who feel injured by a publication to go to court to demonstrate that it violated their civil rights. The potential subjectivity of this approach led MC and the Indiana CLU to challenge the Indianapolis statute in the federal courts. Although the libertarians won in *Hudnut* (1984, 1985), future courts—especially given new appointments and the possible linking of feminist and pro-decency forces—could receive these proscriptive efforts more favorably. This fear led libertarians to commit many resources to the Indianapolis litigation, but precedents, especially those generated by lower courts, are malleable.

These three general political factors further conditioned the post-*Miller* adaptation of material groups. The ACLU's de-emphasis of obscenity litigation forced material groups, for the first time, to take the lead in the legal defense of their interests. The general revival of political conservativism, especially its fundamentalist variant, also changed the context in which they litigated. With society's moral norms conceivably moving away from their position, these groups had to innovate to protect their material interests. The rise of feminist anti-pornography groups and statutes kindled the interest of a new segment of society in the proscription of sex-oriented material: attacks on obscenity now came from the Left as well as the Right. In adapting to the post-*Miller* environment, material groups also had to adapt to these developments. If the right and left wings of the anti-obscenity movement should ever unite, the task of these organizations will become more difficult and important than ever.

CONCLUSION

If the ACLU and the pro-decency organizations were the only ones involved in obscenity litigation, the explanation of organizational adaptation to *Miller* would be simple: winners stay in the game, and losers turn their attention to other goals. But these groups were not the only ones participating in obscenity litigation. Most groups active in this litigation were not general, mass-membership organizations devoted to the furtherance of some political vision but were material groups concerned with protecting the particular and narrow interests of their members. Although generally libertarian and comfortable with the ACLU's obscenity goals, these groups did not follow the ACLU's lead in this realm. Indeed, in the post-*Miller* environment they became the preeminent organizational litigators of libertarian concerns. Material groups, losers in *Miller*, turned to the courts after that decision to minimize their losses and offset the rule changes that disadvantaged their legal, and material, position.

Pluralist group theory suggests that when interests are threatened, groups will mobilize to protect them; in large measure, the obscenity example bears this out. Although the participation in obscenity litigation by the ACLU fell off after *Miller*, that by material groups increased. The explanation for this revolves around the specific perspective of these groups and the threat occasioned by *Miller*. Whereas the interests of purposive, goal-oriented groups are general and somewhat abstract, those of material organizations are tangible and immediate. The latter mobilized after *Miller* to protect material interests central to their organizational existence. This changed the nature of the key organizational litigators. Prior to *Miller*, the arguments and goals of purposive groups of the Right (CDL and MM) and the Left (ACLU) dominated the courts. After the decision, the purposive Right remained active, but the libertarian litigators shifted to those groups possessing and pressing material concerns. In the post-*Miller* context, material groups had an incentive to carry on libertarian litigation, an incentive the purposive ACLU lacked—profits and vocational integrity.

Two distinctions are crucial in understanding this shift in the locus of libertarian litigation. One has to do with the different nature of the libertarian groups active in obscenity litigation. This is the distinction pointed out by Salisbury (1969), Wilson (1973), and Moe (1980, 1981). Purposive and material groups make use of different *kinds* of incentives to attract and maintain their memberships. The former rely on political positions pursued through public channels; the latter depend on particular and exclusive benefits. Both give members a return on their investment, but the returns are much different. These different membership incentives translate into different organizational perspectives on political affairs. Politics is central for purposive groups, whereas for material groups it is tangential unless it touches on matters with a tangible connection to their material interests. Purposive organizations litigate to further general principles; material groups do so to protect narrow interests specific to their members. Because of the relationship between obscenity law enforcement and their material interests, the latter did not have the luxury of an exit option after *Miller*. So closely intertwined was their well-being with the courts that they had little choice but to mobilize. The distinction between purposive and material organizations does much to explain the post-*Miller* shift of the libertarian litigation burden.

A second distinction—the nature and locus of their material concerns—aids in understanding the varied adaptive responses of material groups. A few dimensions are especially relevant here. One is commercial-professional. The more commercial a group's interests, the more inclined it is to focus on the particular aspect of litigation relevant to those interests. The adaptations of MC, MPA, and MPAA illustrate this. The more professional the interests of an organization, the more inclined it is to participate in litigation raising a broader range of obscenity issues (for example, ALA, AL, and FALA). Another dimension encompasses the internal factors that orient a group. Relevant here are the quality and perceptions of its leaders, the disposition of its members, and the clarity of the goals it established for group action. Groups with strong leaders, compliant members, and clearly defined goals are more inclined to undertake concerted litigation to achieve their ends than are those not similarly endowed. The different responses of the AFAA and the other material groups speak to this point.

A group's perception of the external environment it faces, as seen by both leaders and members, is a final dimension useful in explaining the adaptive differences among material groups. Factors relevant here include the comportment of the Supreme Court, the degree of the threat posed to organizational interests, and the general political configuration of the times. When threats are seen as remote, the litigation activity of a group declines. When they are seen as pressing, courts as unsympathetic, and the political culture as hostile, groups continue to litigate to defend their interests. The continuing legal activity of those involved in the printed media bears this out. All of these factors are relevant to the particular adaptive mode chosen by these groups. When the specific reactions of material groups vary, it is because the factors submerged in these three dimensions vary among organizations.

The shift in libertarian litigation from the purposive ACLU to material groups resulted from the *Miller* decision. That decision changed the incentives for libertarian litigation. It also changed the nature of the arguments presented to the courts. Whereas the pre-*Miller* period was characterized by broad and principled claims challenging the constitutionality of obscenity legislation, the post-*Miller* period saw the subordination of those claims in favor of narrow and pragmatic contentions about the permissible extent of regulation. The shift in litigation incentives had a great deal to do with this. A group's perspective on obscenity is conditioned by the position from which it views the issue; where groups stand is influenced by where they sit. The ACLU and the material groups active in this litigation sit at different ends of the libertarian row, and their approaches to this issue are affected accordingly. Given these different vantage points, it is not surprising that their behavioral responses to the 1973 term decisions of the Court differed substantially. After these decisions, those groups with material interests in the issue came to dominate its litigation and definition.

NOTES

1. This is not to suggest that none of these groups have individual members. The difference lies in the nature of those members. Membership organizations such as the ALA, AL, and FALA draw not on the general public but on a specialized professional segment of it.

2. At this point the analysis is pitched in terms of general orientation. As will be seen, the material interests of a group do not necessarily preclude it from also possessing more general, and indeed societal, interests.

3. The AL position on *Miller* is somewhat ambiguous. Its general counsel states that the AL still opposes restrictions on the choice of consenting adults, but its amicus curiae briefs no longer stress this point (Karp letter and AL amicus briefs).

4. All of these groups filed amicus curiae briefs in *Jenkins* (1974). These briefs clearly lay out the nature of their concerns in the legal context created by *Miller*.

5. For example, see the amicus briefs of the AL in *Jenkins*, *Erznoznik* (1975), and *Southeastern Productions* (1975), those of the MPAA in *Erznoznik*, *Huffman* (1975), and *Young* (1976), and that of the DGA in *Jenkins*.

6. For example, see the amicus briefs of the ABA, CPDA, and NATO in *Jenkins* and those of MC in *Jenkins*, *McKinney* (1976), *Smith* (1977), *Lo-Ji* (1979), and *Vance* (1980).

7. For a discussion of these, see the amicus curiae brief of the ABA in *Jenkins*.

8. See the amicus curiae briefs of the AFAA, ALA/FRF, and AAP in *Jenkins*. The FALA has not formally participated in obscenity litigation since 1973, but it opposes the *Miller* doctrine (Gerber letter, Schwarz and Weston interviews, and organizational literature).

9. For example, see AAP amicus curiae briefs in *Butler* (1957), *Ginzburg* (1966), and *Hamling* (1974) and those of the ALA in *Smith* (1963), *Jenkins* (1974), and *Smith* (1977).

10. Interviews with ALA/FRF and FALA officials. Also see the amicus curiae briefs these organizations have filed with the Supreme Court. The decision of the AAP to work to live within *Miller* is manifest in its role in creating and maintaining MC.

11. The exceptions are easily explained. The DMAA has very narrow interests that were only threatened in *Rowan* (1970). It has lacked an incentive to litigate since then. The FALA expends its resources in ways other than organizational litigation. See chapter 2.

12. This was true of the Magazine Publishers Association and the MPAA. Their specific adaptation will be examined below.

13. Interviews with group officials. This is the raison d'être for the existence of MC. To see this shift in argument strategy, examine the pre- and post-*Miller* amicus curiae briefs of any of the material organizations involved in this litigation.

14. "Our primary concern here is with pay television" (MPAA amicus curiae brief in *Pacifica*, 1978). Since MPAA members make films, some of which have sexual

content, that are distributed to pay-television networks, their material interest in the issue raised in this case is apparent.

15. Although *McKinney* (1976) involved the proscription of printed material, it concerned the conditions for a determination of obscenity *vel non*—a point of some interest to a group whose members engage in the national distribution of their products.

16. The broader and more principled approach of these groups is reminiscent of purposive groups. Their incentives to litigate are a mix of material and political. It may be that these purposive incentives are used to assist in group maintenance.

17. This broader orientation is suggested not only by the range of cases in which these groups participate. The AAP and the ALA have standing committees on intellectual freedom (ALA) and freedom to read (AAP). They also jointly established the Freedom to Read Foundation (FRF).

18. Computer searches using Lexis and Westlaw revealed little organizational activity in lower federal courts during this period. Interviews with officials of material groups also suggested that their involvement in lower courts was minimal before *Miller*.

19. Fleishman was the most active private attorney involved in obscenity litigation before his retirement from this field in the mid-1970s. He argued *Roth* (1957) and hundreds of other obscenity cases, and ACLU files are peppered with letters from and references to him.

20. Lexis searches under NATO's name revealed its involvement in only one trial decision, *NATO* v. *Milwaukee* (1971), and none since *Miller*. Its involvement in state cases is unknown, since Lexis searches to determine the participation of material groups there were prohibitive.

21. Its members feel the information it provides to be crucial to the successful handling of obscenity trials (interviews). Pro-decency groups also perceive it to be influential (see chapters 2 and 4).

22. Karp (1977).

23. See *AFAA* v. *Times-Mirror* (1978).

24. The case noted is *Moore* v. *California* (1974). It has financially supported the litigation of individual librarians and that of MC.

25. Its challenges to minors' access, plastic covering, and broadly written obscenity statutes are examples of this activity. Recently it, along with the Indiana CLU, brought the case (*Hudnut*, 1984, 1985) that culminated in the striking, as unconstitutional under *Miller*, of the feminist anti-pornography statute in Indianapolis (*NYT*, 5 May 1984).

26. MC was created to provide its members with information on obscenity law and to give them an entity through which to lobby state legislatures and present occasional amicus curiae briefs to the Court. Its extended litigation activity was in large part the result of the leadership of its first full-time general counsel.

27. This was something they could demonstrate. See data presented in table 5.4.

28. Reitman and Bamberger interviews. Also see the MC amicus curiae brief in *Jenkins* (1974).

29. See chapter 2 for the details of MC's litigation strategy.

30. Interviews with group officials. The leaders and the members of MC are constantly trying to attract new members to the group. The basic information sheet

they circulate to promote this end gives a great deal of attention to the group's litigation achievements.

31. One person close to the organization believes that members do this to help their attorneys. Such a position would lend these attorneys an air of expertise and aid them in attracting more clients (interview).

32. The AFAA has probably had an indirect effect on the development of obscenity law through the advice its co-counsel give to the attorneys of group members.

33. The members of MC act as a constraint on its actions. Because of their varied goals its leaders are limited in the types of arguments they can make and cases they can enter. Were they actively to pursue the abolition of obscenity laws, they would invite membership exit and the potential demise of the group.

34. The FRF is intriguing in this sense because it seems to combine purposive and material incentives. It is a general membership group pledged to protect intellectual freedom, but the bulk of its membership and assistance is library related. See chapter 2.

35. Since this exit the Supreme Court has treated two cases involving the proscription of films, *Ballew* (1978) and *Renton* (1986). MC did not join *Ballew*, even though it was generated by a state prosecution. Its participation in *Renton* was premised not on that case's link to theatrical presentations but to the city's use of zoning statutes.

36. The different general goals of MC's member organizations can be seen in the multiple amicus briefs they presented in *Jenkins*. MC filed a "least common denominator" brief while its members each filed one reflecting their own perspective on *Miller*.

37. Bamberger interview. The sole post-1977 participation in obscenity litigation by the MPAA was in *Pacifica*, where it sought to protect the commercial interests of its members in the realm of cable television.

38. The AAP seems to have both professional and commercial interests. It is a member of MC, and its participation in litigation has not been as broadly based as that of the AL or the ALA, but it holds to a "consenting adults" position and has a Freedom to Read Committee that treats the philosophical aspects of this issue.

39. Interviews with group officials; Karp (1977).

40. The CPDA, DMAA, MPAA, and NATO did not ask the Court to back off its *Roth* approach before 1973. The goals of these groups have always been narrower than those of other material organizations. The ABA and DGA did not participate in Supreme Court obscenity litigation before 1973.

41. For example, see amicus curiae briefs of the AFAA, ALA, AL, CPDA, and MC in *Jenkins* (1974).

42. For example, see amicus curiae briefs of the ABA, AL, CPDA, DGA, MC, and NATO in *Jenkins*.

43. For example, see the amicus curiae briefs of the AL and MC in *Jenkins* and the amicus arguments of MC and VLA in *Pope* (1987).

44. For example, see the argument presented to the Court by the AFAA in *Young* (1976) and the amicus curiae brief presented to it in that case by the MPAA. Note also the arguments of MC and OAA in *Renton* (1986).

45. For example, see the amicus curiae briefs of MC and the ALA in *Smith* (1977).

46. For example, see the amicus curiae brief of MC in *Lo-Ji Sales* (1978) and that of MC in *Maryland* (1985).

47. For example, see the amicus curiae briefs of the AAP, ALA, and AL in *Pico* (1982).

48. For example, see the amicus curiae brief of MC in *Ferber* (1982).

49. For example, see the amicus curiae briefs of MC and VLA in *Pope* (1987).

50. *Pope* (1987) and *Virginia* (1988) cannot be coded as libertarian or proscriptionist because the former dealt with the locus of the definition of "serious value" under *Miller* and the latter was certified back to the Virginia Supreme Court. It is tempting to read Justice White's *Pope* opinion as proscriptionist—the dissenters clearly do—but it is sufficiently ambiguous to merit the designation "other."

51. Interviews with various group officials.

52. Weston, Rosenwein, Fleishman, Bamberger interviews. The Obscenity Law Project (1976) of New York University Law School found that the percentage of appellate court reversals of obscenity convictions declined from 18 percent to 8 percent between 1972 and 1975.

53. See the discussion of its litigation strategy in chapter 2.

54. This concern is reflected in almost all of the amicus curiae briefs presented to the Supreme Court since 1973 by these groups. For example, see those presented in *Jenkins* (1974).

55. Reitman, Okrand, Schwarz, Weston, and Bamberger interviews; Karp (1977) and letter. This perception seems to be supported by the research conducted by the Obscenity Law Project (1976) of the New York University Law School. Although its legal definition is never fully articulated, "hard-core" usually means graphic and explicit presentation of actual sex acts.

56. This lack of enforcement was described in some detail in chapter 3. For a lengthier discussion of this phenomenon, see the Obscenity Law Project (1976) of the New York University Law School.

57. This happened in Fulton County, Georgia. CDL's Paul McCommon, a former prosecutor there, told me that "adult" store operators left the city after persistent prosecution because they knew they would not face the same hassles in other cities.

58. Whether this perception is held independently by MC members or is considerably shaped by MC leaders is unclear.

59. FALA members also handle cases involving prosecutions of "adult" theaters. Although this problem is not sufficient to mobilize the AFAA, it is one that individual theater owners and their attorneys must continue to face.

60. See the Moral Majority publication *How to Clean Up America* (1981) and the March 1983 issue of its *Report*. On Eagle Forum's concerns here see the February 1983 issue of the *Phyllis Schlafly Report*. Pat Robertson's "700 Club" has run numerous program segments on obscenity.

61. MC mobilized to attack the link between this action and the Meese Commission (Blodgett, 1986), but it could do nothing about the retailers' decisions to discontinue the sale of these magazines at their stores.

62. Interviews with group officials. See also the FRF and ALA newsletters. The ACLU, AAP, ALA, and FRF sponsored a "Colloquium on School and School Library Book Censorship Litigation" in 1981 to address these issues. It is interesting to note the ACLU's involvement in *Pico* (1982)—a case involving the removal of "offensive" books from a school library. This is one of the religious Right's major areas of concern.

63. For an interesting discussion of this, see Elshtain (1984). Note, however, the tensions between the pro-decency and the feminist conceptions of the problem (West,

1987). For a brief discussion of feminist anti-pornography organizations, see chapter 2.

64. Such statutes have been introduced in Minneapolis and Indianapolis. The Minneapolis ordinance was vetoed by the mayor, but the Indianapolis measure was signed into law prior to being struck down in *Hudnut* (1984, 1985). See the *Minneapolis Star Tribune*, 6 January 1984, and the *NYT*, 15 May 1984. See also Downs (1989).

6

Conclusion: A Court-Created Context for Organizational Litigation

It is neither realistic nor sound to read the First Amendment as requiring that the people of Maine or Mississippi accept public depiction of conduct found tolerable in Las Vegas, or New York City.

—*Miller* v. *California*, 413 U.S., pp. 32–33 (1973), Chief Justice Burger, majority opinion

Although the Court's affirmance of this conviction represents a logical extension of recent developments in this area of law, it sharply points up the need for a principled re-examination of the premises on which it rests.

—*Smith* v. *U.S.*, 431 U.S., p. 311 (1977), Justice Stevens, dissenting opinion

On the issue of obscenity Richard Nixon got the Supreme Court he wanted. His appointment of Chief Justice Burger and Associate Justices Blackmun, Powell, and Rehnquist added four proscriptionist votes to that of the Warren Court holdover Byron White. This majority, in *Miller* and subsequent decisions, reversed the doctrinal and decisional libertarianism of the Warren Court. Ronald Reagan's appointments maintained this proscriptionist legal shift. Despite the refusal of Justices Brennan, Marshall, and Stevens to join their brethren, the legal change in obscenity law worked by *Miller* has endured.

Miller's recasting of obscenity doctrine also modified the environment in which group litigation occurred. The Warren Court's treatment of these issues put libertarian groups on a favorable footing. In rejecting its predecessor's approach, the Burger Court created new opportunities for organizational action. Formerly disadvantaged pro-decency groups became advantaged as the Court evinced new concern for proscriptionist claims and little patience for traditional libertarian arguments. Not only did it lower judicially created barriers to obscenity enforcement, but it also reduced the probabilities of reversing convictions on appeal.[1]

The *Miller* shift supplies an opportunity to examine the dynamics of organizational litigation. It created a "natural experiment" providing a unique opportunity to investigate how groups active in litigation react when the legal context changes. This raises questions previously unaddressed in the literature. One is seemingly simple: do groups adapt? If so, how and why? This research described adaptive responses ranging from de-emphasis to continuance to mobilization. More difficult than discovering the adaptive behaviors is accounting for them.

The answer to this speaks to the various factors that condition group actions. It is not just a matter of "winners" and "losers," with the former abandoning litigation and the latter continuing it. Although one loser (the ACLU) de-emphasized obscenity litigation, and the winners (pro-decency groups) continued their legal activities, a majority of libertarian groups—losers under *Miller*—increased their legal activity to minimize the threat posed by the new doctrine. Though uniform in their initial mobilization after *Miller*, these groups differed in the form, intensity, and duration of their responses. Their adaptation was the result of group-specific and contextual factors.

The dynamics of group litigation do not lend themselves to simple explanation. No single factor can be adduced to explain the richness of activity that occurs in a dynamic issue environment. However, some generalizations about the litigation behavior of groups in this context can be offered. They are grounded in an empirical examination of group actions, identify pertinent factors that condition specific adaptive behaviors, and suggest the extent to which such behavior will occur. The integration of these factors into a conceptual framework can clarify our understanding of group litigation and provide a more coherent approach to its study.

SUMMARY OF FINDINGS

Group Behavior

Organizational adaptation to *Miller* took three forms: continuance, de-emphasis, and mobilization. Pro-decency groups continued their pre-*Miller* behavior. They made strategic adjustments to the new context, but their underlying goal remained the same: assist in the proscription of obscenity.

Table 6.1
Number of Supreme Court Appearances of the Five Most Frequent
Libertarian Group Litigators, 1957–1973

21	ACLU
11	AAP
8	AL
4	CPDA
3	FALA, MPAA

Data drawn from appendix A.

Citizens for Decency through Law (CDL) expanded its legal activities, and Morality in Media (MM) created the National Obscenity Law Center, marking an intensification of prior activity. *Miller* was seen as a stepping-stone to the achievement of their goals. The strategic modifications they undertook were designed to extend the *Miller* approach to allow localities unfettered control over obscenity. The courts remained the most appropriate avenue for their activities.

Libertarian groups reacted to *Miller* in two ways: exit and mobilization. Prior to 1973, the ACLU was the preeminent libertarian litigator; it was involved in almost twice as many Supreme Court obscenity cases as was the next most active libertarian group (see table 6.1). *Miller* ended this domination. Facing a legal environment not conducive to its obscenity goals, and undergoing an internal shift in issue priorities, the ACLU de-emphasized its litigation. Of its first five post-*Miller* obscenity involvements, only three— *Hamling* (1974), *Young* (1976), and *Ferber* (1982)—raised issues directly involving obscenity.[2] Only in the latter years of the Reagan presidency did the ACLU once again enter this litigation with any vigor. By then, however, it had ceded its dominant status in this arena; as noted in table 6.2, when it disengaged from obscenity litigation, material groups (commercial and professional) mobilized.

This shift in libertarian litigation involved more than behavior and went beyond the Supreme Court. Not only did material groups participate with greater frequency, but they also adapted their goals and arguments to meet the new legal context and came to dominate libertarian litigation. When the Warren Court was liberalizing obscenity doctrine, these groups presented it with two lines of argument. First, they urged the Court to grant legal protection to sex-oriented works by striking obscenity laws, at least when applied to consenting adults, as unconstitutional. Their second goal was more limited: securing procedural safeguards for the activities in which their members

Table 6.2
The Shift in Litigation Burden: Participation of Libertarian Groups in
Supreme Court Litigation

	Pre-Miller (n=88)	Post-Miller (n=31)
ACLU	21	9
Material Groups	20	19

Counts participation as amicus curiae and sponsor.
Numbers listed represent cases in which libertarian groups participated.
Data drawn from appendix A.

engaged. Meeting the first goal would have given them the whole pie—
without obscenity laws there would be no need to protect specific interests.
Failing this, these groups would defend their slice of the pie with narrow
and technical arguments. The Warren Court's liberalization of obscenity law
led these groups to stress the first-order goal and argument. *Miller* negated
this strategy and forced them to rely solely on their secondary arguments.
The whole pie became a memory as groups struggled to protect their slices.

A change in strategy accompanied this change in goals and arguments.
Miller increased the importance of trials by reducing the likelihood of reversals on appeal. This contextual change led to a strategic one: material
groups began to participate in lower court litigation. Some of these groups
had supported this kind of litigation previously,[3] but after *Miller* they and
others intensified this strategy. The most prominent example of this was
Media Coalition (MC), an organization representing the interests of a variety
of material groups before the courts. A primary component of its litigation
strategy involved bringing cases at the trial level; the goal of immediate
victory decentralized its litigation efforts. The American Library Association
(ALA) also increased its attention to trial litigation, giving cash grants to
individuals and groups (MC) involved in trials and bringing a case to contest
California's obscenity statute. After *Miller* the most active material groups
placed heightened importance on trial court participation.

Nathan Hakman, in his critique of the group litigation literature, argued
that most groups engage in narrow, pecuniary, and nonpolitical litigation in
furtherance of private, rather than public, interests (1966, p. 50). Although
this conclusion does not fit the litigation of groups like the ACLU or CDL,
it comes close to capturing that of material organizations. The latter became
heavily involved in obscenity litigation only when the legal environment was
pointedly hostile to the material interests of their members. Their participation was not so much an act of political as of material concern—protection

of *their* members' interests. However, some of the material groups that mobilized after *Miller* were also moved by political concerns. The litigation of the ALA, the Association of American Publishers (AAP), and the Authors League (AL) sprang, at least in part, from principled attachment to the First Amendment, an attachment forged by members' participation in the system of freedom of expression.

Even a partial acceptance of Hakman's conclusion, however, hinges on what one calls *political*. Although material groups litigated to protect private and exclusive interests, their actions *were* political. Not only did they try to influence the government, but they also provided, intentionally or not, a public good. Though moved by concerns different from those of purposive groups, material groups initiated litigation that was political and significant to the development of public policy. The material groups involved in obscenity litigation realized this; indeed, this was why they became involved. The specific threat posed by *Miller* made their provision of a public good—the protection of expression—worth its costs.

The Continuing Politicization of Litigation

It is commonly said that litigation has become more political—courts are being used more frequently by groups to settle disputes traditionally resolved by other governmental institutions (Barker, 1967; Cortner, 1968, 1970; Sorauf, 1976; Vose, 1981; O'Connor and Epstein, 1981–82, 1982; Morgan, 1984; Epstein, 1985; Caldeira and Wright, 1988). It is undeniable that the judiciary is now more deeply involved in political controversies than ever before.[4] Obscenity litigation is a further manifestation of this phenomenon. Groups that felt disadvantaged in other forums increasingly turned to litigation to secure their interests. This led to qualitative and quantitative changes in their use of the courts.

Scholars have argued that groups litigate because they are "disadvantaged" in more traditional political institutions (Cortner, 1968). The literature chronicles their litigation in many policy areas. However, recent studies have demonstrated that disadvantaged groups are not alone in their "political" use of litigation. O'Connor and Epstein (1982)[5] and Epstein (1985) show that conservative groups have long pursued policy goals through the courts.

Obscenity litigation provides support for the disadvantaged thesis, but the thesis must be broadened to include groups not usually considered politically impotent. Some groups did go to court because their obscenity goals were not met by other institutions. For example, the ACLU lobbied elected branches of government, but it chose the courts as a primary avenue of enterprise. This squares with Cortner's thesis: civil liberties issues are traditionally more of an elite- than mass-based concern (see also Casper, 1972b). After *Miller*, material groups felt themselves disadvantaged and in need of favorable judicial rulings, and they too went to the courts. Yet, obscenity law developments in the 1960s also disadvantaged pro-decency groups—they had little chance to secure their goals solely through legislative action because of judicial hostility to the enforcement of obscenity statutes. Given this, and faced with organized libertarian litigators, they turned to the courts. Although Cortner's thesis is underinclusive, all groups involved in this litigation went to the courts, at one time or another, because they were disadvantaged in other arenas.

The literature suggests that group litigation extends to many areas of law and is increasing. The proliferation of organized litigation in areas such as civil rights (Wasby, 1983) and women's rights (Cowan, 1976; O'Connor, 1980) has been well chronicled. The general increase in group litigation, at least at the Supreme Court level, has been noted in the work of O'Connor and Epstein (1981–82, 1982) and of Caldeira and Wright (1988). Obscenity litigation is a further manifestation of development. Once dominated by a handful of groups, its arena now extends to two dozen.

This increase in group litigation is of more than academic interest—it has led to an increase in the centralized control of litigation and the greater professionalism of its conduct. These developments are related. Studies have shown that as groups nationalize litigation they develop considerable expertise (Vose, 1959; Cowan, 1976; Sorauf, 1976). This often leaves local attorneys at an extreme disadvantage and affects the outcome of litigation. The literature is replete with studies of groups that emerged triumphant only after their litigation moved from the local to the national level (Kluger, 1975; Sorauf, 1976; O'Connor, 1980). This expansion of the "scope of conflict" is a useful legal and political strategy (Schattschneider, 1960). First, it reverses the decisions of local judges in the immediate case. Second, it establishes precedents for future decisions. As a result, nationalized group litigation changes the role played by courts and challenges the power of local and state governments to control policies that were once "theirs" alone.

Obscenity litigation is characterized by increased centralization and professionalism. The number of groups active in it increased over the period of this study, but their communication centralized knowledge of their activities and tactics. Before *Miller*, the ACLU served as an information clearinghouse for groups such as the AAP, ALA, and the Motion Picture Association of America (MPAA). After that decision, this service was provided for material groups by MC and for individual defense attorneys by the Adult Film Association of America (AFAA) and the First Amendment Lawyers Association (FALA). Because *Miller* increased the importance of narrow and technical legal arguments, this communication network grew in importance: complex defense strategies put a premium on the organized transmission of pertinent information.[6] This facilitated the development of a specialized bar well prepared to deal with the altered legal environment and helped to frustrate the extension of *Miller*'s promise. The desire of CDL and MM to offset this

Table 6.3
Group Participation in Supreme Court Obscenity Litigation, Pre- and Post-
Miller

| | Pre-Miller | | Post-Miller |
	All	Non-SR*	
Cases with Group Participation	37	32	22
Total Cases	88	46	31
Percentage of Cases with Group Participation	42.0%	69.6%	71.0%

* Not counting cases summarily reversed. In the pre-Miller period there were 42
summary reversals; post-Miller there were none.
Data drawn from appendix A.

centralized libertarian expertise was a primary reason for their continued
litigation.

Some of *Miller*'s effects on group litigation were subtle. In fact, by one
measure the level of group activity remained relatively stable over time;
indeed, the data presented in table 6.3 suggest that it remained roughly
constant during the period under examination. These data, however, hide
three important facets of organized obscenity litigation: they fail to show the
shift in the litigation burden; they reflect only Supreme Court cases and ignore
the *intensity* of group litigation; and they do not speak to the number of
groups involved in any given case—the *density* of litigation. The previous
discussion makes clear the first effect; however, the latter two also increased
after *Miller*.

The literature reports that some groups, especially those that have been
losing elsewhere, intensely involve themselves in litigation. Sponsorship,
though more costly than amicus curiae or monetary support, allows them
greater control over the development of cases and, hence, the law. The
litigation of the NAACP was intense in this sense (Vose, 1959; Kluger, 1975),
as was that of separationist groups in church-state cases (Sorauf, 1976). *Miller*
increased the intensity of organized obscenity litigation by leading libertarian
groups like the MPAA, ALA, and MC to become active in trials. This was
also true for proscriptionists: MM created the National Obscenity Law Center, and CDL increased its provision of assistance to prosecutors. This suggests that an abrupt shift in constitutional doctrine can move groups to more
intense litigation to protect threatened interests or to advance those newly
realized.

Miller also brought about an increase in the density of group litigation.

Table 6.4
The Increasing Density of Group Participation in Supreme Court Obscenity
Litigation, Pre- and Post-*Miller*

	Pre-Miller	Post-Miller
Instances of Group Participation	81	67
Average # of Groups per Case (Counting Summary Reversals)	.920 (n=88)	2.913 (n=23)
Average # of Groups per Case (Not Counting Summary Reversals)	1.761 (n=46)	2.913 (n=23)

Data drawn from appendix A.

This is not uncommon: many areas have seen an increase in group litigators over time (Cowan, 1976; O'Connor and Epstein, 1982; Wasby, 1983). What the literature has not shown is the relationship between court decisions and this development. This study identifies such a relationship, at least in the area of obscenity. In localizing the obscenity determination, *Miller* led to decentralized group litigation. To cover the field once occupied by the ACLU, numerous groups representing narrow interests began to litigate. This is reflected in table 6.4. This increased density was a direct result of *Miller* and suggests that judicial decisions are significant forces shaping the contours and dynamics of the group litigation system.

Increased density can affect the ability of groups to pursue coherent litigation strategies. Studies have shown that the effective management of litigation is lessened by an increase in the number of litigating groups (Sorauf, 1976; Cowan, 1976; Wasby, 1988). This was not so in obscenity; no group officials complained of other, nominally allied groups generating decisions contrary to the interests of their group. This coherence resulted from two factors: homogeneous goals and legal particularization. In one sense, *Miller* prompted the development of common goals—the libertarians' "least common denominator" approach and the proscriptionist concerns of pro-decency groups—as a strategic necessity. In this context, a victory in one area effectively promoted the interests of other groups in other areas by establishing favorable precedent or frustrating (or facilitating) further prosecution. This similarity of goals lessened the ill effects of multiple group litigators described in other studies. In another sense, the particularization of obscenity law provided different material interests a degree of legal autonomy. For example, a legal defeat for a publisher may not hamstring a movie producer because of the differences between their activities. Thus, the density of organized litigators did not impair the pursuit of individual interests.

A dense litigation field can also promote novel legal development. Sorauf (1976) noted that different goals, interests, and strategies occasionally lead groups to litigate different issues and make new arguments, and Stewart and Heck (1981) have hypothesized that multiple litigators with different interests raise different questions. This study supports these contentions: libertarian groups with different interests made different arguments, and this aided the libertarian cause in the wake of the Court shift. Although organizational dynamics and changes in goals removed the ACLU from dominance in obscenity litigation, those of material groups moved them to fill this void. *Miller* made absolutist and consenting adults' arguments anachronistic, but pragmatic arguments designed to protect specific material interests kept the Court from greatly extending the scope of that decision. Thus, the presence of multiple litigators increased the flexibility of group response to this sudden change in legal doctrine.

The literature is largely quiet on the resurgence of groups that initially lose in the courts. This deficiency results from its inattention to the longitudinal dynamics of litigation and the vastness of the group system as it subsumes litigation. There are some exceptions to this. Sorauf (1976) noted the resurgence of the accommodationist bar in the late 1960s, but the time span of his study was too short to track this development. O'Connor and Epstein (1982) suggested that the increased Supreme Court litigation by conservative groups might be attributable to the groups' observation of the litigation success of liberal groups, but they did not test this hypothesis. This research shows that the potential for group resurgence is present in a dynamic legal environment and can be fueled by what former losers learn from their organized foes.

Obscenity litigation is marked by the resurgence of former "losers." CDL, a legal loser under the Warren Court, reasserted itself after *Miller* when it was able to fight libertarian claims on more favorable legal ground. With trial court decisions growing in importance, it increased its activities at this level. This strategic shift put pressure on libertarians at an earlier stage of litigation. Although the libertarian bar was once the only nationally organized body of trial attorneys, CDL and MM countered by developing a "pro-decency" bar. CDL also began to control some cases itself.[7] In short, *Miller* put pro-decency groups in a position analogous to that of libertarians after *Redrup* (1967): on the verge of capturing obscenity law. Learning from libertarian successes, proscriptionists capitalized on this development and projected themselves more forcefully into obscenity litigation.

The post-*Miller* response of libertarian groups is also suggestive of resurgence and organizational learning. The new environment favored local, decentralized enforcement of obscenity law. Prior libertarian strategy—entering a case at the appellate level—became less viable. To accommodate this change, MC mobilized and decentralized libertarian litigation by, in part, bringing cases in trial courts.[8] In so doing, it jettisoned the heavy reliance

on Supreme Court amicus curiae participation that had characterized libertarian litigation prior to *Miller*.[9] This adaptation enabled MC to protect its
interests more readily.

The politicization of the judiciary discussed in the literature on group
litigation is pervasive; Hakman's (1966) attempt to place it into a scholarly
dustbin fails. Group litigation is increasing in both quantitative—density and
intensity—and qualitative—centralization and professionalization—terms. It
is also fluid in a way previously undiscussed—the capacity for resurgence in
dynamic legal environments. However, disposing of Hakman's analysis does
not rectify the deficiencies that plague systematic and comparative analyses
of group litigation. The literature is devoid of an analytic perspective capable
of generalizing our understanding of group use of the courts. This research
suggests the beginnings of such a framework.

TOWARD A CONCEPTUAL FRAMEWORK FOR
GROUP LITIGATION: FACTORS CONDITIONING
LITIGATION CHOICES

The groups examined in this study share a common interest in obscenity,
but beyond this, differences emerge that affect their behavior. Different
organizations reacted to *Miller* in different ways: one dramatically de-emphasized its obscenity litigation; others mobilized; a few, always active in
this area, remained so. The question is whether it is possible to construct a
perspective that can explain, in general terms, this behavior. The findings
of this study suggest it is.

A conceptual framework would identify and weight the factors that shape
the litigation behavior of groups. These are two types: group-specific and
contextual. Group theory suggests that associational type is an important
group-specific variable. Material and purposive groups are formed and maintained in different ways (Wilson, 1973; Moe, 1980, 1981). The latter engage
in political affairs to advance a public interest, but the former do so to enhance
and defend the segment of society they represent. Thus, organizational
reasons for undertaking political activity will differ. The intensity of commitment to an issue is also related to a group's litigation choices; it moves
a group from orientation (general) to action (behavior).[10] Further, contextual
variables interact with these group-specific characteristics to condition litigation choices. This research shows that comportment of the law and perception of threat are primary among these factors. The disposition of the
Supreme Court defines the opportunities for litigation by establishing the
rules of the legal game and the nature of the threat perceived by the group.
If the threat is perceived to be great and can be addressed through litigation,
such behavior may be expected; if not, litigation may be seen as an
extravagance.

A framework integrating these four factors—associational type, intensity of commitment, legal context, and threat—provides a coarse explanation for group litigation of obscenity issues. Because of its traditional commitment to free expression and the increase in sex-oriented material after World War II, the ACLU assumed the lead in litigation to undermine obscenity regulation. Frustrated by the inability of local enforcement agencies to control the spread of obscenity, and angered by the seeming judicial tolerance of it, pro-decency groups formed to pressure governments to stop this trend. As the ACLU's arguments increasingly influenced legal development—protecting ever greater types of sexually oriented works—material groups, their interest secure, allowed it to bear the costs of litigation. Thus, purposive groups dominated obscenity litigation throughout the 1960s.

Miller altered this context. The ACLU, having lost the chance to attain its goals, being intensely committed to other civil liberties issues, and perceiving the proscriptionist threat as minimal in a sexually liberated society, de-emphasized its participation. Material groups, fearing for the profitability and integrity of their vocations, facing prosecutions of major movie and literary efforts, and lacking the protective umbrella previously provided by the ACLU, assumed the cost of libertarian litigation. On securing protection of their commercial interests, some of these groups—for example, the MPAA and National Association of Theatre Owners (NATO)—quickly abandoned their post-*Miller* mobilization. Pro-decency groups, seeing the real possibility of eliminating the legal protections afforded obscenity, being intensely committed to its demise, and realizing that enforcement was required for this end, pressed the courts to remove further obstacles to proscription.

This explanation for the behavior of groups in the dynamic environment of obscenity law finds the interaction of four group-specific and contextual variables to produce a particular pattern of group litigation. However, it does not explain a number of aberrant behaviors. Why did material groups such as the AL and the AAP involve themselves in obscenity litigation before *Miller*? Why did the AFAA—a group solely concerned with the profitability of its members' productions—not engage in the general mobilization observed among other material groups? How could the ACLU turn away from an issue previously given high priority?

To address these questions, the conceptual framework must be expanded. Although the primary factors account for much of the litigation observed, the inclusion of secondary factors broadens the explanatory power of the framework. These secondary variables are again framed in terms of group-specific (relationship between leaders and members, the nature and clarity of organizational goals) and contextual (configuration of groups, general sociopolitical context) factors.

Implicit in the associational types drawn from group theory are assumptions about the ways leaders and members interact. In purposive groups, members have substantial influence over the political decisions of leaders; in material groups, leaders are seen to be more autonomous, at least in their political actions. However, the latter conclusion is too broad. Unlike other material groups, the AFAA did not mobilize after *Miller*. This was not because its leaders felt no need to do so but because its members would not follow their lead—intraorganizational conflict stymied the establishment of a planned litigation campaign. This helps to account for its anomalous—largely passive—response to *Miller*. The presence of the MPAA made MC adopt a broad litigation focus. When the MPAA left MC, it did so because it felt major films were safe from prosecution. With its exit, MC focused on printed material. These examples suggest that even the members of material groups can constrain the political actions of their leaders.

It is true that the political actions of a material group do not *have* to reflect the political concerns of its members, but there is no a priori reason to believe that they will not.[11] The closely related nature of political and material concerns in obscenity matters suggests that leadership decisions to undertake this litigation *were* reflective of membership concerns. In opposing proscription, leaders sought to protect the material interests of their members. The members wanted these interests protected—presumably that is why they joined the group (Olson, 1965). Insofar as the political environment threatened these interests, group action to protect them was consistent with attitudes expressed in the membership decision. It may be that the closer the nexus between the political and the material concerns of groups, the greater the tendency for the political decisions of leaders to be representative of, and sensitive to, specific concerns of members.

The nature and the clarity of group goals also help to explain some seemingly aberrant litigation responses. The nature of a group's goals is usually clear when one identifies its associational type: the interests of material groups are narrowly commercial or professional, those of purposive groups are broadly political. However, the pre-*Miller* litigation of the AAP and the AL shows that their interests were broader than those of their material cohorts. These groups promoted a political principle—access to all expressive material—informed by their vocational posture in a system of information provision. Thus, even ostensibly material groups may have goals that go beyond their exclusive interests. This helps to explain the heavy pre-*Miller* participation of the AAP and the AL: litigation choices grounded in material interests were conceived of in terms of broader political and social significance. This perspective expanded their litigation horizons and led them to participate in a wide range of obscenity cases even before the threat—the danger of prosecution—became acute.

The cases of the AFAA and the ALA demonstrate that clarity of goals also affects a group's litigation strategy. Some AFAA members were comfortable with the minimal threat that *Miller* came to pose: they preferred a consenting adults position, but they believed that *Miller* protected them from potential competitors; others wanted to see *Miller* fall. Because of this division, the group lacked clearly defined goals on which to act. The ALA could not decide whether to focus on cases involving librarians or on those raising more general First Amendment concerns.[12] Ultimately, its leaders opted to go broad by supporting the litigation of MC. These examples suggest that a lack of clarity in organizational goals can lead to anomalous and unexpected behaviors.

Incorporating two other contextual factors also enhances the explanatory utility of the framework: the configuration of group litigators and the general sociopolitical environment. Limited resources make the configuration of other litigators relevant to the litigation choices of groups; the configuration helps to define threat. If no other organized actors had been available to fill the void left by the ACLU, its leaders may have been less inclined to abandon obscenity litigation. Likewise, the decisions of the Directors Guild of America (DGA), MPAA, and NATO to leave this litigation were eased by the knowledge that other libertarian groups would continue their legal efforts. The nonmobilization of the AFAA was softened by the presence of these other litigators as well as the reservoir of experienced lawyers capable of handling members' cases. If a group's interests are protected by others—as was the case for material groups prior to *Miller*—it can use its resources in other areas; if not, or if others challenge those interests, it has an incentive to litigate.

The general sociopolitical environment influences public and group priorities in subtle but significant ways. For example, in the 1960s, social and sexual mores liberalized concomitant with obscenity law development. This further persuaded the ACLU to push the Court for an "end of obscenity" (Rembar, 1968) and assured other libertarian groups that their participation was unnecessary. The same environment stimulated the litigation of pro-decency groups and gave their leaders an argument to attract and maintain membership support—the impending "Romanization" of American culture.

Miller and the growing conservativism of the 1970s and 1980s altered this context. However, perceptions of this environment varied, and this affected group behavior. Because of their members' occupations, the leaders of MC and the ALA saw an increased possibility for the suppression of "offensive" materials; CDL and MM held a similar perception. This perception influenced the litigation strategies they adopted. Other groups perceived the environment differently. Some libertarians saw an increased social and governmental acceptance of sexually explicit material even after *Miller*. Combined with sporadic enforcement, this lessened their fear of prosecution and, hence, their inclination to litigate. This contributed to the anomalous response of the AFAA to *Miller* and reinforced the decisions of the ACLU, DGA, MPAA, and NATO to de-emphasize or abandon litigation. Although subjective and difficult to pin down, groups' perceptions of the larger sociopolitical context affect their understanding of the threat they face and their decisions whether to use litigation to meet it.

Table 6.5 displays the conceptual framework discussed above. It separates

Table 6.5
Factors Conditioning Group Litigation Behavior

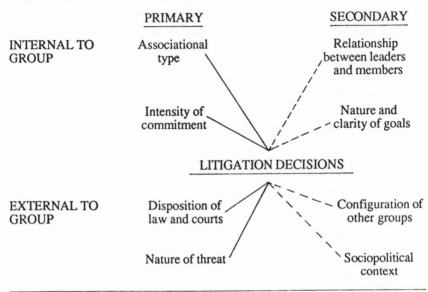

	PRIMARY	SECONDARY
INTERNAL TO GROUP	Associational type	Relationship between leaders and members
	Intensity of commitment	Nature and clarity of goals
	LITIGATION DECISIONS	
EXTERNAL TO GROUP	Disposition of law and courts	Configuration of other groups
	Nature of threat	Sociopolitical context

primary factors—those that explain general trends in the behavior observed—from secondary factors—those that fine-tune the analysis. In most cases, secondary factors buttress the effect of primary factors; in others, they identify reasons for actions seemingly at variance with expected behavior.

CONCLUSION

Past studies of group litigation have examined relatively stable areas of law contested by small numbers of purposive, political groups. Obscenity presents a different case. Twenty-four groups litigated over a 30-year period that saw constitutional law shift from the near acceptance of obscenity to its decisive rejection. The longitudinal design of this study allows it to describe the adaptive patterns prevalent among these organizations in a time of profound legal change, demonstrate the vastness of the group litigation system, and articulate factors that conditioned the observed dynamics. It shows that litigation of public issues is not the sole domain of purposive groups but is an arena in which material groups seek to advance their goals independent of more overtly political concerns. In these ways, the picture of group litigation presented by this study differs from that painted in previous studies.

Miller substantially altered the context of obscenity litigation. It was the catalyst for a radical redistribution of the litigation burden among libertarian groups. The ACLU de-emphasized its involvement, and material groups filled the void it left, although the nature of and reasons for this response varied according to the type of group affected. Some commercial groups formed a new group charged with watching obscenity developments, and all litigated narrow questions of law of immediate importance to their members until they perceived a diminution of threat. Professional groups increased their litigation but went beyond the vocational interests of their members to treat a broader range of issues. They behaved like hybrid purposive-material groups; in a sense, they became the functional equivalent of the ACLU. Purposive, pro-decency groups continued, with greater intensity, their judicial activities. These adaptations demonstrate the nexus between environment and group behavior. Further study is needed to determine whether behavioral differences between purposive and material (commercial and professional) groups are present in other areas.

The research presented here suggests that a conceptual framework can be developed to better describe and explain the underlying dynamics of group litigation. It would include the group-specific and contextual variables that affect litigation decisions—factors such as group type, intensity of commitment, relationship between leaders and members, nature and clarity of goals, disposition of the law, perception of threat, configuration of groups, and sociopolitical context. Further work is needed to clarify the relationships among these factors and to incorporate others found to be relevant. This would facilitate the development and testing of other hypotheses, the analytic treatment of the overtime dynamics of group litigation, and the pointed comparison of the litigation activities of various groups in different issue areas. In short, it would move the study of group litigation from the descriptive and idiosyncratic to the analytic and generalizable.

An example of the kind of analysis this approach could suggest and guide demonstrates its utility. This research found that much group litigation is the result of mobilization to protect material interests from legal threats. However, it is possible that this mobilization is a phenomenon limited to obscenity. Do threats to interests lead material groups to mobilize in other areas? Previous studies have looked at groups that have expressly political purposes and that are working in areas (for example, civil rights and civil liberties) with few connections to material interests. But, as the obscenity example demonstrates, the system of group litigation is more vast than the literature suggests. Characterizing organizational litigation as dominated by purposive groups may distort our understanding of this phenomenon. An examination of other areas of litigation conducive to the participation of material groups would lead to a deeper explanation of organizational litigation. If it disclosed that many organized litigators are of the material type, it would have important implications for our understanding of the forces working on legal development, the reasons groups go to court, and the relationship among organization, law, and policy.

The development of a conceptual framework would also enable us to capture the dynamics of ongoing organizational litigation. One of the reasons that groups become active in litigation is to keep their hands in areas of recurring interest. This provides them an opportunity to shape aspects of the law in a way conducive to their goals and gives them an advantage over litigators that do not have the resources or interest to engage in extended litigation (Galanter, 1974). Court shifts (as in obscenity) provide new opportunities for these actors; they create the potential for a fluid litigation system. There is little literature on the dynamics at work here, but with group use of the courts no longer an isolated phenomenon, this neglect should end.

Scholars have long studied group litigation; we now need to account more systematically for its dynamics and vastness. One of the great strengths of the behavioral revolution was its emphasis on *process*. A conceptual framework articulating factors relevant to the process of group litigation would move the literature beyond case studies to an understanding of a reality that changes. Thinking in these terms would move the study of group litigation from a collection of descriptively rich snapshots to a more generalized level. It would bring previous studies into the web of group theory, and generate a far richer explanation of the dynamics of group litigation.

NOTES

1. This is true not only for cases brought before the Supreme Court (see table 1.1) but also for those treated by appellate courts. See the Obscenity Law Project (1976), p. 921.

2. *Pacifica* (1978) involved "indecent" speech, and *Pico* (1982) involved the removal of "offensive" books from a school library.

3. This participation was indirect and consisted of giving expert legal advice to the counsel of members (AFAA) or training member attorneys in successful strategies (FALA).

4. For an interesting discussion of this phenomenon and its consequences, see Horowitz (1977) and Morgan (1984). A spirited rejoinder to Horowitz's argument was made by Wasby (1978).

5. O'Connor and Epstein (1982) assume that conservative groups are not disadvantaged. This, especially for the 1970s and 1980s, may not be so. However, they do show that group litigators do not represent merely the downtrodden.

6. For example, all FALA members interviewed for this study commented that the group contributed to their legal success.

7. For example, *Flynt* v. *Ohio* (1981)—case dismissed after oral argument—and *Huffman* v. *Pursue* (1975).

8. See chapters 2 and 5 for a discussion of this strategy.

9. It continued to file amicus briefs before the Supreme Court, but only to supplement its own litigation.

10. The intensity of commitment can be assessed independent of the frequency of litigation by an examination of a group's rhetoric and resource allocation.

11. Key (1961) makes the argument that group leaders do not necessarily reflect

the political preferences of their membership. Olson (1965) and Salisbury (1969) extend this to contend that leaders of material groups make no effort to represent the political positions of their members.

12. The ALA's attempted clarification of organizational goals is so vague and multi-faceted as to offer little chance for coherent litigation guidance. See its *Freedom to Read Foundation News* 11, no. 4 (1983).

Appendix A

Organizational Involvement in Obscenity Litigations before the Supreme Court

	Libertarian Involvement*	Pro-Decency Involvement*	Court Outcome	Summary Reversal
Butler v. Michigan, 352 U.S. 380 (1957)	AAP, ACLU, AL		lib.	
Kingsley Books v. Brown, 354 U. S. 436 (1957)	ACLU		pros.	
Roth v. U. S., Alberts v. California, 354 U. S. 476 (1957)	AAP, ACLU, AL		pros.	
Mounce v. U.S., 355 U. S. 180 (1957)			lib.	X
Times-Film v. Chicago, 355 U. S. 35 (1957)	ACLU		lib.	X
One v. Olesen, 355 U. S. 371 (1957)			lib.	X
Sunshine Books v. Summerfield, 355 U. S. 372 (1957)	ACLU		lib.	X
Kingsley Pictures v. Regents, 360 U. S. 684 (1959)			lib.	
Smith v. California, 361 U. S. 147 (1959)	ACLU		lib.	
Times-Film v. Chicago, 365 U. S. 43 (1961)	AAP, ACLU, AL, MPAA		pros.	

	Libertarian Involvement*	Pro-Decency Involvement*	Court Outcome	Summary Reversal
Marcus v. Search Warrant, 367 U. S. 717 (1961)			other	
Manual Enterprises v. Day, 370 U. S. 478 (1962)			lib.	
Bantam Books v. Sullivan, 372 U. S. 58 (1963)	AAP, AL		lib.	
Jacobellis v. Ohio, 378 U. S. 184 (1964)	ACLU	CDL	lib.	
Quantity of Books v. Kansas, 378 U. S. 205 (1964)			lib.	
Tralins v. Gerstein, 378 U. S. 576 (1964)			lib.	X
Grove Press v. Gerstein, 387 U. S. 577 (1964)			lib.	X
Freedman v. Maryland, 380 U. S. 51 (1965)	ACLU		lib.	
Memoirs v. Massachusetts, 383 U. S. 413 (1966)		CDL	lib.	
Ginzburg v. U.S., 383 U. S. 463 (1966)	AAP, ACLU, AL	CDL	pros.	
Mishkin v. New York, 383 U. S. 502 (1966)		CDL	pros.	
Austin v. Kentucky, 386 U.S. 767 (1967)	AAP, ACLU, CPDA	CDL	lib.	
Gent v. Arkansas, 386 U.S. 767 (1967)	AAP, CDPA		lib.	
Redrup v. New York, 386 U. S. 767 (1967)	AAP, CDPA	CDL	lib.	
Holding v. Nesbitt, 387 U. S. 94 (1967)			lib.	X
Keney v. New York, 388 U. S. 440 (1967)			lib.	X
Friedman v. New York, 388 U. S. 441 (1967)			lib.	X
Ratner v. California, 388 U. S. 442 (1967)			lib.	X
Cobert v. New York, 388 U. S. 443 (1967)			lib.	X

	Libertarian Involvement*	Pro-Decency Involvement*	Court Outcome	Summary Reversal
Sheperd v. New York, 388 U. S. 444 (1967)			lib.	X
Avansino v. New York, 388 U. S. 446 (1967)			lib.	X
Aday (West Coast News) v. U.S., 388 U. S. 448 (1967)	AAP, ACLU	CDL	lib.	X
Corinth Publishing v. Westberry, 388 U.S. 447 (1967)			lib.	X
Books v. U.S., 388 U. S. 449 (1967)			lib.	X
Rosenbloom v. Virginia, 388 U. S. 450 (1967)			lib.	X
Quantity of Books v. Kansas, 388 U. S. 452 (1967)			lib.	X
Mazes v. Ohio, 388 U. S. 453 (1967)			lib.	X
Schackman v. California, 388 U. S. 454 (1967)			lib.	X
Landau v. Fording, 388 U. S. 456 (1967)			pros.	X
U.S. v. Potomac News, 389 U. S. 47 (1967)			lib.	X
Conner v. Hammond, 389 U. S. 48 (1967)			lib.	X
Central Magazine v. U.S., 389 U. S. 50 (1967)			lib.	X
Chance v. California, 389 U. S. 89 (1967)			lib.	X
I. M. Amusement v. Ohio, 389 U. S 573 (1967)			lib.	X
Robert-Arthur v. Tennessee, 389 U. S. 578 (1967)			lib.	X
Teitel Film Corp., v. Cusak, 390 U. S. 139 (1968)			lib.	X
Felton v. Pensacola, 390 U. S. 340 (1968)			lib.	X

	Libertarian Involvement*	Pro-Decency Involvement*	Court Outcome	Summary Reversal
Interstate Circuit v. Dallas, 390 U. S. 676 (1968)	ACLU, AL		lib.	
Ginsberg v. New York, 390 U. S. 629 (1968)	AAP, ACLU, AL, CPDA	CDL	pros.	
Rabeck v. New York, 391 U. S. 462 (1968)			lib.	X
Lee Art Theatre v. Virginia, 392 U. S. 636 (1968)			lib.	X
Henry v. Louisiana, 392 U. S. 655 (1968)			lib.	X
Stanley v. Georgia, 394 U. S. 557 (1969)		CDL	lib.	
Carlos v. New York, 396 U. S. 119 (1969)			lib.	X
Milky Way v. Leary, 397 U. S. 98 (1970)			other	
Cain v. Kentucky, 397 U. S. 319 (1970)		CDL	lib.	X
Gable v. Jenkins, 397 U. S. 592 (1970)			pros.	
Rowan v. Post Office, 397 U. S. 728 (1970)	DMAA		pros.	
Bloss v. Dykema, 398 U. S. 278 (1970)			lib.	X
Walker v. Ohio, 398 U. S. 434 (1970)			lib.	X
Hoyt v. Minnesota, 399 U. S. 524 (1970)			lib.	X
Blount v. Rizzi, 400 U. S. 410 (1971)			lib.	
Delta Book (Perez) v. Cronvich (Ledesma), 401 U. S. 82 (1971)			other	
Batchelor v. Stein, 401 U. S. 200 (1971)	ACLU		other	
Byrne v. Karalexis, 401 U. S. 216 (1971)	ACLU		other	
Grove Press v. Maryland, 401 U. S. 480 (1971)	AFAA, MPAA, NATO	MM	pros.	

	Libertarian Involvement*	Pro-Decency Involvement*	Court Outcome	Summary Reversal
Childs v. Oregon, 401 U. S. 1006 (1971)			lib.	X
U. S. v. Reidel, 402 U. S. 351 (1971)			pros.	
U. S. v. 37 Photographs, 402 U. S. 363 (1971)			pros.	
Bloss v. Michigan, 402 U. S. 938 (1971)			lib.	X
Cohen v. California, 403 U. S. 15 (1971)	ACLU	CDL	lib.	
Burgin v. South Carolina, 404 U. S. 806 (1971)			lib.	X
Hartstein v. Missouri, 404 U. S. 988 (1971)			lib.	X
Wiener v. California, 404 U. S. 988 (1971)			lib.	X
Rabe v. Washington, 405 U. S. 313 (1972)	MPAA, NATO	CDL, MM	lib.	
Kois v. Wisconsin, 408 U. S. 229 (1972)			lib.	
California v. LaRue, 409 U. S. 109 (1972)			pros.	
Papish v. Board of Curators, 410 U. S. 667 (1973)	ACLU	CDL	lib.	
Kenosha v. Bruno, 412 U. S. 507 (1973)			other	
Miller v. California, 413 U. S. 15 (1973)	AAP, ACLU, ALA, AL		pros.	
Paris Adult Theatre v. Slaton, 413 U. S. 49 (1973)		CDL	pros.	
Kaplan v. California, 413 U. S. 115 (1973)	ALA		pros.	
U.S. v. 12 Reels of Super 8mm Film, 413 U.S. 123 (1973)	ACLU, FALA		pros.	
U. S. v. Orito, 413 U. S. 139 (1973)	ACLU		pros.	

	Libertarian Involvement*	Pro-Decency Involvement*	Court Outcome	Summary Reversal
Heller v. New York 413 U.S. 483 (1973)		CDL	pros.	
Roaden v. Kentucky, 413 U. S. 496 (1973)	FALA	CDL	other	
Alexander v. Virginia, 413 U. S. 836 (1973)	FALA		pros.	
Kirkpatrick v. N.Y., 414 U. S. 948 (1973)	AAP, ABA, ALA, AL		pros.	
Hamling v. U. S., 418 U. S. 87 (1974)	AAP, ACLU, ALA		pros.	
Jenkins v. Georgia, 418 U. S. 153 (1974)	AFAA, AAP, ABA, ALA, AL, CPDA, MC, MPAA, NATO, DGA	CDL	lib.	
Southeastern Promotions v. Conrad, 420 U. S. 546 (1975)	AL	CDL	lib.	
Huffman v. Pursue, 420 U. S. 592 (1975)	MPAA	CDL	other	
Erznoznik v. Jacksonville, 422 U. S. 205 (1975)	AL, MPAA		lib.	
Hicks v. Miranda, 422 U. S. 332 (1975)			other	
Doren v. Salem Inn, 422 U. S. 922 (1975)			lib.	
McKinney v. Alabama, 424 U. S. 669 (1976)	AAP, CPDA, MC, MPAA		lib.	
Young v. American Mini Theatres, 427 U. S. 50 (1976)	AFAA, ACLU, MPAA		pros.	
Marks v. U. S., 430 U. S. 188 (1977)		CDL	other	
Smith v. U.S., 431 U.S. 291 (1977)	AAP, ABA, ALA, CPDA, MC	CDL	pros.	
Splawn v. California, 431 U. S. 595 (1977)		CDL	pros.	
Ward v. Illinois, 431 U. S. 767 (1977)			pros.	

	Libertarian Involvement*	Pro-Decency Involvement*	Court Outcome	Summary Reversal
Ballew v. Georgia, 435 U. S. 223 (1978)		CDL	other	
Pinkus v. U. S., 436 U. S. 293 (1978)			pros.	
FCC v. Pacifica Foundation, 438 U. S. 726 (1978)	AAP, ACLU, ALA, AL, MPAA	MM	pros.	
Lo-Ji Sales v. New York, 442 U. S. 319 (1979)	AAP, ABA, ALA, CPDA, MC	CDL	other	
Vance v. Universal Amusement, 445 U. S. 308 (1980)	ABA, CPDA, MC	CDL	lib.	
Walter v. U.S., U.S. v. Sanders, 447 U. S. 647 (1980)			other	
Schad v. Mt. Ephraim, 452 U. S. 61 (1981)			other	
New York v. Bellanca, 452 U. S. 714 (1981)			pros.	
Board of Education v. Pico, 457 U.S. 853 (1982)	AAP, ACLU, ALA, AL	CDL	lib.	
New York v. Ferber, 458 U.S. 747 (1982)	AAP, ABA, ACLU, ALA, CPDA, MC	CDL, MM, CH/IYA	pros.	
Maryland v. Macon, 472 U.S. 463 (1985)	ABA, ACLU, ALA, AAP, CPDA, MPAA, MC		pros.	
Brockett v. Spokane Arcades,472 U.S. 491 (1985)	AFAA, ABA, ALA, AAP, CPDA, MC	CDL, MM	pros.	
Renton v. Playtime Theatres, 475 U.S. 41 (1986)	ABA, ACLU, ALA, AAP, CPDA, MC, OAA	NIMLO, NLC, FCF	pros.	
New York v. P.J. Video, 475 U.S. 868 (1986)	VSDA		pros.	
Arcara v. Cloud Books, 478 U.S. 697 (1986)	ACLU	CDL	pros.	

	Libertarian Involvement*	Pro-Decency Involvement*	Court Outcome	Summary Reversal
Newport v. Iacobucci, 479 U.S. 92 (1986)			pros.	
Pope v. Illinois, 481 U.S. 497 (1987)	ABA, ALA, AAP, CPDA, MC, VLA	CDL	other	
Virginia v. American Booksellers Association, Inc., 108 S.Ct. 636 (1988)	ABA, ACLU, AAP, ALA, AL, ASJA, CPDA, MC	CH/IYA, NLF	other	

*Key to Group Abbreviations

Libertarian Groups

AFAA	Adult Film Association of America
ABA	American Booksellers Association
ACLU	American Civil Liberties Union
ALA/FRF	American Library Association/Freedom to Read Foundation
ASJA	American Society of Journalists and Authors
AAP	Association of American Publishers
AL	Authors League of America
CPDA	Council for Periodical Distributors Association
DMAA	Direct Mail Advertising Association
DGA	Directors Guild of America
FALA	First Amendment Lawyers Association
MC	Media Coalition
MPAA	Motion Picture Association of America
NATO	National Association of Theatre Owners
OAA	Outdoor Advertising Association
VSDA	Video Software Dealers Association
VLA	Volunteer Lawyers for the Arts

Proscriptionist Groups

CDL	Citizens for Decency through Law
CH/IYA	Covenant House/Institute for Youth Advocacy
FCF	Freedom Council Foundation
MM	Morality in Media
NIMLO	National Institute of Municipal Law Officers
NLC	National League of Cities
NLF	National Legal Foundation

Appendix B

Citizens for Decency through Law Supreme Court Participation Not Counted in Appendix A

1. Smith v. California, 375 U.S. 259 (1963)

2. Arneberg v. Zeitlin, 375 U.S. 957 (1963)

3. Grove Press v. Flask, 413 U.S. 902 (1973)

4. "Vixen" v. Ohio, 413 U. S. 905 (1973)

5. Michigan v. Bloss, 413 U. S. 905 (1973)

6. Huffman v. U. S. District Court, 413 U. S. 918 (1973)

7. Boyd v. Ohio, 418 U. S. 954 (1973)

8. Smith v. Keator, 419 U. S. 1043 (1974)

9. Fair v. Smith, 421 U. S. 902 (1975)

10. Art Theatre Guild v. Ewing, 421 U. S. 923 (1975)

11. People v. Superior Court, 429 U. S. 1097 (1977)

12. Alabama v. General Corporation, 425 U. S. 904 (1976)

13. Harmer v. "Devil in Miss Jones," 430 U. S. 967 (1977)

14. Harmer v. "Deep Throat," 432 U.S. 907 (1977)

15. East Detroit v. Llewellyn, 438 U. S. 909 (1978)

16. Ricco v. Ohio, 445 U. S. 921 (1980)

17. Flynt v. Ohio, 451 U. S. 619 (1981)

18. Newport v. Fact Concerts, 453 U. S. 247 (1981)

19. Cooper v. Mitchell Brothers, 454 U. S. 849 (1981)

20. Brockett v. Spokane Arcades, 454 U. S. 1022 (1981)

21. U. S. Marketing v. Idaho, 455 U.S. 1009 (1982)

22. Clancy v. Jartech, 459 U.S. 826 (1982)

23. Warner v. Sovereign News, 459 U.S. 864 (1982)

24. Turso v. Cleveland Municipal Court, 459 U.S. 880 (1982)

25. Sovereign News Company v. John T. Corrigan, 459 U.S. 883 (1982)

26. McAuliffe et al. v. Penthouse, 465 U. S. 1108 (1984)

27. Herceg v. Hustler, 108 S.Ct. 61 (1987)

Appendix C

Participation of Groups in Supreme Court Obscenity Decisions: Pre- and Post-*Miller*

Libertarian Groups	Pre-Miller	Post-Miller
Adult Film Association of America (**AFAA**)	1 (2.8%) 1 (3.8%)*	3 (9.7%)
American Booksellers Association (**ABA**)	0 (0%)	11 (35.5%)
American Civil Liberties Union (**ACLU**)	21 (23.9) 18 (39.1%)*	9 (29.0%)
American Library Association/Freedom to Read Foundation (**ALA/FRF**)	2 (2.3%) 2 (4.3%)*	13 (41.9%)
American Society of Journalists and Authors (**ASJA**)	0 (0%)	1 (3.2%)
Association of American Publishers (**AAP**)	11 (12.5%) 10 (22.7%)*	14 (45.2%)
Authors League of America (**AL**)	8 (9.1%) 8 (17.4%)*	7 (22.6)
Council for Periodical Distributors Association (**CPDA**)	4 (4.5%) 4 (8.7%)	11 (35.5%)
Direct Mail Advertising Association (**DMAA**)	1 (1.1%) 1 (2.2%)*	0 (0%)
Directors Guild of America (**DGA**)	0 (0%)	1 (3.2%)

Libertarian Groups	Pre-Miller	Post-Miller
First Amendment Lawyers Association (**FALA**)	3 (3.9%) 3 (12.5%)*	0 (0%)
Media Coalition (**MC**)	0 (0%)	11 (35.5%)
Motion Picture Association of America (**MPAA**)	3 (3.4%) 3 (6.5%)*	7 (22.6%)
National Association of Theatre Owners (**NATO**)	2 (2.3%) 2 (4.3%)*	1 (3.2%)
Outdoor Advertising Association (**OAA**)	0 (0%)	1 (3.2%)
Video Software Dealers Association (**VSDA**)	0 (0%)	1 (10%)
Volunteer Lawyers for the Arts (**VLA**)	0 (0%)	1 (3.2%)

Proscriptionist Groups	Pre-Miller	Post-Miller
Citizens for Decency through Law (**CDL**)	16 (18.2%) 14 (30.4%)*	14 (45.2%)
Covenant House/Institute for Youth Advocacy (**CH/IYA**)	0 (0%)	2 (6.5%)
Freedom Council Foundation (**FCF**)	----------	1 (21.5%)
Morality in Media (**MM**)	2 (2.6%) 2 (4.8%)*	3 (9.7%)
National Institute of Municipal Law Officers (**NIMLO**)	0 (0%)	1 (3.2%)
National League of Cities (**NLC**)	0 (0%)	1 (3.2%)
National Legal Foundation (**NLF**)	----------	1 (2.5%)

---

* Notes participation in cases formally decided (not those summarily reversed).

Data drawn from appendix A.

The number of cases for the pre-Miller period is 88; for the post-Miller period, 31. For groups formed after 1957, the n used to calculate their percentage involvement was adjusted to reflect the cases decided after their establishment.

Appendix D

Table of Cases

ABA, et al. v. Hudnut, 598 F. Supp. 1316 (1984), 771 F.2d 323 (1985), 106 S.Ct. 1664 (1986)

ABA, et al. v. McAulliffe, 533 F. Supp. 50 (1981)

ACLU v. Chicago, 121 N.E. 2d 585 (1954)

Action for the Children's Television v. FCC, 852 F.2d 1332 (CADC, 1988)

Aday (West Coast News) v. U.S., 388 U.S. 447 (1967)

AFAA v. Times-Mirror, 3 Media Law Reporter 2292 (1978)

Alberts v. California, 354 U.S. 476 (1957)

Alexander v. Virginia, 413 U.S. 836 (1973)

Arcara v. Cloud Books, 478 U.S. 697 (1986)

Austin v. Kentucky, 386 U.S. 767 (1967)

Avansino v. New York, 388 U.S. 446 (1967)

Ballew v. Georgia, 435 U.S. 223 (1978)

Bantam Books v. Sullivan, 372 U.S. 58 (1963)

Barenblatt v. U.S., 360 U.S. 109 (1959)

Batchelor v. Stein, 401 U.S. 200 (1971)

Beauharnais v. Illinois, 343 U.S. 250 (1952)

Bloss v. Dykema, 398 U.S. 278 (1970)

Bloss v. Michigan, 402 U.S. 938 (1971)

Blount v. Rizzi, 400 U.S. 410 (1971)

Board of Education v. Pico, 457 U.S. 853 (1982)

Books v. U.S., 388 U.S. 449 (1967)

Brockett v. Spokane Arcades, 472 U.S. 491 (1985)

Brown v. Board of Education, 347 U.S. 483 (1954)

Burgin v. South Carolina, 404 U.S. 806 (1971)

Burstyn v. Wilson, 343 U.S. 495 (1952)

Butler v. Michigan, 352 U.S. 380 (1957)

Byrne v. Karalexis, 401 U.S. 216 (1971)

Cain v. Kentucky, 397 U.S. 319 (1970)

California v. LaRue, 409 U.S. 109 (1972)

Carlin Communications, Inc. v. FCC, 749 F.2d 113 (CA2, 1984)

Carlos v. New York, 396 U.S. 119 (1969)

Central Magazine Sales v. U.S., 389 U.S. 50 (1967)

Chance v. California, 389 U.S. 89 (1967)

Chaplinsky v. New Hampshire, 315 U.S. 568 (1942)

Childs v. Oregon, 401 U.S. 1006 (1971)

Clancy v. Jartech, 666 F.2d 403 (1982)

Cohen v. California, 403 U. S. 15 (1971)

Commonwealth v. Gorden, 66 Pa. D and C. 101 (1949)

Commonwealth v. Holmes, 17 Mass. 336 (1821)

Commonwealth v. Sharpless, 2 S&R 91 (Pa. 1815)

Conner v. Hammond, 389 U.S. 48 (1967)

Cobert v. New York, 388 U.S. 443 (1967)

Corinth Publications v. Westberry, 388 U.S. 448 (1967)

Delta Book (Perez) v. Cronvich (Ledesma), 401 U.S. 82 (1971)

Dennis v. U.S., 341 U.S. 494 (1951)

Dominus Rex v. Curll, 2 Stra. 789 (1727)

Doren v. Salem Inn, 422 U.S. 922 (1975)

Doubleday v. New York, 335 U.S. 848 (1948)

Duncan v. Louisiana, 391 U.S. 145 (1968)

Dyson v. Stein, 401 U.S. 200 (1971)

Erznoznik v. Jacksonville, 422 U.S. 205 (1975)

FCC v. Pacifica Foundation, 438 U.S. 726 (1978)

Felton v. Pensacola, 390 U.S. 340 (1968)

Flynt v. Ohio, 451 U.S. 619 (1981)

Fort Wayne Books, Inc. v. Indiana, 109 S.Ct. 916 (1989)

Freedman v. Maryland, 380 U.S. 51 (1965)

Friedman v. New York, 388 U.S. 441 (1967)

FW/PBS v. City of Dallas, 648 F.Supp. 1061 (1986), 837 F.2d 1298 (CA5, 1988)

Gable v. Jenkins, 397 U.S. 592 (1970)

Gent v. Arkansas, 386 U.S. 767 (1967)

Ginsberg v. New York, 390 U.S. 629 (1968)

Ginzburg v. U.S., 383 U.S. 463 (1966)

Grove Press v. Gerstein, 378 U.S. 577 (1964)

Grove Press v. Maryland, 401 U.S. 480 (1971)

Hamling v. U.S., 418 U.S. 87 (1974)

Hartstein v. Missouri, 404 U.S. 988 (1971)

Heller v. New York, 413 U.S. 483 (1973)

Henry v. Louisiana, 392 U.S. 655 (1968)

Herceg v. Hustler, 108 S.Ct. 61 (1987)

Hicks v. Miranda, 422 U.S. 332 (1975)

Holding v. Nesbitt, 387 U.S. 94 (1967)

Hoyt v. Minnesota, 399 U.S. 524 (1970)

Huffman v. Pursue, 420 U.S. 592 (1975)

I. M. Amusement v. Ohio, 389 U.S. 573 (1967)

Interstate Circuit, Inc. v. Dallas, 390 U.S. 676 (1968)

Jacobellis v. Ohio, 378 U.S. 184 (1964)

Jenkins v. Georgia, 418 U.S. 153 (1974)

Jones, et al. v. Wilkinson, Attorney General of Utah, 661 F.Supp. 1099 (1985), 800
     F.2d 989 (1986)

Kaplan v. California, 413 U.S. 115 (1973)

Keney v. New York, 388 U.S. 440 (1967)

Kenosha v. Bruno, 412 U.S. 507 (1973)

Kingsley Books v. Brown, 354 U.S. 436 (1957)

Kingsley Pictures v. Regents, 360 U.S. 684 (1959)

Kirkpatrick v. New York, 414 U.S. 948 (1973)

Kois v. Wisconsin, 408 U.S. 229 (1972)

Landau v. Fording, 388 U.S. 456 (1967)

Lee Art Theatre v. Virginia, 392 U.S. 636 (1968)

Liles v. Oregon, 425 U.S. 963 (1976)

Lo-Ji Sales v. New York, 442 U.S. 319 (1979)

Lynch v. Donnelly, 465 U.S. 668 (1984)

McKinney v. Alabama, 424 U.S. 669 (1976)

Manual Enterprises v. Day, 370 U.S. 478 (1962)

Mapp v. Ohio, 367 U.S. 643 (1961)

Marcus v. Search Warrant, 367 U.S. 717 (1961)

Marks v. U.S., 430 U.S. 188 (1977)

Maryland v. Macon, 472 U.S. 463 (1985)

Mazes v. Ohio, 388 U.S. 453 (1967)

Memoirs v. Massachusetts, 383 U.S. 413 (1966)

Milky Way v. Leary, 397 U.S. 98 (1970)

Miller v. California, 413 U.S. 15 (1973)

Mishkin v. New York, 383 U.S. 502 (1966)

Moore v. California (1974), unpublished federal district court opinion

Mounce v. U.S., 355 U.S. 180 (1957)

NATO v. Milwaukee, 328 F.Supp. 6 (1971)

Near v. Minnesota, 283 U.S. 697 (1931)

Newport v. Iacobucci, 479 U.S. 92 (1986)

New York v. Bellanca, 452 U.S. 714 (1981)

New York v. Ferber, 458 U.S. 747 (1982)

New York v. P.J. Video, 475 U.S. 868 (1986)

New York Times v. Sullivan, 376 U.S. 254 (1964)

One v. Olesen, 355 U.S. 371 (1957)

Papish v. Board of Curators, 410 U.S. 667 (1973)

Paris Adult Theatre v. Slaton, 413 U.S. 49 (1973)

Penthouse v. McAulliffe, 436 F.Supp. 1241 (1977), 610 F.2d 1353 (1978), 465 U.S.
     1108 (1986)

Pinkus v. U.S., 436 U.S. 293 (1978)

Plessy v. Ferguson, 163 U.S. 537 (1896)

Pope v. Illinois, 481 U.S. 497 (1987)

Potomac News v. U.S., 389 U.S. 47 (1967)

Quantity of Books v. Kansas, 378 U.S. 205 (1964)

Quantity of Books v. Kansas, 388 U.S. 452 (1967)

Rabe v. Washington, 405 U.S. 313 (1972)

Rabeck v. New York, 391 U.S. 462 (1968)

Ratner v. California, 388 U.S. 442 (1967)

Red Bluff Drive-in v. Vance, 648 F.2d 1020 (CA5, 1981)

Redrup v. New York, 386 U.S. 767 (1967)

Regina v. Hicklin, 3 QB 360 (1868)

Renton v. Playtime Theatres, 475 U.S. 41 (1986)

Roaden v. Kentucky, 413 U.S. 496 (1973)

Robert-Arthur Management Corp. v. Tennessee, 389 U.S. 578 (1968)

Rosen v. U.S., 161 U.S. 29 (1896)

Rosenbloom v. Virginia, 388 U.S. 450 (1967)

Roth v. U.S, 354 U.S. 476 (1957)

Rowan v. Post Office, 397 U.S. 728 (1970)

St. Martin's Press v. Carey, 605 F. 2d 41 (1979)

Schackman v. California, 388 U.S. 454 (1967)

Schad v. Mt. Ephraim, 452 U.S. 61 (1981)

Sheperd v. New York, 388 U.S. 444 (1967)

Skokie v. National Socialist Party, 69 Ill.2d 605 (1978)

Smith v. California, 361 U.S. 147 (1959)

Smith v. California, 375 U.S. 259 (1963)

Smith v. U.S., 431 U.S. 291 (1977)

Southeastern Promotions v. Conrad, 420 U.S. 546 (1975)

Splawn v. California, 431 U.S. 595 (1977)

Stanley v. Georgia, 394 U.S. 557 (1969)

Sunshine Books v. Summerfield, 355 U.S. 372 (1957)

Teitel Film Corp. v. Cusak, 390 U.S. 139 (1968)

Times-Film v. Chicago, 355 U.S. 35 (1957)

Times-Film v. Chicago, 365 U.S. 43 (1961)

Tinker v. Des Moines, 393 U.S. 503 (1969)

Tralins v. Gerstein, 378 U.S. 576 (1964)

U.S. v. Dennett, 39 F.2d 564 (CA2, 1930)

U.S. v. Kennerley, 209 F.119 (1913)

U.S. v. Levine, 83 F.2d 156 (1936)

U.S. v. Nixon, 418 U.S. 683 (1974)

U.S. v. Orito, 413 U.S. 139 (1973)

U.S. v. Potomac News, 389 U.S. 47 (1967)

U.S. v. Reidel, 402 U.S. 351 (1971)

U.S. v. Sanders, 447 U.S. 647 (1980)

U.S. v. 37 Photographs, 402 U.S. 363 (1971)

U.S. v. 12 Reels of Super 8mm Film, 413 U.S. 123 (1973)

U.S. v. Two Obscene Books, 99 F.Supp. 760 (1951)

U.S. v. Ulysses, 5 F.Supp. 182 (1933), 72 F.2d 705 (1934)

U.S. Marketing v. Idaho, 455 U.S. 1009 (1982)

Vance v. Universal Amusement Company, 445 U.S. 308 (1980)

Virginia v. American Booksellers Association, Inc., et al., 108 S.Ct. 636 (1988)

Virginia State Board of Pharmacy v. Virginia Citizens Consumer Council, 425 U.S. 728 (1976)

"Vixen" v. Ohio, 413 U.S. 905 (1973)

Walker v. Ohio, 398 U.S. 434 (1970)

Walter v. U.S., 447 U.S. 647 (1980)

Ward v. Illinois, 431 U.S. 767 (1977)

Whitney v. California, 274 U.S. 357 (1927)

Wiener v. California, 404 U.S. 988 (1971)

Winters v. New York, 333 U.S. 507 (1948)

Young v. American Mini Theatres, 427 U.S. 50 (1976)

Younger v. Harris, 401 U.S. 37 (1970)

Bibliography

BOOKS

Allison, Graham T. 1971. *Essence of Decision: Explaining the Cuban Missile Crisis*. Boston, Mass.: Little, Brown.

Attorney General's Commission on Pornography. 1986. *Final Report*. Washington, D.C.: U.S. Government Printing Office.

Ball, Howard. 1980. *Courts and Politics*. Englewood Cliffs, N.J.: Prentice-Hall.

Bentley, Arthur F. 1908. *The Process of Government*. Cambridge, Mass.: Belknap Press of Harvard University.

Bickel, Alexander. 1970. *The Supreme Court and the Idea of Progress*. New York: Harper and Row.

———. 1975. *The Morality of Consent*. New Haven, Conn.: Yale University Press.

Boyer, Paul S. 1968. *Purity in Print: The Vice Society Movement and Book Censorship in America*. New York: Charles Scribner and Sons.

Broun, Haywood, and Margaret Leech. 1927. *Anthony Comstock: Roundsman of the Lord*. New York: Albert and Charles Bon.

Cardozo, Benjamin M. 1921. *The Nature of the Judicial Process*. New Haven, Conn.: Yale University Press.

Casper, Jonathan. 1972. *Lawyers Before the Warren Court*. Urbana: University of Illinois Press.

———. 1972b. *The Politics of Civil Liberties*. New York: Harper and Row.

Comstock, Anthony. 1880. *Frauds Exposed: How the People Are Deceived and Robbed, and Youth Corrupted*. New York: J. Howard Brown.

―――. 1967. *Traps for the Young*. Cambridge, Mass.: Belknap Press of Harvard University.

Cortner, Richard C. 1970. *The Apportionment Cases*. Knoxville: University of Tennessee Press.

Downs, Donald. 1989. *The New Politics of Pornography*. Chicago: University of Chicago Press.

Dworkin, Andrea. 1981. *Pornography*. New York: Putnam.

―――. 1987. *Intercourse*. New York: Free Press.

Emerson, Thomas I. 1965. *Toward a General Theory of the First Amendment*. New York: Vintage Books.

―――. 1970. *The System of Freedom of Expression*. New York: Vintage Books.

The Encyclopedia of Associations. Detroit: Gale Research Company, yearly.

Epstein, Lee. 1985. *Conservatives in Court*. Knoxville: University of Tennessee Press.

Ernst, Morris L. 1940. *The Censor Marches On*. New York: Doubleday.

―――. 1964. *Censorship: The Search for the Obscene*. New York: Macmillan Company.

Frank, Jerome. 1950. *Courts on Trial*. Princeton, N.J.: Princeton University Press.

Gardiner, Harold C. 1958. *Catholic Viewpoint on Censorship*. Garden City, N.J.: Hanover House.

Gibson, James L., and Richard D. Bingham. 1985. *Civil Liberties and Nazis*. New York: Praeger.

Goldstein, Michael J., Harold S. Kant, and John J. Hartman. 1973. *Pornography and Social Deviance*. Berkeley: University of California Press.

Haney, Robert W. 1960. *Comstockery in America: Patterns of Censorship and Control*. Boston: Beacon Press.

Hirschman, Albert O. 1970. *Exit, Voice, and Loyalty*. Cambridge, Mass.: Harvard University Press.

Horowitz, Donald I. 1977. *The Courts and Social Policy*. Washington, D.C.: Brookings Institution.

Key, V. O. 1961. *Public Opinion and Public Policy*. New York: Knopf.

Kluger, Richard. 1975. *Simple Justice*. New York: Knopf.

Levin, Martin. 1977. *Urban Politics and the Courts*. Chicago: University of Chicago Press.

Levine, James P. 1968. *The Bookseller and the Law of Obscenity*. Ph.D. diss., Northwestern University.

Levy, Leonard. 1974. *Against the Law*. New York: Harper and Row.

McIlhany, William H. III. 1975. *The ACLU on Trial*. New Rochelle, N.Y.: Arlington House Publishers.

Meiklejohn, Alexander. 1948. *Free Speech and Its Relation to Self-Government*. New York: Harper.

Moe, Terry M. 1980. *The Organization of Interests*. Chicago: University of Chicago Press.

Morgan, Richard E. 1968. *The Politics of Religious Conflict: Church and State in America*. New York: Pegasus.

―――. 1984. *Disabling America: The "Rights Industry" in Our Time*. New York: Basic Books.

Murphy, Paul L. 1972. *The Constitution in Crisis Times*. New York: Harper and Row.

Murphy, Walter. 1964. *Elements of Judicial Strategy*. Chicago: University of Chicago Press.

Neier, Aryeh. 1979. *Defending My Enemy*. New York: E. P. Dutton.

O'Connor, Karen. 1980. *Women's Organizations' Use of the Courts*. Lexington, Mass.: Lexington Books.

Office for Intellectual Freedom/American Library Association. 1983. *Censorship Litigation and the Schools*. Chicago: Office for Intellectual Freedom/American Library Association.

Olson, Mancur. 1965. *The Logic of Collective Action*. Cambridge, Mass.: Harvard University Press.

Olson, Susan. 1984. *Clients and Lawyers*. Westport, Conn.: Greenwood Press.

Pivar, David J. 1973. *Purity Crusade: Sexual Morality and Social Control*. Westport, Conn.: Greenwood Press.

President's Commission on Obscenity and Pornography. 1970. *Report*. New York: Bantam Books.

Pritchett, C. Herman. 1968. *The American Constitution*. New York: McGraw-Hill.

Rembar, Charles. 1968. *The End of Obscenity*. New York: Simon and Schuster.

Rhode, David, and Harold Spaeth. 1976. *Supreme Court Decision-Making*. San Francisco, Calif.: W. H. Freeman and Company.

Rubin, Eve R. 1987. *Abortion, Politics, and the Courts*. Revised edition. Westport, Conn.: Greenwood Press.

Schattschneider, E. E. 1960. *The Semi-Sovereign People*. Hinsdale, Ill.: Dryden Press.

Schauer, Frederick. 1976. *The Law of Obscenity*. Washington, D.C.: Bureau of National Affairs.

Sorauf, Frank J. 1976. *The Wall of Separation: Constitutional Politics of Church and State*. Princeton: Princeton University Press.

Tribe, Laurence. 1978. *American Constitutional Law*. New York: Foundation Press.

Truman, David. 1971. *The Governmental Process*. 2d ed. New York: Alfred A. Knopf.

Trumbull, Charles Gallandet. 1913. *Anthony Comstock: Fighter*. New York: Fleming H. Revel Co.

Vose, Clement. 1959. *Caucasians Only*. Berkeley: University of California Press.

———. 1972. *Constitutional Change*. Lexington, Mass.: Lexington Books.

Walker, Samuel. 1990. *In Defense of the ACLU*. New York: Oxford University Press.

Warren, Earl. 1977. *The Memoirs of Chief Justice Earl Warren*. New York: Doubleday and Company.

Wasby, Stephen L. 1976. *Continuity and Change: From the Warren Court to the Burger Court*. Pacific Palisades, Calif.: Goodyear Publishing Company.

———. 1988. *The Supreme Court in the Federal Judicial System*. Chicago: Nelson-Hall.

Wilson, James Q. 1973. *Political Organizations*. New York: Basic Books.

Woodward, Bob, and Scott Armstrong. 1980. *The Brethren*. New York: Avon.

Zurcher, Louis A., and R. George Kirkpatrick. 1976. *Citizens for Decency*. Austin: University Of Texas Press.

ARTICLES

Armstrong, O. K. 1965a. "Must Our Movies Be Obscene?" *Reader's Digest*, November, pp. 154–56.

———. 1965b. "The Damning Case against Pornography." *Reader's Digest*, December, pp. 131–34.

————. 1966. "Filth for Profit: The Big Business of Pornography." *Reader's Digest*, March, pp. 73–76.

————. 1967a. "Victory over the Smut Peddlers." *Reader's Digest*, February, pp. 147–54.

————. 1967b. "Landmark Decision in the War on Pornography." *Reader's Digest*, September, pp. 93–97.

Barker, Lucius J. 1967. "Third Parties in Litigation: A Systematic View of the Judicial Function." *Journal of Politics* 29:41–69.

Berns, Walter. 1971. "Pornography vs. Democracy: The Case for Censorship." *Public Interest*, Winter, pp. 3–24.

Bickel, Alexander. 1971. "Dissenting and Concurring Opinions." *Public Interest*, Winter, pp. 25–28.

Bishop, Joseph W. 1971. "Politics and the ACLU." *Commentary*, December, 52:50–58.

Bodgett, Nancy. 1986. "Porno Blacklist." *ABA Journal*, 1 July, pp. 28–29.

Bork, Robert. 1971. "Neutral Principles and Some First Amendment Problems." *Indiana Law Review* 47:1–35.

Brennan, William. 1965. "The Supreme Court and the Meiklejohnian Interpretation of the First Amendment." *Harvard Law Review* 79:1–20.

Brest, Paul, and Ann Vandenberg. 1987. "Politics, Feminism, and the Constitution: The Anti-Pornography Movement in Minneapolis." *Stanford Law Review* 39:607–61.

Caldeira, Gregory A., and John R. Wright. 1988. "Organized Interests and Agenda Setting in the Supreme Court." *American Political Science Review* 82:1109–28.

Casper, Gerhard, and Richard Posner. 1974. "A Study of the Supreme Court's Caseload." *Legal Studies* 3:339–75.

Chayes, Abraham. 1976. "The Role of the Judge in Public Law Litigation." *Harvard Law Review* 89:1281–1316.

Clor, Harry M. 1971. "Science, Eros, and the Law: A Critique of the Obscenity Commission Report." *Duquesne Law Review* 10:63–76.

Corn, David. 1990. "Dirty Bookkeeping." *New Republic*, 2 April, pp. 14–16.

Cortner, Richard. 1968. "Strategies and Tactics of Litigants in Constitutional Cases." *Journal of Public Law* 17:287–307.

Cowan, Ruth B. 1976. "Women's Rights through Litigation: An Examination of the ACLU Women's Rights Project." *Columbia Human Rights Law Review* 8:373–412.

Downs, Donald. 1987. "The Attorney General's Commission and the New Politics of Pornography." *American Bar Foundation Research Journal* 1987:641–80.

Edwards, Deryl M. 1981. "How to Clean Up America by Eliminating Pornography—Step 1." In *How You Can Help Clean Up America*, ed. Jerry Falwell. Washington, D.C.: Moral Majority.

Elshtain, Jean Bethke. 1984. "Women, Politics, and Pornography." *New Republic*, 25 June, pp. 15–20.

Engdahl, David. 1969. "Requiem for *Roth*." *Michigan Law Review* 68:185:236.

Fuller, Lon. 1978. "The Forms and Limits of Adjudication." *Harvard Law Review* 92:353–409.

Galanter, Marc. 1974. "Why the 'Haves' Come Out Ahead: Speculations on the Limits of Legal Change." *Law and Society Review* 9:95–160.

Goldstein, Tom. 1978. "The ACLU Finds Another Issue: Itself." *New York Times Magazine*, 23 April.

Gottschall, Jon. 1986. "Reagan's Appointments to the U.S. Courts of Appeals." *Judicature* 70:50–54.

Hakman, Nathan. 1966. "Lobbying the Supreme Court: An Appraisal of Political Science Folklore." *Fordham Law Review* 35:15–50.

Hall, Clarence W. 1964. "Poison in Print—And How to Get Rid of It." *Reader's Digest*, May, pp. 94–98.

Halpern, Steven C. 1976. "Assessing the Litigative Role of ACLU Chapters." In *Civil Liberties*, ed. Stephen L. Wasby. Lexington, Mass.: Lexington Books.

Heck, Edward. 1983. "Consensus and Conflict on the Supreme Court." Paper presented at the Midwest Political Science Association Annual Meeting, Chicago.

Henkin, Louis. 1963. "Morals and the Constitution: The Sin of Obscenity." *Columbia Law Review*. 63:391–414.

Hertzberg, Henrick. 1986. "Big Boobs." *New Republic*, 14 and 21 July, pp. 21–24.

Janos, Leo. 1983. "The Adult Film Industry Goes Hollywood." *Cosmopolitan*. January.

Karp, Irwin. 1977. "From *Roth* to *Rohauer*: Twenty Years of *Amicus* Briefs." *Bulletin: Copyright Society of the U.S.A.* 25:1–18.

Katz, Al. 1969. "Privacy and Pornography: *Stanley* v. *Georgia*." *Supreme Court Review* 1969:203–17.

Keating, Charles H. 1971. "The Report That Shocked the Nation." *Reader's Digest*, January, pp. 37–40.

———. 1972. "Attacking Obscenity: What Parents Can Do to Stem the Flood of Pornography." *Parents Magazine* 47:16.

———. 1974. "Green Light to Combat Smut." *Reader's Digest*, January, pp. 147–50.

Kobylka, Joseph F. 1987. "A Court-Created Context for Group Litigation: Libertarian Groups and Obscenity." *The Journal of Politics* 49:1061–78.

Krislov, Samuel. 1963. "The Amicus Curiae Brief: From Friendship to Advocacy." *Yale Law Journal* 72:694–721.

———. 1968. "From *Ginzburg* to *Ginsberg*: The Unhurried Children's Hour in Obscenity Litigation." *Supreme Court Review* 1968:153–98.

Kristol, Irving. 1972. "Pornography, Obscenity, and the Case for Censorship." In *On the Democratic Ideal in America*, pp. 31–47. New York: Harper, Row, Publishers.

Latham, Earl. 1952. "The Group Basis of Politics: Notes for a Theory." *American Political Science Review* 46:376–97.

Levine, James P. 1970. "Methodological Concerns in Studying Supreme Court Efficiency." *Law and Society Review* 4:583–611.

Lockhart, William. 1975. "Escape from the Chill of Uncertainty." *Georgia Law Review* 9:533–87.

Lockhart, William, and Robert C. McClure. 1954. "The Law of Obscenity." *Minnesota Law Review* 38:295–395.

———. 1960. "Censorship of Obscenity: The Developing Constitutional Standards." *Minnesota Law Review* 45:5–121.

Lukas, J. Anthony. 1978. "The ACLU against Itself." *New York Times Magazine*, 9 July, pp. 9ff.

MacKinnon, Catherine. 1984. "Not a Moral Issue." *Yale Law and Policy Review* 2:321–45.

———. 1985. "Pornography, Civil Rights, and Speech." *Harvard Civil Rights–Civil Liberties Review* 20:1–70.

Magrath, C. Peter. 1966. "The Obscenity Cases: The Grapes of *Roth*." *Supreme Court Review* 1966:7–77.

Mann, Jim. 1978. "Hard Times for the ACLU." *New Republic*, 15 April, pp. 12–15.

Meiklejohn, Alexander. 1961. "The First Amendment is an Absolute." *Supreme Court Review* 1961:245–66.

Minneapolis Star-Tribune, 30 December 1983–9 January 1984.

Moe, Terry M. 1981. "Toward a Broader View of Interest Groups." *Journal of Politics* 43:531–43.

Murphy, Paul L. 1975. "Communities in Conflict." In *The Pulse of Freedom*, ed. Alan Reitman, pp. 1–39. New York: W. W. Norton.

Newsweek. 1985. "The War Against Pornography." 18 March, pp. 58–67.

New York Times, various.

Note. 1966a. "More Ado about Dirty Books." *Yale Law Journal* 75:1364–1415.

Note. 1966b. "Obscenity and the Supreme Court: Nine Years of Confusion." *Stanford Law Review* 19:167–89.

Note. 1969. "Obscenity from *Stanley* to *Karalexis*: A Backdoor Approach to First Amendment Protection." *Vanderbilt Law Review* 23:369–87.

Note. 1969–1970. "Obscenity from *Stanley* to *Karalexis*: A Backdoor Approach to First Amendment Protection." *Vanderbilt Law Review* 23:369–86.

Note. 1971a. "The Application of a Local or National Standard of Decency in the Use of the *Roth-Memoirs* Obscenity Test." *Washington University Law Quarterly* 1971:691–95.

Note. 1971b. "The Geography of Obscenity's 'Contemporary Community Standards.' " *Wake Forest Law Review* 8:81–92.

Note. 1974a. "Constituent Elements of Tripartite Definition of Obscenity to Be Determined by Applying Contemporary Community Standards, Not National Standards." *Emory Law Journal* 23:551–65.

Note. 1974b. "Pornography, the Local Option." *Baylor Law Review* 26:97–107.

Obscenity Law Project. 1976. "An Empirical Inquiry into the Effects of *Miller* v. *California* on the Control of Obscenity." *New York University Law Review* 52:810–939.

O'Connor, Karen, and Lee Epstein. 1981–82. "*Amicus Curiae* Participation in United States Supreme Court Litigation: An Appraisal of Hakman's 'Folklore.' " *Law and Society Review* 16:311–19.

———. 1982. "The Rise of Conservative Interest Group Litigation." Paper presented at the Midwest Political Science Association Meetings, Chicago.

———. 1983. "Court Rules and Workload: A Case Study of Rules Governing Amicus Curiae Participation." *Justice System Journal* 8:35–45.

Olson, Susan N. 1981. "The Political Evolution of Interest Group Litigation." In *Governing through Courts*, ed. Gambritta, May, and Foster. Beverly Hills, Calif.: Sage Publications.

Orren, Karen. 1976. "Standing to Sue: Interest Group Conflict in the Federal Courts." *American Political Science Review* 70:723–41.

Pilpel, Harriet. 1974. "Dirty Business in Court." *The Civil Liberties Review* 1:30–41.

Rowland, C. K., Donald Songer, and Robert A. Carp. 1988. "Presidential Effects on Criminal Justice Policy in the Lower Federal Courts: The Reagan Judges." *Law and Society Review* 22:191–200.

Salisbury, Robert H. 1969. "An Exchange Theory of Interest Groups." *Midwest Journal of Political Science* 13:1–32.

Schauer, Frederick F. 1978. "Reflections on 'Contemporary Community Standards': The Perpetuation of an Irrelevant Concept in the Law of Obscenity." *North Carolina Law Review* 56:3–28.

Shugrue, Richard E., and Patricia Zieg. 1974. "An Atlas for Obscenity: Exploring Community Standards." *Creighton Law Review* 7:157–81.

Slough, M. C., and P. D. McAnany. 1964a. "Obscenity and Constitutional Freedom, Part I." *Saint Louis University Law Journal* 7:279–367.

———. 1964b. "Obscenity and Constitutional Freedom, Part II." *Saint Louis University Law Journal* 8:449–532.

Stewart, Joseph, Jr., and Edward V. Heck. 1981. "Lawyers, Interest Groups, and the Attack on Civil Wrongs." Paper presented at the Meetings of the American Political Science Association, New York.

Teachout, Terry. 1987. "The Pornography Report That Never Was." *Commentary*, August, pp. 51–57.

Tribe, Laurence. 1980. "The Puzzling Persistence of Process Based Constitutional Theories." *Yale Law Journal* 89:1063–80.

Vance, Carole S. 1986. "The Meese Commission on the Road." *Nation*, 2 and 9 August, pp. 1, 76–82.

Vines, Kenneth N. 1964. "Federal District Judges and Race Relations Cases in the South." *Journal of Politics* 26:337–57.

Vose, Clement. 1958. "Litigation as a Form of Pressure Group Activity." *Annals of the American Academy of Political and Social Science* 319:20–31.

———. 1981. "Interest Groups and Litigation." Paper presented at the American Political Science Association Meeting, New York.

Wasby, Stephen L. 1978. "Review of Horowitz's *Courts and Social Policy*." *Vanderbilt Law Review* 31:727–61.

———. 1983. "Interest Groups in Court: Race Relations Litigation." In *Interest Group Politics*, ed. Allan Cigler and Burt Loomis, pp. 251–73. Washington, D.C.: Congressional Quarterly Press.

West, Robin. 1987. "The Feminist-Conservative Anti-Pornography Alliance and the 1986 Attorney General's Pornography Report." *American Bar Foundation Research Journal* 1987:681–712.

Witcover, Jules. 1970. "Civil War over Smut." *Nation*, 11 May, pp. 550–52.

Zurcher, Louis A., Jr., and R. George Kirkpatrick. 1971–72. "The Anti-Obscenity Campaign: A Symbolic Crusade." *Social Problems* 19:217–38.

———. 1973. "Ad Hoc Anti-Pornography Organizations and Their Active Members: A Research Summary." *Journal of Social Issues* 29:69–94.

Index

ABA, et al. v. *Hudnut* (1984; 1986), 45, 61, 90, 144, 147
ABA, et al. v. *McAulliffe* (1981), 45
ACLU v. *Chicago* (1945), 31
Adult Film Association of America (AFAA), 16, 35, 40–41, 42, 43–44, 56, 57, 127, 129–30, 132, 134, 135, 141, 142–43, 144, 145, 149, 160, 165–66, 166–67; goals, 43–44, 129, 141, 142–43, 145; leadership, 135, 136–37, 138–39, 141, 145, 166; membership, 136–37, 138–39, 141, 145, 166; range of interests, 41, 132; response to *Miller*, 129–30, 132, 134, 141, 145; strategies, 43–44, 129–30, 132, 134, 141, 144
Agnew, Spiro, xiii
Alberts v. *California* (1957), 4, 25
Allison, Graham T., 125
American Booksellers Association (ABA), 16, 41, 42, 88, 128–29, 132, 134, 143; goals, 42, 129, 143; range of interests, 41, 132; response to *Miller*, 128–29, 132, 134; strategies, 44–45, 129–30, 132, 134
American Civil Liberties Union (ACLU), 11, 12, 16, 24, 25, 27–34, 35, 36, 41, 42, 44, 45, 46, 51, 61, 71–95, 97–98, 104–5, 108, 110, 114, 119, 125, 126, 127, 128, 131, 132, 134, 135, 136, 146, 147, 148, 149, 156, 157, 158, 159, 160, 162, 163, 165, 167, 168; feminist perspectives, 84–85; goals, 30–33, 71–73, 74, 75–76, 79–81, 84, 86, 90, 92, 148, 163; Ku Klux Klan, 83, 84, 92; leadership, 76–81, 82, 83–84, 85, 86, 87, 88, 90, 91–92, 167; membership, 76–77, 81, 82–85, 90, 91, 92; range of interests, 30–31, 78–79, 81, 86, 91, 92; response to *Miller*, 73–76, 128; Skokie Nazis, 30, 83, 84, 91, 92; strategies, 32–34, 72, 73, 74–76, 81, 86
American Jewish Congress, 88
American Library Association/Freedom

to Read Foundation (ALA/FRF), 16, 35–40, 75, 88, 128, 129, 132, 134, 135, 138, 139, 140–41, 142, 144, 145, 147, 149, 158, 159, 160, 161, 166–67; goals, 37–39, 129, 140–41, 142; leadership, 135, 138; membership, 138; range of interests, 35–38, 132, 140–41, 145, 149, 166–67; response to *Miller*, 129–30, 132, 134, 140, 144; strategies, 38–40, 129–30, 132, 134, 138, 140, 144

American Society of Journalists and Authors (ASJA), 35

amicus curiae, 13–14, 15, 17, 33, 57–58, 128, 161, 164

Arcara v. *Cloud Books* (1986), 59, 75, 86, 112

Association of American Publishers (AAP), 16, 25, 35–40, 44, 86, 129, 132, 134, 136, 138, 139, 140, 142–43, 159, 160, 165, 166; goals, 37–39, 129, 140, 142–43; leadership, 138; membership, 138; range of interests, 35–38, 132, 166; response to *Miller*, 129–30, 132, 134, 139, 140; strategies, 38–40, 129–30, 132, 134, 138

Attorney General's Commission on Pornography (1986), xiii, 112, 116, 146

Austin v. *Kentucky* (1967), 98, 99

Authors League of America (AL), 16, 25, 35–40, 44, 128–29, 134, 138, 139, 140, 142, 145, 149, 159, 165, 166; goals, 37–39, 129, 142; leadership, 138; membership, 138; range of interests, 35–38, 140, 145, 149, 166; response to *Miller*, 128–29, 134; strategies, 38–40, 129–30, 134, 138

Ballew v. *Georgia* (1978), 51, 97

Bamberger, Michael, 43, 57

Bantam Books v. *Sullivan* (1963), 39

Barker, Lucius J., 10, 12, 159

Bentley, Arthur F., 10

Bingham, Richard D., 77, 91

Bishop, Joseph W., 78, 79, 81

Black, Hugo, 6, 99

Blackmun, Harry A., 111, 155

Board of Education v. *Pico* (1982), 51, 75, 86, 90

Boyer, Paul S., 24

Brennan, William, 3, 4, 5, 6, 7, 43, 86, 89, 99, 129, 155

Brockett v. *Spokane Arcades* (1985), 59, 111, 112

Brown v. *Board of Education* (1945), 25

Burger, Warren E., 6, 53, 74, 155

Burstyn v. *Wilson* (1952), 31

Bush, George, 112

Butler v. *Michigan* (1957), 3, 25, 35, 38

Caldeira, Gregory A., 11, 14, 159, 160

Carp, Robert A., 146

Casper, Jonathan, 12, 159

Chaplinsky v. *New Hampshire* (1942), 3

Citizens for Decency through Law (CDL), 16, 18, 47, 49–59, 61, 63, 64, 72, 92, 97–123, 126, 148, 157, 158, 161, 163, 167; goals, 52–56, 98, 101–2, 104, 105, 107–8, 109, 112, 118, 119; leadership, 103, 104–8, 114, 116–17, 118; membership, 108–10, 118; range of interests, 51–52, 104–5, 110–11, 118; response to *Miller*, 100–104; strategies, 49, 56–59, 100, 102–4, 105, 106–7, 112, 113–14, 117–18, 163

Clancy, Carol, 107

Clancy, James J., 23, 49, 53, 58, 97, 107

Coalition for Better Television, 116

Cohen v. *California* (1971), 51

Comstock, Anthony, 3, 24

Cortner, Richard C., xiii, 10, 12, 159, 160

Council for Periodical Distributors Association (CPDA), 41, 43, 88, 125, 128–29, 132, 134, 136, 139; goals, 43, 129; range of interests, 43, 132; response to *Miller*, 128–29, 132, 134, 139; strategies, 44–45, 129–30, 132, 134

Covenant House/Institute for Youth Advocacy (CH/IYA), 47–49, 51, 52–53, 54, 58, 62, 98, 103; goals, 52–53,

54; range of interests, 51; strategies, 58

Cowan, Ruth B., 11, 12, 13, 79, 160, 162

Direct Mail Advertising Association (DMAA), 40, 42, 131, 132, 139
Directors Guild of America (DGA), 35, 128–29, 131, 132, 139, 140, 143, 145, 167
Douglas, William O., 6, 7, 111
Dworkin, Andrea, 60, 61, 63

Eagle Forum, 116, 146
Engdahl, David, 6
Ennis, Bruce J., 84
Epstein, Lee, 11, 12, 13, 159, 160, 162, 163
Ernst, Morris L., 77
Erznoznik v. *Jacksonville* (1975), 40, 111, 140, 145

FCC v. *Pacifica Foundation* (1978), 40, 52, 59, 75, 86, 111, 112, 132
Falwell, Jerry, 116
"feminist" antipornography statutes, xii, 45, 76, 144, 145, 146, 147
First Amendment Lawyers Association (FALA), 40–41, 42, 56, 87, 114, 129, 131, 134, 142, 144, 145, 149, 160; goals, 41, 129, 142, 144; range of interests, 41, 149; response to *Miller*, 129–30, 134, 144; strategies, 41, 129–30, 134, 144
Fleishman, Stanley, 87, 132–33
Flynt v. *Ohio* (1981), 58
Ford, Gerald, 83
Fortas, Abe, 53, 99
Fraenkel, Osmond K., 77
Frankfurter, Felix, 3
Fraser, Donald, 60, 61
Freedom Council Foundation (FCF), 47, 51, 52, 55, 61, 62, 98, 103; goals, 52, 55; range of interests, 51; strategies, 55

Galanter, Marc, 170
Gauer, Raymond J., 49

Gent v. *Arkansas* (1967), 43, 99
Gibson, James L., 77, 91
Ginsberg v. *New York* (1968), 72, 99
Ginzburg v. *U.S.* (1966), 39, 57, 98
Goldberg, Arthur, 6
Goldstein, Michael J., 79
Gottschall, Jon, 146

Hakman, Nathan, 10–11, 158–59, 164
Hall, Clarence W., 49
Hamling v. *U.S.* (1974), 73, 74, 75, 81, 85–86, 88, 99, 111, 117, 142, 157
Harlan, John Marshall, Jr., 4, 25, 99
Heck, Edward V., 163
Henkin, Louis, 3
Hill, Morton A., 50, 54, 107, 109, 115
Hirschhorn, Joel, 87
Hirshman, Albert O., 77, 108, 135
Huffman v. *Pursue* (1975), 58, 112

International Periodical Distributors Association (IPDA), 136
Interstate Circuit, Inc. v. *Dallas* (1968), 40

Jacobellis v. *Ohio* (1964), 5, 6, 7, 74
Jenkins v. *Georgia* (1974), 40, 42, 106, 111, 112, 117, 118, 125, 127, 129, 131, 140, 143, 145, 146
Johnson, Lyndon B., xii, 50, 54

Karp, Irwin, 38, 39–40
Katz, Al, 6
Keating, Charles H., 49, 50, 53, 54, 100–101, 107
Kennedy, Anthony, 7
Kluger, Richard, 11, 12, 13, 14, 15, 160, 161
Krislov, Samuel, 4, 13, 14

Levine, James P., 89
litigation density, 161–62
litigation intensity, 161
Lo-Ji Sales v. *New York* (1979), 112
London, Ephraim, 32, 77
Lukas, J. Anthony, 77, 79, 84
Lynch v. *Donnelly* (1984), 51

McGeady, Paul J., 51, 56, 107, 109
McKinney v. Alabama (1976), 132
MacKinnon, Catherine, 60, 61, 63
Magazine Publishers Association
  (MPA), 134, 136, 138, 139, 149
Magrath, C. Peter, 6
Mann, Jim, 77, 79, 80, 82–83
Manual Enterprises v. Day (1962), 5, 25
Mapp v. Ohio (1961), 25
Marks v. U.S. (1977), 112
Marshall, Thurgood, 7, 112, 155
Maryland v. Macon (1985), 75, 86
material groups, 16, 17, 18, 27, 34–46,
  47, 63, 82, 87, 91, 119, 125–54, 157–
  59, 160, 164–68, 169; commercial
  groups, 16, 27, 35, 40–45, 46, 63, 88,
  125–54, 157–59, 165, 166, 169; "least
  common denominator" approach,
  128, 129–30, 132, 137, 140, 142, 162;
  professional groups, 16, 27, 34–40,
  41, 43, 44, 45, 46, 63, 88, 125–54,
  157–59, 166, 169; response to Miller,
  128–34
Media Coalition (MC), 16, 39, 41–42,
  45, 52, 57, 61, 75, 76, 86, 88, 128,
  134, 135, 136, 137, 138, 139, 140,
  142, 143, 144, 145, 147, 149, 158,
  160, 161, 163–64, 166, 167; goals,
  42, 136, 139, 140, 142; leadership,
  136, 167; membership, 138, 139,
  167; range of interests, 41–42, 132,
  136, 140, 166; response to Miller,
  132, 134, 136, 140, 143, 144; strategies, 45, 132, 134, 136, 140, 142,
  143, 144, 163–64, 166
Meese, Edwin, xiii, 112, 116, 146
Meiklejohn, Alexander, 4
Memoirs v. Massachusetts (1966), 5–6, 7,
  43, 55, 72, 74, 98, 99
Miller v. California (1973), xii, xiii, 2,
  6–8, 17, 18, 19, 25, 26, 27, 33, 34,
  39, 42, 43, 44, 45, 46, 55, 59, 64, 71,
  73, 74, 76, 81, 82, 84, 85, 86, 87, 88,
  89, 90, 91, 92, 97, 99, 100–104, 105,
  106, 107, 108, 109, 110, 111, 112,
  113, 114, 115, 117, 118, 119, 126,
  127, 128–34, 135, 136, 138, 139, 140,
  141, 142–44, 145, 146, 148, 149,
  155–59, 160–64, 165, 166, 167, 168
Mishkin v. New York (1966), 98
Moe, Terry M., 16, 27, 77, 82, 90,
  108, 126, 135, 137, 148, 164
Morality in Media (MM), 16, 47, 49–
  59, 61, 63, 64, 92, 97–123, 126, 148,
  157, 161, 163, 167; goals, 52–56, 98,
  101–2, 104, 105, 106, 107–8, 112;
  leadership, 104–8, 110, 111, 114,
  116–17, 118; membership, 108–10,
  111, 118; National Obscenity Law
  Center (NOLC), 53–54, 58, 59, 100,
  103, 106, 115, 118, 157, 161; range
  of interests, 51–52, 104–5, 110–11,
  118; response to Miller, 100–104;
  strategies, 49, 56–59, 102–4, 105,
  106, 108, 112, 113–15, 118
Moral Majority, 61, 89, 116, 146
Morgan, Charles, 83
Morgan, Richard E., 10, 159
Motion Picture Association of America
  (MPAA), 40, 41, 42, 43, 88, 128–29,
  132, 134, 136, 138, 139, 140, 145,
  149, 160, 161, 165, 166, 167; goals,
  42, 129, 140, 145; leadership, 138,
  139, 145; membership, 139; range of
  interests, 42, 132, 140, 145; response
  to Miller, 128–29, 132, 134, 139, 140;
  strategies, 43, 129–30, 132, 134, 145

National Association for the Advancement of Colored People (NAACP),
  10, 11, 12, 13, 33, 161
National Association of Theatre Owners
  (NATO), 40, 42–43, 128–29, 131,
  134, 139, 140, 145, 165, 167; goals,
  42–43, 129, 145; range of interests,
  42–43, 132, 145, 165; response to
  Miller, 128–29, 132, 134, 139; strategies, 43, 129–30, 132, 134, 145
National Coalition Against Censorship,
  88
National Council of Churches, 88
National Institute of Municipal Law
  Officers (NIMLO), 47, 51, 52, 54–
  55, 58, 62, 103, 105; goals, 52, 54–

55; range of interests, 51; strategies, 58

National League of Cities (NLC), 47, 51, 52, 54–55, 58, 62, 103, 105; goals, 52, 54–55, range of interests, 51, strategies, 58

National Legal Foundation (NLF), 47, 51, 52, 55, 61, 62, 98, 103; goals, 52, 55; range of interests, 51; strategies, 55

National Legion of Decency (NLD), 24, 105

National Office for Decent Literature (NODL), 24, 105

National Organization for Women (NOW), 60, 61, 85

Near v. *Minnesota* (1931), 31

Neier, Aryeh, 12, 77, 83, 84

New York v. *Ferber* (1982), 36, 47, 49, 51, 52–53, 59, 75, 86, 111, 112, 142, 157

Nixon, Richard M., xiii, 6, 49, 54, 64, 72–73, 79, 82–83, 84, 99, 155

obscenity: constant definitional approach, 4, 101; *Miller* test, 6–7; pandering, 6, 99; *Roth* test, 3–6; variable definitional approach, 4, 51, 53, 55, 59, 98, 101, 106, 117

"obscenity bar," 87–88, 111, 114–15, 118–19, 160–61, 163, 167

Obscenity Law Project, 89, 133

O'Connor, Karen, 11, 13, 159, 160, 162, 163

O'Connor, Sandra D., 7, 11

Olson, Mancur, 15, 97, 126, 135, 137, 166

Olson, Susan, 11, 12

organizational maintenance, 81, 82, 100, 106, 109, 113, 117, 119, 135, 140, 141

organizational type, 16–17, 18, 164–68, 169

Outdoor Advertising Association (OAA), 40

Papish v. *Board of Curators* (1973), 51

Paris Adult Theatre v. *Slaton* (1973), 7, 43, 86, 89, 129

Pilpel, Harriet, 32, 77, 88

Pivar, David J., 24

Plessy v. *Ferguson* (1896), 11

pluralism, 10–19, 148–49

Pope v. *Illinois* (1987), 59, 112, 142

Powell, Lewis: 111, 155

President's Commission on Obscenity and Pornography (1970), xii-xiii, 5, 30, 34, 38, 49, 50, 54, 64, 109, 114–15

purposive groups, 16, 17, 18, 26, 27–34, 46, 50–51, 61, 62, 63, 76–77, 78, 81, 82, 83, 85, 90, 91, 97–98, 100, 104, 108, 110, 118, 119, 125–28, 135, 141, 144, 148–49, 159, 164–68, 169

Rabe v. *Washington* (1972), 43

Reagan, Ronald, 7, 112, 116, 146, 155, 157

Red Bluff Drive-in v. *Vance* (CA5, 1981), 138

Redfield, Emanuel, 77

Redrup v. *New York* (1967), 6, 7, 53, 59, 72, 74, 98, 99, 102, 125, 143, 163

Regina v. *Hicklin* (1868), 2–3, 4

Rehnquist, William, 155

Reitman, Alan, 30, 71

Rembar, Charles, 6, 167

Renton v. *Playtime Theatre* (1986), 47, 58, 75, 86, 90, 111, 142

Rhine, Joseph, 87

Rice, Elmer, 32

Robertson, Pat, 51, 61, 116, 146

Rosenwein, Samuel, 87

Roth v. *U.S.* (1957), xii, 2, 3–6, 7, 25, 31, 32, 34, 35, 37, 38, 46, 53, 55, 63, 64, 71, 72, 74, 98, 99, 102, 129, 142

Rowan v. *Post Office* (1970), 72

Rowland, C. K., 146

Rubin, Eva R., 11, 13

St. Martin's Press v. *Carey* (1979), 36

Salisbury, Robert H., 16, 77, 80, 82, 90, 108, 119, 126, 135, 148

Scalia, Antonin, 7

Schattschneider, E. E., 160

Schauer, Frederick F., 7, 99

Scheingold, Stuart, 15

Schwartz, Arthur M., 87
Schwarz, Ralph J., 87
Skoilrood, Robert K., 51
Smith, Robert E., 87
Smith v. *California* (1959), 38
Smith v. *U.S.* (1977), 112, 155
Songer, Donald, 146
Sorauf, Frank J., xiv, 11, 12, 14, 15,
    159, 160, 161, 162, 163
Southeastern Promotions v. *Conrad*
    (1975), 40, 111, 112
Splawn v. *California* (1977), 112
Stanley v. *Georgia* (1969), 2, 6, 7, 34,
    72, 74, 99
Stevens, John Paul, 112, 155
Stewart, Joseph, Jr., 163
Stewart, Potter, 6, 7, 39, 111

Taylor, Bruce A., 51, 57, 58, 102, 107,
    109, 114, 116
"test case" (sponsorship) strategy, 12–
    13, 15, 17, 33, 128, 134, 136, 161,
    163
Truman, David, 10, 16

U.S. v. *Reidel* (1971), 72
U.S. v. *37 Photographs* (1971), 72
U.S. Marketing v. *Idaho* (1982), 112

Valenti, Jack, 43
Video Software Dealers Association
    (VSDA), 40

Virginia v. *American Booksellers Associa-
    tion, Inc., et al.* (1988), 47, 49, 51,
    75, 86, 90
Volunteer Lawyers for the Arts (VLA),
    30
Vose, Clement, 10, 11, 12, 13, 14, 15,
    159, 160, 161

Walker, Samuel, 12, 31, 77, 78, 79, 83,
    84
Wallace, DeWitt, 49
Warren, Earl, 4, 6, 99
Wasby, Stephen L., 7, 12, 160, 162
Weston, John H., 87
White, Byron, 6, 155
Wilson, James Q., 16, 27, 50, 77, 82,
    90, 104, 108, 126, 135, 137, 148, 164
Women Against Pornography, 60, 62
Women Against Violence Against
    Women, 60, 62
Women Against Violence in Pornogra-
    phy, 60, 62
Women's Organizations, 25–26, 59–63,
    111
Wright, John R., 11, 14, 159, 160
Wulf, Melvin, 71, 78, 79, 83

Yates v. *U.S.* (1957), 25
Young v. *American Mini Theatres* (1976),
    42, 75, 86, 111, 142, 157